Margins
of the
Mind

Frank Musgrove

with the assistance of
Roger Middleton and Pat Hawes

Methuen & Co Ltd

First published by Methuen & Co Ltd
11 New Fetter Lane, London EC4P 4EE

© 1977 Frank Musgrove
Photoset by Red Lion Setters, Holborn, London
Printed in Great Britain by
Richard Clay (The Chaucer Press), Ltd, Bungay, Suffolk

ISBN (hardbound) 0 416 55040 1
ISBN (paperback) 0 416 55050 9

Contents

Author's note

The material on which the arguments of this book are based is principally the transcripts of tape-recorded interviews which were carried out under the author's general direction as follows: Chapters 3, 6 and 7 by Pat Hawes; Chapters 4 and 9 by Roger Middleton; and Chapters 5 and 8 by Frank Musgrove. The responsibility for the conception and design of the study, for the selection and organization of the material, and for the interpretation and speculation that appear in this book, rests solely with the undersigned.

F. Musgrove.

1 | Aspects of change in adult life

Psychology *and stability*

Psychologists generally see adult identity as finished and relatively closed; some contemporary sociologists see it (at least in advanced modern societies) as endlessly open and even peculiarly conversion-prone. Deep-seated change in adult life occurs especially, they think, in the 'marginal situations' which abound in a complex, pluralistic world. For most psychologists adult identity is massively stable; for many contemporary sociologists it remains endlessly fugitive. It is always fragile and precarious, and modern man is a chameleon.

This is a book of seven ethnographic case studies of change in adult life. Its purpose is to make a contribution to our understanding of the problems and processes of adult resocialization. Change is examined principally in terms of a modification of consciousness. The seven groups of people selected for study had moved into unusual, extreme or abnormal positions in contemporary English society. Their positions could be described as 'marginal'. The focus of this book is the modification of consciousness in adult life through the experience of marginality.

Two groups were selected for study because they have been placed in marginal positions through misfortune: they are men and women who have gone blind in adult life, and people who have contracted incurable physical disabilities and entered a Cheshire Home. Other groups of people who have taken up their marginal positions from choice were selected for comparative purposes: self-employed artists; late entrants to the Anglican ministry; a Sufi commune; Hare Krishna devotees; and (although the notion of choice is somewhat problematic) adult homosexuals. These groups were studied in order to suggest an answer to the question: Can adults really change?

The view that adults cannot 'really change' (unless, perhaps, they undergo a prolonged course of psychoanalysis) is a very dispiriting conclusion for anyone concerned with the re-education of adults in either 'developing' or rapidly changing modern societies. And it is because of the author's long-standing interest in the problems of 'marginal men' and lifelong learning[1] that the studies reported in this book were undertaken. The production of retreads for changing fields of industrial employment is a comparatively minor, technical problem for 'l'éducation permanente'. The current debate on continuing education is conducted in a context of profound ignorance of the ways and circumstances in which adults can 'really change' when life calls for deep-seated and creative readjustments and perhaps radical redefinitions of self and reality.

For we have no psychology of adulthood in the sense in which we have a child psychology.[2] It is true that we have some systematic knowledge of the adult years from demographic data (we know that as we grow older we are more inclined to suicide and less inclined to crime); and simple (and sometimes misleading) 'directory research' tells us something about the peak years of achievement in different fields of endeavour.[3] Psychologists have mapped out developmental stages for the first fifteen to twenty years; but thereafter life is a blank. Half a century of adult life remains psychologically speaking, an unchartered waste.

Some attention has been given to the social and psychological significance of the menopause (and its importance as a stage in the life-cycle of women greatly de-emphasized[4]); but there are few well-established psychological landmarks in the forty years after twenty. Sociologists have not made any systematic contribution to studies of the life-cycle, and even those who have been interested in age-classification as an aspect of social structure have little to say about the fifty years between youth and old age.[5]

The psychologist's 'stages' are usually based on the work of Piaget and Freud. They end abruptly with adulthood and 'maturity'.[6] Kohlberg's stages of moral reasoning extend into the twenties,[7] and Keniston, drawing on Kohlberg's work, sees a post-conventional morality marking a new stage of the life-cycle for some (mostly highly educated) people in post-modern societies, interposed between adolescence and full adulthood: 'a previously unlabeled stage of development is opening up.' [8] Only a minority will ever achieve this post-adolescent but pre-adult stage, which is characterized by adherence to personal principles, often stated at a very high level of generality, and frequently involving conflict with existing concepts of law and of the social contract. A prolonged period of disengagement from the institutions of adult society appears to facilitate this level of moral development. It is from this 'stage' that the adherents of the counter culture (in both its activist and mystical forms) appear in the main to be drawn.

But there has been little advance on Erik Erikson's tentative exploration of adult change and development more than twenty years ago. Erikson gave us eight ages of man: five related to the first twenty years of life, three to the remaining fifty. Indeed, his eighth stage ('ego integrity versus despair') is the stage of 'maturity' and appears to extend over the whole of life after thirty.[9] Erikson's stages are defined by conflicts which have to be resolved before the next stage can be reached: they are steps which are predetermined in the growing person's readiness to interact with a widening social sphere, but are 'encouraged' by society to unfold at their proper rate and in their proper sequence.

The case for the stability and continuity of adult personality rests not on stages and sequences that have been explored, but on general theories of personality and the evidence of longitudinal follow-up studies. The interests and values of 'gifted' Californians have been followed up for half a century and show remarkable stability;[10] 'deeper' personality characteristics at thirty have been shown to be substantially the same as twelve years previously — though the experience of war, marriage and adult careers had intervened.[11] Benjamin Bloom's celebrated and highly influential recent study points in the same direction. Bloom's collation and interpretation of extensive research on stability and change generally confirms the picture of massive continuity, although Bloom concedes that this is not necessarily 'natural' and inevitable, but may be a reflection of a stable social environment.[12]

Sociology and flux

For the 'symbolic interactionists' all is openness and flux: adult identity is provisional and tentative, open to far-reaching 'transformation' and redefinition. Identity is produced, sustained and transformed by the fleeting patterns of human interaction.[13]

The author has elsewhere discussed the psychological stage as a social invention;[14] and others have pointed to its significance as a social rather than a psychological fact.[15] This book does not attempt to establish psychological stages for the adult years: it examines change not as the outcome of maturation, but of socialization. But it does not dismiss 'stages' as having no reality or explanatory value. The materials in this book are used to comment on stage theories where this is appropriate. In particular, the account of the two religious communes (Chapters 8 and 9) are interpreted in part as manifestations of Kohlberg and Keniston's stage of post-conventional morality.

Socialization is the process by which men are moulded by their society and the social relationships in which they are involved. A distinction is commonly made between primary socialization in the early years of life, principally in the family, and subsequent secondary socialization into an occupation, marriage, parenthood and community life. Through primary socialization the individual apprehends a reality which appears inevitable and has 'a peculiar quality of firmness';[16] secondary socialization, to be effective, must be congruent with this first conception of the world. The process of socialization has often been conceived (following the seminal writing of G.H. Mead) as the learning of social roles. 'Mind presupposes and is a product of the social process', said Mead; and through language and play the young child enters society by 'taking the role of the other'.[17]

G.H. Mead was at one with Freud in emphasizing the importance and permanence of these early childhood experiences; but the neo-Meadian 'symbolic interactionists' of recent years focus attention on later stages of life and see socialization as much more provisional. Indeed, there is about it an artificiality which seems to make change not only relatively easy but perhaps desirable. Berger and Luckmann describe primary socialization as 'the most important confidence trick that society plays on the individual ...'[18]

Artifice, staginess and collusion are central to Goffman's conception of self. Personal identity is a conspiracy, the individual defines himself and his situation with the provisional agreement of others who are prepared to suspend disbelief while he gives his 'performance'. In this dramaturgical conception of social roles the self is not immutable, but depends on 'agreement as to whose claims concerning what issues will be temporarily honoured'.[19] But 'performances' are not merely theatrical pretence: 'the very structure of the self can be seen in terms of how we arrange such performances in our Anglo-American society.'[20]

Sociologists reject the notion of socialization as an inexorable unfolding which leads to completeness or maturity. Ethnomethodologists reject this deficit view of personal development: when they enter into the social world of the child (or anyone at an 'inferior' or 'lower' stage of development) they find a culture which is entirely meaningful in its own terms; and change arises not from development to a higher stage, but from culture contact. Attention shifts from long-term sequences to short-term interaction with another culture.[21] Parents and teachers are enjoined to treat children not as incomplete adults but simply as cultural strangers.[22]

The emphasis among both ethnomethodologists and symbolic interactionists is upon a greater openness of individuals to change. Psychologists talk of personality development; more dramatically symbolic interactionists talk of transformations of identity. Unlike 'development', transformation does not imply sequence or change in any particular direction, towards some defined state of maturity, completeness or fulfilment; it is intended to capture 'the open-ended, tentative, exploratory, hypothetical, problematical, devious, changeable, and only partly unified character of human courses of action.' [23] Psychologists with a psychoanalytical orientation may emphasize not only basic stability but deny any 'real change' at all: apparent changes are merely variations on a theme. By contrast interactionists explore the ever-shifting 'situational adjustments' of social life and argue that stability (or change) need not rest on interests, values and deeper personality traits, but simply on 'structural' circumstances — by which is meant social rewards and punishments, the 'coercion' of people by circumstances. Commitment, it is conceded, may indeed impede behavioural change, but commitment is unnecessary;[24] and in a modern pluralistic world we are all chameleons.[25]

The importance of marginality

This is Peter Berger's view: in modern highly diverse (or pluralistic) societies, if men are not chameleons, they are at least conversion-prone. Modern man invites and experiences fundamental transformations of identity. The influential sociological writing of Berger has elaborated this central theme for a decade. It is Berger's key propositions about modification of consciousness and change in adult life that the present study was designed to test.

In a series of striking and very popular books Berger develops the theme that in modern societies identity is open, precarious, fragile,

liable to fundamental transformations. These can happen 'with frightening speed', thus 'The intellectual becomes a slob after he is
kidnapped by the army'.[26] Modern man is singularly conversion-
prone,[27] but 'To have a conversion experience is nothing much. The
real thing is to be able to go on taking it seriously ...'[28] Identities are
socially bestowed, but 'They must also be socially sustained, and fairly
steadily so'.[29] This is one of Berger's key propositions which is tested
and examined in this book.

Berger's notions of adult change and transformation of consciousness are closely related to his conception of 'marginality'. (When
people move into marginal positions, as many do in complex societies,
familiar props for their identity are lost.) Indeed, the concept of
marginality, after an inconclusive history following the pioneer writing
(in the 1920s and '30s) of Stonequist and Park,[30] has assumed a new
significance in recent years in discussions of socialization. It is perhaps
people in marginal situations — in the anterooms of life — who are
most open to change?

Three different lines of sociological thought converge today to
highlight the importance of marginality in studies of personal change.
In the early years of this century Emile Durkheim's sociology of
religion dealt with the social bases of the sacred and the profane: the
home and origin of the sacred was the 'effervescent', non-routine or
marginal phase of social life.[31] Arnold Van Gennep distinguished
three main phases or stages in rites of passage: rites of separation,
marginality (or liminality), and finally aggregation to a new condition,
or reaggregation to the old.[32] In more recent times Schutz's phenomenological approach to the sociology of knowledge has posited
multiple realities, with marginal realms or 'sub-universes of meaning'
surrounding, challenging and subverting the paramount reality of
everyday life.[33]

Three very popular contemporary writers draw respectively on these
distinctive sociological traditions to develop further the idea of
marginality: Mary Douglas draws heavily on Durkheim,[34] Victor
Turner on Van Gennep,[35] and Peter Berger on Schutz.[36] But they
are alike in emphasizing the potency and transfiguring properties of
marginality. Victor Turner and Mary Douglas draw on exotic anthropological data, but Peter Berger's highly dramatic view of marginality
— with its promise of terror and ecstasy — is based on observation of
ordinary, everyday life in the West.

Few would nowadays subscribe to the psychological notion of
'marginal man' as a distinctive personality type; but the marginal

position, which is ambiguous, not fully institutionalized, and removed from what most people would see as society's central institutions and values, has considerable utility.[37] The marginal situation can be defined subjectively (in the phenomenological perspective of Schutz) as people experience it from inside: it is change from a former position which was accepted as self-evident and normal, which was taken for granted, and presented itself as not in need of further analysis. Change to a marginal position brings into question three basic ingredients of reality: time, typicality, and preconstituted (recipe) knowledge. Marginal situations, at least when first encountered, make time, types and recipes problematical.

The former normal position was firmly anchored in time, like the 'proper' stage of life or career; but now temporality is disordered, or life is lived by a different timetable or clock. And in the marginal situation no-one fades into the background, anonymous, typical: events, relationships and people cannot be unreflectingly noted, absorbed and dismissed. And formerly trustworthy recipes which were reliably used for interpreting and manipulating the world no longer work. The marginal situation calls for new recipes, timetables and types; and they too may finally appear self-evident constituents of a congealed reality.

Seen objectively, from the outside, change from one position to another is far from abnormal: it is in fact a constant of social life; but some changes are of an unusual order of magnitude. Social positions stand close into, or further removed from, society's 'centre', which may be defined as Shils has defined it, in terms of values and power. [38] It is where most people — and according to Shils a growing number — spend most of their everyday adult lives. But marginal positions stand off to a degree that is discontinuously greater than the ones next in line. And at the centre of contemporary Western societies there is heterosexual marriage, secular employment in industrial-bureaucratic organizations, and good health.

For Peter Berger marginality is first and foremost a threat to man's primary socialization, and for Victor Turner and Mary Douglas it has comparable powers of transfiguration. It was their assertions regarding the potency of marginality in adult resocialization which prompted the studies reported in this book.

Thresholds symbolize the beginnings of new statuses, new ways of feeling and action; and in Western society the bridegroom traditionally carries his bride over the threshold of their new home. Mary Douglas and Victor Turner draw on a wealth of more exotic anthropological data to argue, after Van Gennep, the significance of liminality or the threshold state.

Mary Douglas draws heavily on her fieldwork with the Lele of Central Africa and illustrates the power, danger and essential ambiguity of marginality in the treatment of the pregnant woman and her unborn child: persons in a marginal state 'are people who are left out of the patterning, who are placeless ... their status is indefinable.' [39] (Mary Douglas also follows Durkheim in his view that concepts — of time, causality and space — are modelled on the shape, boundaries and margins of society, and develops the thesis of the symbolic replication of the social state.[40] This book alludes to his theory where appropriate, but does not claim to use it or to test it.)

Victor Turner draws on his fieldwork with the Ndembu tribe and illustrates the concept of marginality (or liminality) from the installation rites of their chiefs. The liminal or threshold state of the chief-elect is one of abasement, and yet it is one of danger and power: 'The attributes of liminality or of liminal *personae* ("threshold people") are necessarily ambiguous, since this condition and these people elude or slip through the network of classifications that normally locate states and positions in cultural space.'[41] But Turner agrees with Mary Douglas that liminality is charged with remarkable power: 'The powers that shape the neophytes in liminality for the incumbency of new status are felt, in rites all over the world, to be more than human powers, though they are invoked and channelled by representatives of the community.'[42]

The rites of passage that Van Gennep described were ritualized, with clearly defined and elaborate behaviour for everyone involved: they were means of control, of maintaining order in perilous conditions of transition, and of ensuring an entirely predictable outcome for the individual who had embarked upon the passage. But Victor Turner elaborates the stage of liminality as a semi-autonomous zone of social reality, and his account of it is very similar to Shutz's 'enclaves' of experience which are full of concrete, immediate, idiosyncratic encounters and devoid of 'typifications'.

For Turner liminality expands into what he calls 'communitas', an unstructured, counter state or phase of social existence: 'Essentially communitas is a relationship between concrete, historical, idiosyncratic individuals. These individuals are not segmented into roles and statuses, but confront one another rather in the manner of Martin Buber's "I and Thou".'[43] It is not a state of incompleteness or repression, but of liberation and fulfilment. 'Spontaneous communitas has something magical about it. Subjectively there is a feeling of endless power.'[44] Turner recognizes that in fact 'Communitas itself soon develops a structure':[45] even the reality of anti-structure becomes congealed. But above all, he claims, this unstructured side of social experience — and in our own times Turner instances such marginal groups as the hippie and digger communities of California — produces not segregation and belittlement, but a sense of oneness with humanity.

Peter Berger's conception of marginality is no less dramatic, but he arrives at it by a different route (through a phenomenological approach to the sociology of knowledge) and locates it in a more familiar, everyday world of assistant managers in ladies' underwear departments, and the like. But for Berger marginality is ecstasy — literally *ek-stasis*: standing outside the taken-for-grantedness of everyday life. Marginality is what surrounds the 'middle ground' of ordinary existence. To move into the margins is to experience ecstasy. It is also to experience terror. For '... all human societies and their institutions are, at root, a barrier against naked terror.'[46]

Margins are still related to the centre — they are not an utterly separate sphere; and Berger gives considerable attention to the 'overarching symbols' which bracket or embrace both marginal and central realms. 'What is particularly important, the marginal situations of the life of the individual (marginal, that is, in not being included in the reality of everyday existence in society) are also encompassed by the symbolic univers.'[47] This symbolic order enables the person in the marginal situation to regain a foothold in sanity which always, in Berger, seems to be slipping away. Marginality is conceived as crisis, and the 'purest' example is being confronted by death.

> But even when the world of everyday life retains its massive taken-for-granted reality *in actu*, it is threatened by the marginal situations of human experience that cannot be completely bracketed in everyday activity. There is always the haunting presence of metamorphoses, those actually remembered and those only sensed as sinister possibilities.[48]

Marginality of this melodramatic kind is a threat to the very primary socialization of men. A minor shift in the definition of reality would suffice for a man to go to the office without his tie; only a major shift would enable him to go in the nude.[49] But such major shifts are the very stuff of true marginality which is a powerful agency of resocialization. It is the source of counter realities and identities when it is experienced in sub-worlds in which it is possible 'to build for oneself a castle of the mind in which the day-to-day expectations of society can be almost completely ignored'.[50]

It is important to note that Berger makes no distinction between involuntary (and stigmatized) marginality, and marginality which is voluntary (and high status). The only basic requirement appears to be permanence. When 'counter individuals' such as cripples, lepers, bastards and idiots congregate in socially durable groups, there occurs 'a more complex distribution of knowledge', new societies are constructed on the basis of deviant and detached definitions of reality, and counter identities are born.[51]

In spite of the massiveness of the 'taken-for-granted', marginality appears to be omnipresent and powerful. There are rituals to assuage even while they represent the terror of the margins. But marginality is not simply terrifying; it is liberating and transforming:

> Both in practice and in theoretical thought, human life gains the greatest part of its richness from the capacity for ecstasy, by which I do not mean the alleged experiences of the mystic, but any experience of stepping outside the taken-for-granted reality of everyday life, any openness to the mystery that surrounds us on all sides.[52]

In Berger's writing socialization and marginality are quite explicitly linked within a historically specific social context. Berger's ideas of marginality and the 'openness' of personal identity even in full adult life are tied closely to the circumstances of complex modern industrial (and secularized) societies. The distinctive and relevant feature of such societies is their 'pluralism'. Earlier, more unified societies are contrasted with 'the plurality of life-worlds in which the individual typically lives in a modern society'.[53]

One of the basic and characteristic divisions in modern life is between the public and the private: private life seems to be seen by Berger as a form of marginality, a separate reality, a realm of discrepant meanings, in which traditional religion, plucked from the public sphere, and new and exotic cults may be found. It is in these 'interstitial areas', Berger suggests, that new and satisfying identities may be formed.

Modern societies are not mass societies, as an extensive sociological literature argued twenty years ago; they are marked by an extreme division of labour and diversity of life-styles and values. There are diverse systems of honour, and socialization stresses proficiency rather than commitment. It is in these conditions of modern pluralism, argued Berger, that personality even in adult life is susceptible to sudden and deep-seated change:

> Modern identity is peculiarly open ... Not only does there seem to be a great objective capacity for transformations of identity in later life, but there is also a subjective awareness and even readiness for such transformations. The modern individual is not only peculiarly 'conversion-prone'; he knows this and often glories in it. Biography is thus apprehended both as migration through different social worlds and as the successive realization of a number of possible identities. The individual is not only sophisticated about the worlds and identities of others but also about himself. This open-ended quality of modern identity engenders psychological strains and makes the individual particularly vulnerable to the shifting definitions of himself by others.[54]

It is the two key propositions embedded in this passage — that modern identity is ever poised for transformation, and that modern man is highly sensitive and responsive to the shifting definitions of himself by others — that the studies reported in this book are concerned to test.

An inquiry into the transformation of consciousness

The case studies reported in this book were undertaken as inquiries into the 'transformation of consciousness'. The aspects of consciousness which were selected as relevant to this study were principally those on which Peter Berger focuses our attention (especially in the book, *The Homeless Mind*). They are six in number: rationality, secularization, temporality and future-planning; the sharp separation between the public and the private, and a comprehensive stock of reliable recipe knowledge.[55]

The world which supports these aspects of consciousness is experienced as a normal and plausible world: within it the individual makes sense of his life in terms of rational, rule-regulated conduct of affairs; decisions taken with little reference to divine assistance; a life-plan which is constantly reviewed and revised; timetables which order and mark the steady and uniform progression of time; and established recipes which enable the usual routines of life to be lived with the minimum of conscious reflection; and a private world where he can 'really be himself'. These six aspects of consciousness are both the structure of plausibility and the source of modern identity.

They are subverted by marginality. Marginal situations were selected for this study because they were expected to subvert at least one of these props of modern consciousness. The blind and the disabled residents in a Cheshire Home were selected principally because it was envisaged that their former recipe knowledge would be useless and their structuring of time would become acutely problematical. Parsons and artists were chosen partly because they were not 'at home' in a secular, industrial and rational-bureaucratic society, but also because, in the daily conduct and organization of their lives, the distinction between public and private spheres seemed likely to be ill-defined, and their non-bureaucratic careers might change their ordering of time. The homosexuals were selected because their socio-sexual 'typifications' were likely to be shifting and ambiguous, and because in their own homosexual world social recipes which had worked on the 'outside' might have a more dubious utility. The two communes — the supreme manifestation of the contemporary demodernizing impulse — seemed likely to subvert all the six major components of modern identity. They were selected primarily because they clearly run counter to the modern secularized consciousness and (most explicitly in the case of 'Krishna Consciousness') were quite deliberately and systematically concerned to transform the consciousness of modern Western man.

The fieldwork (shared by the author and his two research assistants) was carried out in 1974 and 1975 through participant observation and extended, very lightly structured interviews. The (tape-recorded) interviews were usually carried out in the homes or institutions of the respondents and lasted for two or three hours. Interviewees were invited to talk about their lives, explaining what had led up to their present situation; to say in what ways their lives had changed, and what they felt they had lost or gained from the change. They were asked whether they now made distinctions of any kind which formerly they could not have made, or whether distinctions they had formerly made now seemed unimportant or invalid. They were asked whether the things they considered important had changed. Questions were directed towards social relationships and to their daily activities and routines. They were asked what they looked forward to and whether they felt in any way cut off from life. Replies were generally full and circumstantial; they were also very thoughtful, and great care was taken in disentangling changes in outlook and circumstances that might have occurred in any case, simply through growing older, from changes that could be directly attributed to moving into the 'marginal situation'.

Of course people may lie. Or they may elaborate their stories. And less deliberate distortions are equally possible. Anselm Strauss has written about the 'management' of personal histories, and points out that 'Each person's account of his life, as he writes or thinks about it, is a symbolic ordering of events'.[56] But aspects of a life will be ordered either by an external observer or the person who lives it, if it is to make sense. The rapport established with interviewees seemed sufficient assurance that they were not telling lies; and it was the whole point of making this study to re-order and interpret the ordering of life as it was presented by the subjects. The 'inside view' of respondents is given as extensively as possible; but the terms in which they told their stories, the categories they chose to talk about themselves, provided clues to their current self-conceptions and important changes that might have occurred. When a paralyzed man of fifty who had not worked for more than twenty years talked about himself as a truck driver, his choice of categories for describing himself seemed to indicate a real sense of continuity in personal identity. The interest then lay in accounting for such change or continuity: and the subject's social context and his relationships with immediate, 'significant others' were expected, in the light of neo-Meadian social psychology, to offer the key.

Conclusion

To go blind in adult life; to be stricken by multiple sclerosis and enter a Cheshire Home; to leave work in a mill to become an artist, or work as an engineer to become a priest; to accept that one is a homosexual; and to enter a commune of Eastern mystics — all are changes of considerable magnitude and even high drama. It seemed likely at the outset of this inquiry that all would provide evidence of major transformations of identity in adult life.

They did not. The evidence of these studies suggests that adults are capable of more fundamental change than many psychologists will admit; but that 'consciousness', 'identity' and 'the self' are far more resilient and resistant to change than important contemporary schools of sociology and social psychology will concede. We are not, in fact, chameleons.

But there are endless and obvious pitfalls in studying and talking about 'real change' and the 'essential self'. 'Real change' is a question not only of magnitude and direction, but of what it is precisely that is changing. It is possible to have significant change in behaviour without corresponding changes in values and meanings one gives to the world; and values and meanings may change although corresponding behavioural changes are impossible.

With all due caution, and in the light of all the evidence presented in this book, the author suggests that 'real change' from a former self occurred in five of the seven groups that were studied. The change was greatest and most dramatic in the case of the two communes and the homosexuals.

But significant change can occur less dramatically and suddenly, incrementally, by accretion, scarcely noticed, but steadily cumulative over many years;[57] the parsons especially, but also the artists, provided evidence of marked continuity in self-conceptions, and yet they 'really changed'.

The parsons had not experienced 'conversion' but had usually changed many of their priorities since they became parsons; and they had abandoned rational life-planning while listening for signals of transcendence (even though these often came to them through the machinery of the ecclesiastical bureaucracy). The artists in their intensely private worlds often stood on the brink of personal dissolution, and sometimes went over.

The blind and the residents of the Cheshire Home are remarkable for the persistence and continuity of their self-conceptions over many years and even decades of extreme and grievous 'marginality'. Finding new recipe knowledge does not necessarily sustain a new reality: it supports and even strengthens the old.

The studies also disabuse us of the simplistic view that some social psychologists hold that assuming new 'roles' means creating a new self.[58] All the people in this study had moved to a new status and a new role, but 'real selves' often remained latent though undimmed and available for recall. All new roles in modern life do not involve personal transformation: the post-parental stage of the life-cycle, which is a novelty of our times, clearly does not involve remaking oneself, but subsiding thankfully and comfortably into being one's 'real self' after twenty years of unremmitting child care.[59] 'Real selves' may be saved up and carefully maintained for forty years awaiting retirement — as in the case of one of the artists described in this book. Retirement is well worth a study as the phase or stage of life when 'real selves' are disinterred after fifty years of camouflage.

The 'consciousness' with which this book is concerned is a

relationship between the observing, knowing and reflecting self and the surrounding social world: it is the sense a man makes of his experience, the terms in which he defines himself and his circumstances. Consciousness changes when this relationship between self and social experience is reinterpreted and seen in a new light: when what was formerly taken for granted, unremarkable, scarcely visible, becomes obtrusive and problematical, when old and well-worn distinctions and categories lose their usefulness and new typifications and definitions are brought into play. These changes (it is claimed by contemporary subjective or idealist schools of sociology) are 'negotiated' as men creatively respond to the shifting circumstances and relationships of life: they try out and test their new ways of presenting themselves and accounting for what befalls them, and new 'negotiated realities' are accomplished as they enter into new inter-individual transactions and accommodations.

But new typifications and categories can be minimized and isolated, accommodated to old structures of meaning, leaving former definitions of the self and the world substantially intact. Of course some modification of consciousness occurs when a housewife goes blind and henceforth divides mankind into two basic categories: the sighted and the blind; and when a schoolmistress contracts multiple sclerosis, suffers extensive paralysis, and now typifies herself as 'just a nuisance'. But what is remarkable is the extent to which such modifications of consciousness can be contained: the blind housewife denies that her husband deserted her because of her blindness; and the paralyzed schoolmistress negotiates with her nurses that she is not 'just a nuisance' after all.

Even extreme marginality does not lead easily and automatically to the dissolution of an estbalished self and a fundamentally reconstructed reality. Intellectuals who are kidnapped by the army are in fact unlikely to become slobs, at least at the speed and with the inevitability that Berger imagines. Common sense suggests that people who find themselves in marginal and stigmatized situations against their will are likely to strive for 'normality', but that those who turn deliberately to a new life are more likely to change. This book supports this common sense conclusion.

But there are complications. 'Transformations of identity' are most apparent in three groups described in this book: the members of the Sufi and Hare Krishna communes and the homosexuals. While members of the communes have voluntarily embraced their marginality, voluntariness is a less clear-cut notion when applied to the homosexuals; and while members of the communes have no doubt that they are a spiritual elite, the homosexuals are deeply aware that they are still severely stigmatized people (and a prison record may be a less serious social disability). But unlike the other extremely marginal and stigmatized groups (the blind and the paralyzed), the homosexuals actively and creatively negotiated new selves and definitions of the world.

Psychologists' stage theories of personal development were briefly considered above, and a limited role suggested for them in accounting for transformations of identity. The response to marginality probably varies with age, and in particular the voluntary and semi-voluntary movement into marginal situations and interest in reformulating the relationship between self and society, may characterize developmental stages in early adult life. The Sufis, the Krishna devotees and the homosexuals who decided to accept their homosexuality were predominantly in their twenties. The possible explanatory value of stage theories of development is examined in the final chapter of this book.

2 | Orientations to the centre: passing and coming out

The idea of 'marginality' overlaps the ideas of 'subculture' and 'sect'; but it does not, like the latter, necessarily imply religious commitment; and it does not, like the former, necessarily imply shared values and an organized set of social meanings. But in their varying relationships to the 'centre' marginal positions, subcultures and sects pose similar problems of sociological analysis.

Peter Berger often uses the notion of marginality in a way that is indistinguishable from subculture. The marginal world of a leper colony may indeed develop subcultural characteristics, but it would be difficult to talk about a subculture of the blind. Nevertheless, the problem of the relationship of marginal position to 'centre' is similar to the problem of the relationship of subculture to culture and of sect to society. When does a subculture (for instance of blacks) become a social movement?[1] When does a revolutionary sect (like the Quakers) become 'introversionist'? When do marginal people who may have hitherto tried to 'pass' decide to 'come out'?

Sects have been classified according to their response to the world and a distinction drawn, for example, between introversionist, revolutionary and utopian sects.[2] This is not a ready-made classification to be applied to marginal positions, but varieties of marginality can be distinguished by the same criterion. A simple four-fold classification would distinguish between 'convergers', 'quietists', 'utopians' and 'separatists'.

The convergers play down, hide or deny any real difference between their position and the centre: thus the blind often tried to pass as sighted, and the parsons declared that they were 'ordinary folk' and tended to remove their dog-collars when they went out to enjoy themselves. The quietists (like the residents in the Cheshire Home and some homosexuals who had found congenial networks) accepted that they were in some way marked off from the centre but found a haven in their enclave of marginality. The utopians — like the Sufis, the Hare Krishna devotees and some political homosexuals — stood deliberately and even self-consciously outside normal society but hoped in some way to change it; but the separatists — the artists and the homosexuals who 'came out' simply asserted their distinctive (and superior) values and style of life. The homosexuals are to be found in all four categories and their varied response to the centre is a problem which will be examined in the conclusion of this book.

In this chapter different orientations to the centre will be illustrated from blind people who attempted to 'pass' and homosexuals who decided to 'come out'. The blind person who tries to pass is resisting resocialization and redefinitions of reality; the homosexual who decides to come out has accepted and proclaimed a new self. The interest from the point of view of socialization theory is the extent to which maintaining one's former identity or finding a new one was dependent on the support and perhaps the collusion of 'significant others' in one's immediate, contemporary world.

Sociologists have paid much more attention to passing than refusing to pass (even when this would be quite easy). The strategies of passing have been examined in studies of deviance, although the subjective side of passsing — holding firm to mainstream definitions of reality — has been discussed (for instance by Berger) in the context of the 'microsociology of knowledge'. In the former perspective passing is essentially a matter of 'information management' (that is, lying or masquerade) by persons labouring under some form of stigma; in the latter perspective it is the 'processing of reality' through conversation with supportive family members or friends.

The stigmatized person who is passing must live with great deliberation. 'What are unthinking routines for normals can become management problems for the discreditable.'[3] Passing may involve a skilful and selective reconstruction of one's personal biography — as Garfinkel illustrates in his account of 'Agnes', a boy who underwent a sex-change operation and successfully conveyed a continuous female identity. Even before her operation she had functioned as a girl and had even had a boyfriend. Her female identity required constant and careful management: 'Her claims (to normal femininity) had to be bolstered and managed by shrewdness, deliberateness, skill, learning, reflectiveness, test, review, feedback, and the like.'[4] Agnes developed 'management devices' such as suppressing specific information by talking in generalities.

Information may need to be strategically distributed. A person may pass in all areas of life, his secret being known only to himself; but more commonly he enlists the aid of close associates. Passing tends to be conspiratorial.

> A very widely employed strategy of the discreditable person is to handle his risks by dividing the world into a large group to whom he tells nothing, and a small group to whom he tells all and upon whose help he then relies; he co-opts for his masquerade just those individuals who would ordinarily constitute the greatest danger.[5]

It is not only practical help in social encounters that he requires of them, but confirmation in his sense of social reality, and reassurance that he is 'really' normal.

Goffman has suggested that there may be a 'natural cycle' of passing. Of course the extent of passing can vary, from temporary and partial to continuous and total. But there may be a progression of stages, from unintended passing ('that the surprised passer learns about in mid-passage'), through passing in non-routine activities, such as vacations, to passing in daily routine activities, such as work, and finally 'disappearance' — complete passing in all areas of life.[6] But throughout his discussion of passing, Goffman makes the assumption that it is something carried out before others. This chapter will first illustrate from one of the interviews precisely this process; but it will then describe a striking instance of passing before oneself.

Passing before others

Mrs Johnson was interviewed for two hours in her council house home on a large housing estate in 1975. She was then forty-one years of age and had been blind for twenty-five years. During that time she had married, had three children, and had been deserted by her husband ('but not', she insisted, 'because of my blindness'). Her closest relationship was with her neighbour, Mabel, a sighted woman of about the same age, but also deserted by her husband. Mabel is a crucial conspirator in Mrs Johnson's resolve to pass before others as normal. Mrs Johnson is poor and primly respectable. A major part of the problem of passing for normal is to keep up appearances, to achieve levels of material well-being customary in her neighbourhood.

She is bitter and has a strong sense of deprivation, but appears to have struggled for 'success' without faltering for twenty-five years. She now hopes for success through her children, and is uneasily aware that she is placing them under undue pressure. Her major attempt to pass as normal was through dancing in a public dance-hall. Her world collapsed when she discovered, inadvertently, that everyone knew she was blind.

Mrs Johnson showed the interviewer into her sitting room, where her small son was playing. She explained that he could not go to school at present because she was waiting for some money to buy him some shoes. The room was tidy, but the furniture was badly worn. There was a large television set in one corner and an ironing-board in another. She talked about her personal circumstances: her three children, her inadquate husband, her retraining prospects and problems. She spoke in a careworn voice and had a rather harrassed air. She seemed to be asking the interviewer to make decisions for her: should she retrain as a telephonist? It would mean uprooting the family for three months. She smoked heavily.

Interviewer: *How has going blind affected you?*

My early education was fouled up, because of the war. I was evacuated when I was five, and I was pushed from pillar to post in about seven different homes. I wanted to improve myself and went to night-school when I was fifteen. But my sight was beginning to fail. I wanted to learn French, but it was impossible. I couldn't read the text-books. So I just had to plod on and do ordinary jobs. I couldn't do anything to improve myself because there was nobody there to help or guide me. I haven't been able to read since I was sixteen. So I've always had to do jobs like nurse's aid — nothing needing reading and writing.

My blindness was caused by a disease. They don't know the cause of it. It's not hereditary, thank God. The children haven't got it. But it's given me an awful complex all my life. I'm still fighting it, because I will insist on competing with sighted people.

Did your interests change after you went blind?

The thing that embittered me was that I couldn't read. I did love reading. And more and more I turned to music. Because I can't read I've become attached more to things to do with sound. And my sense of touch ... I mean, you should see me on a dance floor. I would have liked to do amateur acting because I was good at it, but

I couldn't do that, so I took up dancing, the next-best form of self expression.

But it's made me very bitter that I can't read. Perhaps I wouldn't have raised myself up much, even if I'd kept my sight, but I would have liked to go further in life than just doing menial jobs. I had to be glad that I could work at all, really. I'm now being recommended for training as a telephonist, in London, but I say to myself, 'Who the hell wants a forty-five-year-old telephonist?' I couldn't do the training for a year or two, when the children are old enough to leave. Perhaps I'm over-protective with them...

Have your ideas about people changed?

Yes. I'm bitter there, too, Mabel says that if I don't get things into perspective, I'll crumble. Some people ignore you altogether. You can't keep up with the Joneses, and they know this. And they look at the house — I know it's tidy and everything, but just look at the carpet. Other people can replace things, they work to improve their standards of living, but I can't. Mind you, we're not neglected. The children are well fed. Of course, I smoke. If I didn't, that would save something. I was supposed to be trying to give up, this week actually. That is as far as I've got — making the decision that I'm going to try.

I value reading more now that I can't read. That's why I spend so much time getting it into these children that their best friend is a book. I'm a bit of a fanatic about it. I think that because you're a failure you put your children under a lot of pressure to make them a success. They're under too much pressure from me, really, because I want them to be what I can't be. It's wrong, I suppose, but I can't help it. It comes out in what the children say. My son Herbert will tell me that he's passed such a boy at school, because he knows that that's what I want. I know it's wrong to make them so competitive, I know I'm doing it...

I'm very conscious that I can't afford to buy things for the house. Like when Jane brings her friends home, I'm conscious the carpet's worn away. I feel it for them then, you know. I suppose I'm over-sensitive. Perhaps that's what blindness does to you. My friend Mabel advises me to try living from day to day. It's a good policy if you can do it, but I can't. I can't help getting emotional about things. We've both been let down by bad husbands, so we're able to understand each other's problems.

Mabel is vital to Mrs Johnson in constructing and sustaining a sense of reality. She has the role which husbands commonly take in maintaining what Berger and Kellner have called the 'maritally-based sub-world' from which the outer world is perceived, interpreted and processed through the marital conversational apparatus:

> Each partner ongoingly contributes his conceptions of reality, which are then 'talked through', usually not once but many times, and in the process become objectivated by the conversational apparatus. The longer this conversation goes on, the more massively real do the objectivations become to the partners. In the marital conversation a world is not only built, but it is also kept in a state of repair and ongoingly refurnished. [7]

Mrs Johnson 'battles' with Mabel over the processing and interpretation of experience and her collusion in her passing as sighted. They wrestle for an agreed version of their world and for Mrs Johnson's precarious hold on her sense of normality:

> Even now I'm battling with my friend Mabel, across the road. She says, 'You're the same as me. For God's sake stop saying you're not. You come out with me and everyone accepts you as the same.' But I say, 'How can I be the same? There is a difference. Some people show fear of you when they know there's something wrong. Other people show too much pity. It's very difficult.' But Mabel says, 'It's you — you've got this complex'. I've always had this terrible complex about it. Some people drop you altogether when they know there's something wrong. Some people pay you too much attention and say, 'Oh, you poor thing' — that kind of approach.
>
> We used to go dancing with some friends. We'd sit with the same people every week. They're elderly people, mainly. It's very respectable. It's not a fly-by-night place, don't get me wrong. And then one night an elderly man came over to me and said: 'How are you, young lady? How are those eyes?' — in such a sympathetic way. And I just wanted to get up and go straight home. I know it's silly, because the man was being kind. But I thought I was escaping, and nobody could tell, you see, and I was brought right down to earth, that people did know. I just try to pass myself off as the same as anyone else, but they won't let me: I didn't think anybody knew, but apparently they all did. It's me trying to put my head in the sand. I suppose it's wrong to try to pass myself off. And Mabel keeps saying to me, 'You must stop this. If people can't accept you

for what you are they're not worth knowing.' But I shan't go dancing at that place again.

Passing before oneself

Mrs Johnson passed before others who unwittingly or conspiratorially accepted her definition of herself. Mrs Allen, who is described below, is remarkable in that for thirty years she passed before herself.

There is considerable pressure on the blind of both a formal and informal kind to redefine themselves and accept a marginal role. The blind described in this book have all been officially registered as blind: they are persons to whom a deviant label has been successfully and officially attached. What is remarkable is the extent to which they resist the label, although they are aware that the sighted ascribe to them a generalized incapacity and it would be very easy for them to play up to a 'sick man' role.

Lemert has questioned the more extreme formulations of 'labelling theory' and has opposed to it the notion of the 'countervailing self': 'In more extreme labelling theory the process of becoming deviant appears inelectable; deviants lose individuality and become like empty organisms who are successfully labelled by others.' Drawing on the evidence of Goffman's work (in *Stigma*), Lemert points out that there are wide variations in response by individual deviants, and refers to the countervailing self 'who is resigned to deviant status ascription but seeks to nullify or mitigate its impact through information control and reduction of the visability of deviance. The resulting interaction takes on qualities of a contest or game'.[8] Lemert's new term doesn't actually explain anything, but it helps to point up the inadequacy of labelling theory in its grosser forms[9] and the pitfalls of sociologistic determinism.

Both Goffman and Berger make the individual unreal and unsubstantial outside his immediate, face-to-face social relationships. Reality and personal identity are agreement, even collusion, with others directly and currently known. Goffman examined the structure of social encounters in dramaturgical terms, conceiving the individual's social behaviour as a 'performance' enacted in the immediate, physical presence of others, 'the audience'.[10] The performer needs the audience to confirm his definition of the situation, to enter into a 'real agreement', or at least a 'working consensus'.

Older interactionist theories of socialization gave greater emphasis to the enduring influence of early 'internalization'.[11] G.H. Mead saw the self (as formed in early childhood) as itself constituting a social system, in which 'I' constantly interacted with 'me'. Mead realized that the 'me' in his system was virtually the same as Freud's superego or 'censor' in its genesis and constitution,[12] and might show a similar persistence. The 'I' was the impulsive self but the 'me' was the generalized other which kept the 'I' under control. 'Me' was a critical audience before which 'I' performed and acquitted itself.

Mrs Allen is sixty years of age and has lived a desperately lonely life in a well-to-do middle-class neighbourhood since she went blind twenty-seven years ago. She has a husband and one (mentally retarded) son, but she has little social contact with her wider family who live at a distance, and none with her neighbours. She has little contact with the Blind Centre and feels an outsider there because, she says, the regulars are in any case partially sighted. But she has sustained over nearly three decades an intense ambition and has to her credit formidable cultural, musical and academic attainments. She appears to have no 'reinforcement' from any face-to-face contacts, she is playing to no immediate, contemporary audience. Her intense will to achieve shows no sign of weakening. She is now learning Greek. For thirty years she has resolutely passed before herself. In a four-hour interview she typically passed before someone else.

Mrs Allen opened the door of her semi-detached house and led the interviewer down a dark hallway into an expensively furnished but drab sitting room. She was a small, neat person, young-looking for her age, wearing dark glasses and an incongruous ginger wig. She smoked occasionally, experiencing some difficulty lighting her cigarettes, but refusing help. She kept saying how much it meant to her to have someone call.

> I wanted to train as a singer when I was young, but my father died. Ironically, I became an optician. But recently I've taken up singing again, and I've now done a recording for the BBC. I've been interviewed on the radio.
>
> I'm now starting on another new venture. I took English Literature last year. I had to do it orally. I can read braille but I can't write it. That doesn't bother me because I don't know any blind people, so there's no point in it. I can touch-type fairly well. Anyway, I got a huge write-up in the paper when I passed my exam, because half the students failed. I was the only blind student and I passed. So now I'm turning to the Classics and learning Greek.

Are you completely blind?

Yes. A bit or residual vision would make all the difference. I have absolutely no mobility. Oh, it is difficult. But I do all my own work. I have no help whatsoever, but I'm absolutely hopeless at mobility.

Can you remember what effect it had on you, going blind?

I have found that people have tended to avoid me. That hurts me very much. I think it's a form of embarrassment — that's all I can put it down to. I was blind when I came here so of course I couldn't recognize people in the street. But I knew the person who moved in next door before I went blind. She used to work in a shop that I went to. When I knew she was moving in I thought it would be splendid. But the only time she's ever approached me was when we had a burglary and she knocked at the door to get to know the details. And she said to my husband, 'Is Alice quite blind? Oh, I am a rotten neighbour. I will come in. She must be terribly lonely.' Believe me, no-one ever comes in here, ever. No-one. Because I've no relations living here. All my relations and old friends live in Blackburn. Well, she said she'd come in, but that is six years ago. She's never been near. She'll speak to my husband and to my son, but never to me. And it hurts terribly. And I can't understand why. I wouldn't ask her to do anything. I wouldn't ask anyone. I'd rather die than do that.

Once when I hung out the washing in the garden I got lost. I just couldn't find my way back, and I was crawling on my hands and knees round and round the garden. People were outside, I could hear them talking. And do you know, there wasn't one asked if they could help me. They must have seen me. Things like that I've got to put up with. When I'm out with my husband he'll say, 'There's Mrs So-and-So, I bet she crosses the road before she reaches us'. And, you know, he's right. All this hurts me so much, but I know that nothing and nobody will be able to alter it. It's like animals — if there's one different, the others will shun them and tear them to pieces. I think if someone's deaf, they're tolerated more. You can catch their eyes, you see ...

I've been along to the Blind Centre, but only twice. The people there are nearly all partially sighted, and they run the place, and a blind person is just frozen out. They will not admit you to the circle. The only thing I can find to give me satisfaction is to set out to do something and achieve it. That is the pleasure that I get out of life.

English Literature was very difficult because you have to keep so many quotations in your mind. Greek will be more difficult, because I'll have lots of proper nouns to spell out. But I like an end in view. There must be an achievement at the end of it, I think, because it isn't as though I'm in companionship with anyone else. I'm working alone all the time.

You have spoken on other people's attitudes. Have your own attitudes changed?

Yes. I'm afraid it's made me very bitter. I never was a strong church-goer, I'm not saying that I was. But it's altered that, too. I don't know whether I'm an agnostic or even further along the road. I'm beginning to compare Christianity with the religion of Homer. It's no better. I put Christianity on a par with Homer's gods. The gods come down from Olympus and they have their favourite mortals, and they help whichever mortal they favour ... and they call upon the immortals to help them if they're under stress or pressure, if they want anything ... And of course in Greek tragedy it's all Fate. Fate is destiny ... I worry a lot about the future because I haven't a single soul to whom I can turn. I have a son, but unfortunately he's not very bright...

One thing I treasure is that I have an excellent memory, and that helps me. It's funny, but when I first went blind, I used to dream ordinarily, but all at once I found that everything was dark in my dreams. And then it changed again: instead of dreaming in ordinary colour it was in poster colour. And all the most unlikely things happened. Everything was larger than life, and more brilliant. It was all an absolute contrast. That went on for a few weeks, and then there was nothing. It didn't come back any more. I still dream, but it's all in darkness. I often dream of being in a room and I just can't find an exit. I'm all tangled up in it...

I no longer form visual images of people. I get an image of their character. I can tell very quickly whether I'm going to like a person. I make a quick decision. It isn't often I have any reason to change my mind. I can tell whether a person's sensitive or not, perhaps because I'm supersensitive myself.

Another thing I don't like comedy. That's why I like the examination syllabus — I can avoid Aristophanes. I like all tragedies, and that's something that's developed. I don't know why it is. If I find anything funny, it's got to be dry humour, very ironic. That's why Oedipus is my favourite play — because it's sheer dramatic irony all through.

The one thing that beats me is going out. I have this sensation of movement all the time — it's as though I'm sitting in a car. And I can't move in a straight line, because it's only moving on one side. It's all a series of shades of grey, moving across my field of vision. It's like being in a thick white fog most of the time.

Coming out

Both Mrs Johnson and Mrs Allen were 'convergers' in terms of our four-fold typology of marginality. They continued to define themselves as normal in spite of their grievous disabilities. Some of the homosexuals were at the opposite pole in their orientation to the 'centre': they were 'separatists' and even 'utopians'. Far from attempting to 'pass', they had decided to 'come out'.

In refusing to pass as normal or 'straight', even when they might easily do so, stigmatized people re-align their loyalties and proclaim separate systems of honour. Changes in the law and organized, militant movements may help them to take their defiant stand, but at the microsociological level of analysis their refusal to pass can be interpreted (in Lemert's term) as 'secondary deviation'. It may be a solution to some of the deepest personal problems of marginality.

By secondary deviation Lemert refers to the organization of life around deviant characteristics such as physical defects and incapability, prostitution, and mental disorder. The stigma is not covered up but exposed and even magnified. 'Whereas Goffman addresses himself to the question of how persons manage stigma and mitigate its consequences, secondary deviation concerns processes which create, maintain, or intensify stigma.'[13]

Life is built around the stigma, and the moral problems of stigmatization 'become central facts of existence for those experiencing them, altering physical structure, producing specialized organization of social roles and self-regarding attitudes. Actions which have these roles and self attitudes as their referents make up secondary deviance.'[13]

But once more Lemert has usefully labelled a form of social behaviour without explaining it. Secondary deviance may be rewarded:

Thus becoming an admitted homosexual ('coming out') may endanger one's livelihood or his professional career, but it also absolves the individual from failure to assume the heavy responsibilities of marriage and parenthood, and it is a ready way of fending off painful involvements in heterosexual affairs.[14]

Lemert is not in fact satisfied with such simple arguments from rewards, or even more sophisticated learning theories. He falls back on 'identity-crises' and suggests that: 'In a general way it can be shown that modern mass society is characterized by a shrinking inventory of life situations in which identities can be stabilized.'[15] This curious argument — that modern societies have so little privacy and complexity that homosexuals and other 'deviants' are virtually forced onto the public stage — is only possible in terms of a naive 'mass society' theory which flies in the face of all the evidence. Berger more reasonably argues precisely the opposite: that we are a plural and not a mass society, and for this very reason modern man is afflicted by a permanent crisis of identity:[16] he is spoilt for choice by the bewildering range of pockets of alternative reality in which to hide.

The organizer of a regional branch of the Campaign for Homosexual Equality (CHE) — a woman graduate social science research student in her mid twenties — is fully aware of the ambiguities of 'coming out' and the difference between marginality which is secluded and cosy, and marginality which presses on the boundaries of society and modifies its shape and contours. Her aim is to promote the latter. She recognizes — and indeed insists — that the refusal to pass is not only a personal, but a political, act.

When she was interviewed in 1975 she explained the origins of CHE in the wake of the 1967 Law Reform Act, its growth in numbers and militancy while Gay Lib Front had declined. GLF was narrow and elitist and so 'cut off from the vast majority of gay people who hadn't reached that stage of liberation or acceptance of their sexuality'. But CHE had developed from a highly circumspect middle-class movement into a militant association whose members — and notably the women — dared to 'come out'.

CHE does for homosexuals what the Court formerly did for debutantes: it presents them to the world, announces their availability, and affirms their status.

> We've started what we call an 'Activist Register', a register of gay people who've come out, with the things that they're involved in. And they're going to spearhead CHE's political activities. We've circulated groups for people who'll go on to the register. It will be available to anyone who wants to get in contact with gay people. It will go to newspapers, *Gay News*, television companies, local radio ... Over half the people on the register are gay women. When you consider that only fifteen per cent of CHE's members are

women ... it isn't because they're involved in Women's Lib. There are very few women in CHE who are involved in Women's Lib.

She is aware that 'coming out' can have many meanings:

It's a descriptive term, for a start. A lot of people simply mean that they're meeting other gay people. But the way we use it, it's a very specific phenomenon where you just stop pretending and lying about your sexuality, and you just declare yourself as gay every time it's a suitable thing to do. And you don't, sort of, not say things. You are just totally open and honest about it. I don't mean gratuitously stopping people in the street, but I do mean wearing a badge. But certainly if you were going for a job, say, and they asked you if you were going to get married, you would say, 'No, I'm homosexual', rather than say, 'No, I don't believe in marriage'.

Complete coming out is a form of honour: 'You stop being frightened and become proud'. It is inevitably a political act:

Some people just stick and say, 'I've got what I want — other gay people'. But it isn't enough to stick with your own little group. I don't see why we shouldn't be able to walk down the street, or tell people, or come out at work. If you haven't any political awareness you get into a situation which is very comfortable; you know if you want to meet other gay people, you know where to go, and so on. So it's no longer an issue with you. Many people who have contact with a group go that way, they develop their own little circle, and that's that. There is really no such thing as 'adjustment' for homosexuals — only change, total change for society. That's the ultimate adjustment. I would say, to smash society ... The aim of CHE is not to choose between political action and self-liberation, but to combine the two. They're really inseparable.

Refusing to come out is furtive, dishonouring and degrading:

They go to the clubs. They're frightened or hung-up about being gay. They're only gay on two or three evenings a week — Friday night, Saturday night and Sunday morning, and the rest of the time they wouldn't talk to each other if they met in the street. And it's a very sexually competitive atmosphere, because if you're only going to be homosexual two nights a week, you don't have time for friendship or love. All you have time for is sex.

But coming out is not without penalties:

When they know a woman is gay, they assume she is so ugly that she can't get any sort of man. Of course we have publicized our organization and our phone number, and we get literally hundreds of phone calls from heterosexual men saying, 'Here I am, I've got a cock. You can stop being gay now.' And they get very angry indeed when you say, 'I'm sorry, I'm not interested'. They think that all they've got to do is pick up a phone and say they're a man and you'll jump at them. They say, 'Oh, come on, having sex with a man is the real McCoy', and you say, 'I've had sex with men, and it isn't. It's much better with a woman.' They get very angry. Had lots of murder threats. They tell you in graphic detail how they're going to stick a knife up you and up you right up the front. And I quite often say, 'I think you're a very sick man, and I can refer you to a good psychiatrist'.

There are also unanticipated consequences:

We've been finding for the past year that we've become a sexual counselling services. Not just for homosexuals, but for anyone who has any sort of sexual hang-up. Apart from the obscene phone calls we have all sorts of people ringing up because they have nowhere else to turn — girls who want abortions, girls having trouble with their parents, boys who don't know how to have sex with women, and so on. I spoke to a guy for an hour-and-a-half who's a knicker fetishist. Who else? People who just don't function sexually in the way that society says they should. They see our posters. They have nowhere to go for help, no-one to talk to.

Her own personal problems of 'coming out' have not been painless. At the end of the two-hour interview she said:

I'm going to make some more coffee. I'm feeling a bit shattered today. I went to see my parents up in Newcastle and I came back unexpectedly because I got thrown out. They've known for about three years that I'm gay, but they've never talked about it before. They sort of said, 'Ssh, the neighbours' or 'Yes, dear'. But I forced them to talk about it, and they forbade me to tell anyone at all that I'm gay, but it's a bit late, really, because there aren't many people who don't know. And they say, 'You've been on television', and 'Oh, the newspapers'. And they said I was not to bring anyone that I was having an affair with or that I loved or was living with to their home. And yet my sister-in-law goes there with my brother and they hate her guts. But that's all right, you see. So I said if I couldn't

take people I wouldn't go, and they said, 'Right, never darken our
door again'. I said, 'Fine'. And having driven four hundred miles
in one direction I walked out and drove four hundred miles in
the other.

New forms of honour call for courage and tenacity as well as political
organization.

In the moral career of one homosexual interviewee refusing to pass
was certainly a way of extricating himself from social and sexual
demands which he felt incapable of meeting — it was a reward
precisely as Lemert has argued. It was also the discovering of personal
integrity. But it was not simply the solution of a personal problem: it
was in the true sense a political act, a contribution to a social
movement.

Harry is in his late twenties, a Cambridge graduate now a social
worker in London. He joined the interviewer in a bar, as arranged. He
was rather conspicuous. His hair was long and untidy, his ear-ring and
his rings made him look rather like a gypsy. He was wearing faded
blue jeans, a mauve T-shirt, and a beige linen jacket with a 'gay love'
badge sewn on. He was carrying a rucksack and some newspapers —
the *Guardian*, *Gay News* and other underground magazines. He went
with the interviewer to continue the interview in a quiet room.

He sketched in his background and gave an account of his
education, his long years of latency, self-discovery, covering up, and
the falsity of passing:

I was born in a small village in the north-east of England. My father
was a surveyor — he's retired now. He was very heavily working-
class — left school when he was thirteen. My mother was very
heavily middle-class — left school when she was eighteen and
married at nineteen. I'm their third child, at the very end of their
child-bearing years.

I went to the local C. of E. primary school, then to the grammar
school and got an exhibition to Cambridge. After I took my degree
I went to India for eighteen months, then back to Cambridge to
train for social work. I've been a social worker for a year.

I became a Catholic at Cambridge, when I was twenty. Most of
the things that have happened to me, I would say, are the result of
my sexuality. A very large percentage of Catholic converts are gay —
that's something that you notice, and of course a large number of
High Churchmen also.

Do you want to know why I did that? You see Catholicism has a very coherent way of condemning something that you feel guilty about, something that you're told is very wicked and sick and abnormal. I was never in contact with any liberal middle-class people. They just didn't exist in my northern village. Folk there reacted to homosexuality either with sniggers or moral outrage; but it was so appalling you didn't talk about it. It was so sick and twisted you never wanted to meet one. So what I did in those days was to believe heavily in the idea that gay guys were sick, middle-aged men in shabby, gabardine macs flashing down to the local 'cottage' (public lavatory). And I thought it was a terrible fate and I must do everything I could not to succumb to it.

Catholicism provides the only respectable alternative to marriage in this country, and to that extent I still have a sneaking admiration for the Catholic Church in that priests are social drop-outs. My parents had a terrible hang-up about Catholic priests because they're celibate. As a priest you can escape from being married and disguise your homosexuality.

But first I became High Church. I went to a very High Church college at Cambridge, and it was quite noticeable that the chapel crowd were homosexuals. I became scared to death, because the whole of my life was bent towards cloaking this and denying it to myself. So I began to find it intolerable to be an Anglo-Catholic, because it tarred you with the suspicion of being a homosexual, which was the one thing I was most at pains to avoid.

So I became a Catholic, after my first term at Cambridge. I got a great kick out of being one, because the Catholic Church is so socially diverse: you get almost as many men as women, younger, basically working-class Irishmen, Spanish waiters, God knows who — the whole social mix. And it was nice to feel normal, and to feel that you're told to go to confession, have to do it reluctantly, rather than the pious Anglican begging the priest to hear your confession.

I believed very heavily and thought that I'd changed, that I had wanted to be heterosexual all the time. And I used to inflame any possible interest I had in women, and lie out of all proportion to myself. And then I met a girl who was almost attractive to me and I fell in love and lived with her for nearly two years. I was within four weeks of marrying her when I finally jacked out.

For the first two years it was me pretending to myself that everything was all right. I didn't want particularly sexual pleasure for myself — just to be able to make it often enough to keep her happy.

It sounds dreadful but it's true. But from my earliest years I had split off romantic love which I felt for women, from simple sex which I wanted with men. It was really a very sick split in me. I think it happens with heterosexual women, too: they have romantic fantasies which are very innocent and lacking in sexual content. Women's magazines exploit this. It's a corrupt and degrading thing. The sort of pornography I would not allow to be distributed are *Women's Own*, *Marilyn* and *Date*, the ones that pretend that romantic love has nothing to do with fucking.

I hadn't the courage, while I was with Jane, to go to the 'cottages' or gay bars — I was too scared. But more and more I would put myself in a position where maybe ... I knew I'd be powerless to resist if ever a man did approach me, I'd be so overwhelmed. As I say, I was putting myself more and more in a situation where I was sort of looking at beautiful guys and following them around.

When it happened, 'coming out' had the suddenness, the beauty and the drama of revelation:

Then the miracle happened. I was shopping for the evening meal — nice little domestic set-up that we had in the suburbs — and this very beautiful Spanish boy, about twenty — I bought my groceries and wandered off to the butchers and there he was again. And I began to think, 'Oh, my God', and when I went to the tobacconist's, there he was again! I could barely stand, and I thought I would never dare to do such a thing — I didn't know how gays behaved — I knew nothing about 'cruising' or 'cottaging'. I just offered him a cigarette without thinking about it. And we started to speak French, which made it that much easier because it wasn't so direct. And then ... he invited me back to his room and we sat there talking, and I didn't dare do anything because I didn't believe he was anything than just a friendly student. In any case I'd always assumed that gays were ugly — basically that it was because you can't get women that you're gay. Yet here was this handsome young Spaniard, small, stocky and hairy, and also highly intelligent and very funny — and completely amoral. He would shoplift, and was often drugged up to the eyeballs. He just didn't conform in any way to my ideas of what a gay was.

The sex we had together was totally delerious. And it was proper sex, screwing, not like the pathetic wanking experience I'd had in the backs of cars that I felt guilty about. That night I stopped believing in God. Anyone who tries to tell you that religious belief and sexual guilt aren't linked — I know from that that they are. I carried on being a heavy Catholic for quite a long time, but I didn't really believe it all.

Well, that's one thing that happened. The other was that I was happy for the first time in my life. I was extremely, deleriously happy, and I couldn't wait to try it again. That was the beginning of my coming out. It was a dramatic thing. And so I told Jane who I was engaged to — that was the first time I'd admitted to myself that this is what I was, and it was nice. It was really a 'Road to Damascus' thing...

But the new reality had to be negotiated with people important in his life: they had to accept and support it. First he had to negotiate his new reality with his fiancée, then with his close friends, and finally his parents. He was defying the 'straight' world but he needed allies within it. His allies in passing were traitors:

Jane and I went to France two days later, and I told her I was gay — I was drunk on Chablis. But obviously a lot of my emotional invest-ment was in her still, and I said we'd work against it. We had the most anguished year after that, when I started to come home late, a year of terrible lying and deception when I tried to pick men up — and failing because people only came out after ten o'clock and of course I had to be home by then. I lived with her and slept with her and there was no way really of not accounting for my movements. We had terrible scenes and I told her our sex life wouldn't be much good, and she'd say it didn't matter. Then I'd say that maybe there'd be no sex at all. And she still said it wouldn't matter. I said I'd go after men, and she still said it didn't matter.

So we arranged the wedding. And it was within four weeks of the wedding that I said, 'No, I just can't. I simply don't want to marry you.' It was a dreadful thing to do to anyone, but what did it was all those people who'd colluded with me in trying to fight what I was — all the priests, and the whole unspoken thing that if you're gay you really ought to be dead.

The shame that I had when I 'came out' was in telling my friends, who thought they knew me. They didn't know me at all. And so what a lying relationship it had been. I'd posed as the arch-hetero, always randying around, preserved by my Catholicism from actually having to screw women. But suddenly to be known for yourself — it's the most exciting thing you can imagine.

My parents were devastated. I know my parents love me, I've

never doubted that. And it's one of the most important things anyone can have in life. So I knew that if I went home and said I was a child strangler, they'd still love me. Now to them, being gay was about of that order, it was about as bad. They were very upset, and reacted with all the wrong things, like sympathy. My father was hurt and told me to get out, but I knew he'd do that for a bit. I went out, came back, pinned him against the wall and told him everything about myself, all the things one never talks about with parents, about sex and guilt and wanking and going to confession.

In the course of all this some skeletons came out of their own cupboard. And then came this totally honest relationship — very exciting for all of us. And finally they've come to accept it. They've met two of my boyfriends and thought they were very nice indeed. Only three weeks ago my father was bringing tea up on a tray to William and me in bed. My parents have accepted it because they've had their stereotypes destroyed by me presenting them with gays. And yet each time they say, 'Is he really like that? He can't be like that', because I suppose he's not a mincing fairy or whatever.

It did something for my parents. I was tempted not to tell them about myself because it would hurt them. But it would have been a very unloving gesture because it would have meant that the focus of my life would be something they knew nothing about. And they would have been denied the choice, if I'd not told them, of knowing me. This period has got to be worked out: you've got to go through a period where finally it becomes very boring to say I'm gay and you're straight, and then you can continue to have a relationship.

But whether you like it or not, you're in the public eye. For instance, when William went to America, I kissed him at the airport for about half a minute in front to two policemen. I was really sad that he was going away and wanted to kiss him, but inevitably it was a defiant political gesture as well. Or every time we hold hands walking down the street — you're conscious that you're striking a blow for Gay Lib. And that can spoil it, but there's no way out of it. Even carrying *Gay News* — if I hide it inside my newspaper I think, 'God, I'm being timid', and yet if I display it openly, I think, 'God, I'm flaunting it'. So I don't know where to put it. That's something I haven't resolved, though I suppose I err on the side of extremism. I suppose I quite enjoy that.

Conclusion

This chapter has dealt with 'convergers' on the one hand, and 'separatists' (and 'utopians') on the other — two sharply contrasted orientations to society's centre. It poses two related problems: the importance or otherwise of immediate 'audiences' for a sense of identity, resocialization and the reconstruction of reality; and the circumstances under which stigmatized people who might quite easily pass as normal or 'straight' refuse to do so. These two issues are closely related: re-orientation to society's centre and resocialization are two sides of one coin.

Mrs Johnson was sustained by immediate others, but Mrs Allen was able to sustain a strong sense of identity with very little direct external support. The decision of homosexuals to come out enlisted the support of others only after it had been made.

It seems likely that Berger's contention that 'every identity requires specific social affiliation for its survival' may need some revision. Berger's argument is emphatic:

> One cannot be human all by oneself and, apparently, one cannot hold on to any particular identity all by oneself ... For example, a man turned overnight from a free citizen into a convict finds himself subjected at once to a massive assault on his previous conception of himself. He may try desperately to hold on to the latter, but in the absence of others in his immediate environment confirming his old identity he will find it almost impossible to maintain it within his own consciousness. With frightening speed he will discover that he is acting as a convict is supposed to, and feeling all the things that a convict is expected to feel.[17]

Nevertheless one of the most remarkable contemporary accounts of resocialization illustrates not the speed and ease of the process once the familiar world has dissolved, but the continuity of identity that persists through the internal conversation between 'I' and 'me'. Carlos Castaneda is a young American who, as a university postgraduate student in his early twenties, apprenticed himself for five years in the early 1960s to a Yaqui Indian, Don Juan. He tried quite deliberately to find a new reality and a new self, and he has described the process he experienced as one of resocialization. He tried to gain access to Don Juan's 'system of sensible interpretation', and 'Such an accessibility, in this case, was equivalent to a process of resocialization in which new ways of interpreting perceptual data were learned'.[18]

His experiences were deeply disturbing and even terrifying, for eventually the teachings of Don Juan began 'to pose a serious threat to my "idea of the world". I had begun to lose the certainty, which all of us have, that the reality of everyday life is something we can take for granted.' But for a long time an alternative reality eluded him, and his mentor explained why: 'You talk to yourself too much ... we maintain our world with our internal talk ... Whenever we finish talking to ourselves the world is always as it should be. We renew it, we kindle it with life, we uphold it with our internal talk.' Castaneda had to become a warrior, and 'A warrior is aware that the world will change as soon as he stops talking to himself...'[19] (Mystics have always known that meditation stops internal dialogue, dissolves the self as a social system and makes it available to new realities.)

The preconditions of resocialization are perhaps less problematical than decisions to seek and publicly proclaim a new self. A number of studies of passing have suggested that people who can easily pass (like light-skinned negroes and Indians) will be inclined to do so.[20] The refusal of stigmatized persons to pass when they might do so with ease has been relatively little explored (even through the historical records of martyrdom): its referents have not been established in social structures. This book will attempt at least to suggest the structural contingencies related to identity crisis and change through a comparative study of the experience of different varieties of marginality.

3 | Becoming a parson: change of life-plan and the voice of God

A study of late entrants to the Anglican ministry was undertaken to throw light on five questions arising from current theories of marginality and identity: Did their experience illustrate or lend credence to Berger's contention that modern man is conversion-prone? Did their deliberate change of career illustrate rational life-planning as a source of modern identity? Did their marginality seriously challenge the taken-for-granted reality of their former lives? Were 'significant others' crucial to their re-orientation to self and career? And what were the consequences of their move into a marginal situation for their self-conceptions and ways of looking at the world?

Secularization and the marginality of clergymen

The contemporary parson has often been seen as a marginal man. He is the victim of secularization. The sacred cosmos is now segregated from the rest of life and those who interpret it are set apart. It was decided to interview parsons who had entered the ministry from established secular careers. It appeared that instead of moving into a marginal world, they had rejoined society. The meaning they found in their change of position was a wider and more inclusive social involvement. The dog-collar and occasional visits to the local pub were links with the world; but above all they had rejoined the living by burying their dead. It was in funerals that they found a sense of significance. By presiding over death they found unity with the living.

There is general agreement among sociologists of religion that modern industrial societies experience a process of secularization. One sociologist, it is true, claims that on the contrary the very concept of secularization can be demolished,[1] and attention has been drawn to the persistence of religious ritual in such 'rites of passage' as baptism, marriage and burials. (Some 80 per cent of children are baptized with religious ritual, 70 per cent of non-divorced people marry in church, and virtually 100 per cent of burials are accompanied by religious ceremonial.) But the significance of these rites is almost certainly social rather than religious, and finds an explanation in the ties of kinship and family solidarity rather than religious conviction.[2]

The result of secularization, it is said, is that religion moves from the centre of life to a highly marginal position. 'Church-oriented religion has become a marginal phenomenon in modern society', says Luckmann[3] and Wilson defines secularization as 'the process whereby religious thinking, practice and institutions lose social significance'.[4] The parson has moved into the margins of society along with his Church. He is 'alienated'. 'The alienation of the clergy', Wilson maintains, 'is one of the most remarkable phenomena of the Church in modern times'. It is argued moreover, that the very basis of the parson's professional position in an 'expert' society is an anachronism, for the clergyman is made, not qualified, and in consequence 'The clergyman is the odd-man-out in any sociological analysis of his position. He has a social position ... (which is) fundamentally irrelevant to contemporary social structure'.[5] He is not the victim of science; he is the outcast of a highly professional society.

The American experience has been an embarrassment to the secularization thesis, but sociologists have now easily dealt with it. Over the past eighty years, as religious adherence and church attendence have sharply declined in Europe, church membership and attendance have sharply increased in America. This apparent divergence, we are assured, is an illusion, because in America religion itself has been secularized. It has not been relegated: it has been absorbed. Luckman is confident that the American experience 'does not represent a reversal of the trend toward secularization', and Wilson agrees with him. To join a church is to join the nation.[6]

Secularization sharpens the division between the secular and religious spheres of life and belief, which represent separate and autonomous zones of reality. Peter Berger thinks we may still hear rumours of angels if we open ourselves to the signals of transcendance — but he concedes that the rumours are somewhat disreputable.[7] Law, education, economic and political life have been largely evacuated by religion — imprisonment for blasphemy still occurred in

1912, but Bury was not alone in regarding this as an outrage.[8] Churches become sects, religion is privatized, the parson finds it difficult — but by no means impossible — to account for his very position,[9] declines in status, and becomes a marginal man.

The modern parson, it seems, has moved far from the central position and high social status which he occupied in post-Reformation England. Although there is considerable controversy about the precise power, status and incomes of late-sixteenth-century clergymen, it seems that the status of the secular clergy rose after the dissolution of the monasteries, and they became, in effect, a branch of the gentry. 'We speak easily of the rise of the gentry; it would be equally accurate to speak of the rise of the parish clergy'.[10] The incomes of rectors rose and a university man could do much worse than take up an ecclesiastical career. 'The medieval priest had been a peasant among peasants. The parson in 1600 was a gentleman among gentlemen.'[11]

And he had now joined society by getting married and raising a family. But in the nineteenth century the parson's family tied him to the major institutional orders of British society, for it had become the main channel of social mobility. His sons everywhere occupied the highest offices: in Government, the law, medicine, the armed forces and imperial services. The sons of the clergy spread, via the universities, into other occupations with a minimum of concentration. The universities merely promoted circulation within the upper-middle and upper-classes; it was the clergy who were 'the primary channel for change of status'.[12] By the 1930s this was no longer the case. Studies of Oxford and Cambridge students showed that the clergy had 'lost their earlier role as a channel of mobility and have become an inbred group'.[13] In the course of the twentieth century Anglican clergy have become older, their numbers have diminished while the population has increased,[14] and they have lost the pivotal position as a channel of social mobility which gave them close family ties with the major secular institutions of society.

In the mid 1960s the Paul Report on the deployment and payment of the clergy concluded that not only is the priest a man set apart by God, but he is imprisoned in his parish and isolated from his community by the impersonal and anonymous character of our mass society. The parish system means both the legal and geographical isolation of the clergy: 'It is in the nature of geographical territories not to overlap and for that sheer physical fact to separate one ministry from another, one clergyman from another with a kind of finality.' The priest today may not have a semi-magical status, but he appears to have some status that is more than social or professional. Ordination gives a man power to fulfil his office, and this power is of Christ. 'How it separates a man from the laity and from the world, or even why, is arguable. But the world and the clergy have always felt the cleric to be a man set apart.'[15]

Marginal men at the centre

In 1974 twelve Anglican parsons were interviewed in a diocese in the industrial Midlands. They were all the 'late-entrants' to the ministry in that diocese; two had been architects, five engineers, one chief clerk, one graduate textile chemist, one business man, one plumber and one policeman. Their average age was forty-six (the oldest was seventy and the youngest thirty-six). The average age at which they were ordained was thirty-nine. Four were curates (average age forty-three) who had been ordained on average for one year; eight were vicars (average age forty-seven) who had been ordained on average for ten years. Six were of middle-class origin, whose fathers had been company directors or professional men; six were from working-class backgrounds, had attended elementary or secondary modern schools and made their way in life through part-time engineering or business courses. All were married with children, and four had working wives (two schoolteachers and two social workers); all lived in predominantly working-class areas, the vicars in large vicarages with large gardens, the curates on council estates or in terraced houses in working-class streets.

The interviews were carried out in the clergymen's homes and lasted for between two and three hours. They were all asked to 'go through your career up to becoming a clergyman', to say how entering the ministry had changed their outlook and social relationships, and to say what they felt they had lost or gained. All had a long history of religious interest and involvement; none had made a dramatic move from atheism or sin to a Christian life, and mostly they emphasized gradualism in their progression to the priesthood — although three described experiences akin to conversion. One had been a bishop in the Mormon Church for six years, and ten had been lay readers.

None had any sense of losing social status by becoming a parson — indeed, some clearly felt they had gained, although they were at pains to emphasize that they were still ordinary people and shopped at Tesco. A decline in material living standards had been common: when Mr Ford, the textile chemist, told his daughters that he had decided to become a parson, 'they cried and howled and said "we're going to be poor" — which was quite true'. He had to sell his house to help his family during his two years at a theological college (and he has no hope of ever buying his own house again). But he considers that becoming a parson has been 'a great privilege'.

A curate in his late forties, who was ordained two years ago, lives in a terraced house in a mining town. He stresses his working-class origins: his father was a cotton worker and unemployed in the 1930s. He is aware of his special socio-moral status (although his income has declined) but does not feel socially isolated because of it. The test of his social normality is that he can 'take a drink'. He is 'just an ordinary chap' and insists that this is what he will continue to be:

How did you come to take Orders?

I had thought about Orders, but didn't think I'd be accepted. It was the rector who suggested in 1970 that I might go along to the selection conference. So I went along, and much to my surprise, I was selected and given a place at a theological college. I was surprised because I'm just an ordinary chap, not blessed with a great amount of academic success.

How has it changed your life? Are there any things you can't do now because you're a clergyman?

My philosophy is to be myself. I spend a lot of time at the British Legion. I take a drink and it doesn't bother me at all. Some people may frown on the idea of a clergyman drinking — but I don't get drunk. Maybe I don't swear as much as I used to.
The thing is to be yourself and not put yourself on a pedestal. This is the danger, of course — not that you put yourself on a pedestal, but that other people do. There's no doubt about it — one does get a certain amount of respect as a clergyman. You get in what you may call exalted company. So I try to be myself.

Do you feel you have lost anything?

I suppose one has to talk about money, and I suppose I'm about five hundred pounds a year down; one is earning far less. But it's more than a job, it's a calling. Fortunately my wife teaches.

What do you think you have gained?

I think ... more security. It's a gain that I've got what I really wanted. I've achieved what is not an apparent ambition, but one that's appeared slowly. This is what God wants me to do. Often it takes a long time, and I think my case is an illustration of this. This is what God wants me to be, and that's the security. It has its frustrations of course. What I enjoy is just going about the back streets into the homes of the people, sitting down and chatting about just ordinary things. And after a while you get used to the idea of just walking in: the door's open. Just going in and saying, 'Curate's here'. Sometimes, when I get fed up with the administrative side, I go round the back streets and sit down and talk. It's really wonderful, really lifts you up. A lot of people call me 'Father' or 'Reverend'. I encourage them to call me Peter and most people do. I expect the bishop would have a heart attack.

Do you see things differently at all since you became ordained? Have your ideas changed in any way?

I don't think so, really. No, I don't think so. I've always been concerned with the world, concerned for people. I think that concern has always been with me. No, I'm much the same chap.

The 'pedestal-theme' runs through the interviews. But pedestals can be counteracted by pubs. Another curate answered the question, 'How has your social life changed?' by saying:

I don't have that much social life anyway. There's not time. The big change, I suppose, is that people expect you to be whiter than white. This is crucial. Up to a point I suppose I try to live up to their expectations. I find I drive a lot slower now, that's for certain. The thought of being hauled over the coals by the magistrates...

Do you feel apart from things because of this?

No. Not really. If I want to go to a pub for a pint, I do.

As they moved from secular to ecclesiastical careers, they struggled to remain 'just the same person — just an ordinary chap', but found strong expectations that they should be otherwise:

I try to change as little as possible. But no matter what you do personally, people will put you where they want to put you. Some put you on a pedestal, some say you're not part of the ordinary mass of people now.

We modern clergymen no longer want to be seen as a professional class of people out on a limb somewhere, and not really part of this world. We want to be seen as ordinary people, ordinary human beings, no different from anybody else. All we've got is one of these collars, which is the badge of our profession. But trying to get this over to people is difficult — because of history, I suppose, old images ... It's easier to break it down in a town like this than in a rural situation where things are more deeply rooted. The good thing about the clergyman is that he does live in his situation. I live here in an ordinary council house on an estate, and while I'm a curate this works pretty well and people accept me. But when I'm an incumbent of a parish ... you're forced to have various meetings in your house: you just couldn't do it in this kind of house. You're forced by circumstances to have a largish house, which always seems to set you apart from them.

The collar and the large vicarage (especially in a working-class area) both set the parson apart and strengthen his ties with the community. One vicar — who was interviewed in his study which contained a grand piano and several uprights — observed that his house and garden were something of an embarrassment: 'it is not only the largest but the only garden in the area.' He spoke of the problems of living 'in a grotty area like this', and sends his children away to private schools. But he values living among his parishioners and feels that social workers, doctors and other professional people 'who are concerned with the problems of deprivation' are less effective because 'they don't live here — they live well away, in some nice place, you see'. But his large house is in fact a focus for the community (with consequent problems for his private, domestic life): 'Your house is your office. It's where you do most of your work. Your church is only used for services, not for meetings, or interviewing engaged couples.' And the parson's collar similarly both marks a boundary and helps to surmount it: 'I don't always wear my collar, especially if I'm just going out to enjoy myself. People tend to react according to their own suppositions. But I've never felt it was a tremendous problem. In fact in many ways the collar is a passport.'

The parsons had a problem of social isolation, but it was not a problem arising from the sacred nature of their office, or from the low regard in which the contemporary church is held. On the contrary, their problem was that of many men occupying a special and highly esteemed status in any organization or community — the problem of being seen to have no favourites. Like the colonel, the managing director or the headmaster, the parson must not have special, close friends. He must be indiscriminate in his social relationships. The oldest interviewee, who had been a parson for more than twenty years, was acutely aware of this:

> You can't make close friends. You can make good friends when you leave a parish, but not while you're there. You don't have time and it's not advisable to make close friends when you're in a parish, because it divides a parish up. People would accuse you of favour-itism. It's possible only when you leave. I think what you've lost by entering the ministry is a sense of knowing where you belong. Where do I belong? Where do I call home? I'm not really rootless: anywhere I hang my hat ... In business people are settled, they've bought a house, a great many of their friends are around them. With myself, I have a great many associates, but now, at the age of seventy, where can I say, 'Right, this is my home'. My wife has a half-share of a house in Eastbourne, but otherwise, where do I go? Other people can say, 'We'll plan ahead, buy this, and pay off the mortgage'. I can't do that.

So you've lost a sense of belonging?

> Yes. And bishops are reluctant to let you retire into the parish you've just been serving, because it's not fair to your successor. Where for ten years or so you've had all your friends. It upsets the new man who's coming in because people whom you baptized want you to marry them and so on. Always calling on the old man and not giving the new man a chance.

But his collar opens up endless social possibilities: 'They always told me that the dog-collar would divide you and separate you off. I find it's a door-opener. It is no barrier at all. I can talk to all sorts of people I couldn't talk to otherwise. And I can smile at pretty girls and they don't think I'm trying to get off with them...'

The former textile chemist is acutely aware of the dangers of forming special relationships with both individuals and organizations:

> Usually, if you're going out for a drink, you tend to drink outside the parish simply because it's difficult to treat all pubs equally. It would be no good if the vicar had his own particular pub. It's the same with the shops you patronize, and with politics in a similar way. Some sections of the community would be alienated if you declared your politics and your favourite brand of beer. It is very difficult to align yourself with anything remotely controversial.

What about problems of having close friends?

I think you have to be prepared to accept your relationship as vicar to parishioner, which means that sometimes you've got to put people on the right road. This is difficult, if friendship gets in the way. It is impossible to avoid liking some people more than others, but you can't act on this. I think it would be a mistake for us to go out regularly with a limited number of people. You can't let go as much as you'd like. I'm pleased to see it doesn't happen with the children. There's a danger that vicarage children can be labelled as odd.

His relationships with people may have to remain comparatively shallow, but they are also less manipulative than they were when he was an industrial manager, and he considers this a great gain: 'Before, although relationships with people were important, I was conscious of using them and manipulating them. If you were the chief chemist and had to see the foreman, you were nice to him because you wanted a job done. I don't think I approach people in that way now. I hope I don't.' The quality of interpersonal relationships has changed in the direction of greater honesty and openness.

A curate who was formerly an engineering draughtsman is learning quickly that his new status influences the kind of relationships he can form:

You can have really good friendships only with people you knew before. The longer you go on in the ministry, the smaller the circle becomes, because very rarely do you make new friends once you put this collar on, simply because people think they ought not to be that friendly with a minister, or that a minister ought not to be that friendly with people. I personally feel it's very sad, but you've got to weigh in the balance the fact that you're in a position where it's fatal to show any kind of preferential treatment, favouritism, or anything like that — or you're finished. In some respects you're forced to live a very lonely life — which it is, really, you know. But that's one of the things you have to live with.

And yet it would be totally false to present him as either socially isolated or 'alienated'. It is true that he sees himself as 'a bit of a loner, I suppose. That is why loneliness doesn't bother me. Philosophically I've lived a lonely life for a long time. You get used to living in your own mind.' But the great gain he has made by entering the ministry — 'something I consider very precious, which is entirely by virtue of the job' — is precisely 'an inroad into so many people's lives'. He has no regrets about his change of occupation. He is without close friends, but a wide world of people has opened up to him:

> You see, now I can do what I've always wanted to do. My friends at work envy me. They say, 'Edward, you're the only one we know who's doing what he really wanted to do.' Well, what I've always wanted is, not to interfere, but to be in a position where I could deal with people, help people. This is something I really enjoy. This is the ultimate in job-satisfaction for me. I feel I am at last doing something that really matters.

An escape from the division of labour

Modern industrial societies are plural societies, based on the division of labour and a sharp distinction between the public and the private. [16] They are also highly professionalized societies, and professional roles tend to be effectively neutral and specific and restricted rather than diffuse. The clergy, it is said, are the victims of these inter-related modernizing processes.

Religion becomes a separate and specialized activity within clear-cut organizational boundaries,[17] and the parson's previously diffuse role is restricted to the narrow professionalism of a liturgical specialist. Towler claims that the parson is the victim of his own history, for 'the clergy as such never constituted an occupation, let alone a profession. Even the post-Reformation parson's position in society was more akin to that of the squire than that of the physician.'[18] Wilson argues that his problem is not that he is not a professional, but that he is one; as a religious specialist he stakes out his particular areas of narrow professional concern, the administration of church affairs, and 'a greater stress on their distinctive liturgical competence'.[19] The parson is a modern man after all.

The twelve parsons who were interviewed were not entrapped in a highly specialized division of labour: they were escaping from one, and very aware that this was the case. They were moving from confinement and restriction to the open spaces of life outisde the tidy technical definition of a specialized trade. And their conceptual categories appeared to change along with their de-restricted vocational and social roles. Although in general they emphasized continuity with their former selves and attitudes and values, the changes they did concede were towards more embracing social and religious categories. Social and religious distinctions they had previously thought important now seemed illusory. Changes in social position seemed to be mirrored in changes in consciousness.

They emphasized their role as generalists and co-ordinators rather than technical specialists; and it was attempts to treat them simply as technical specialists (for instance by crematoria) that they most strongly resisted. The meaning of their change of occupation for them was they they transcended occupational distinctions. And that fundamental distinction of modern life, between the public and the private, was obliterated too. Erstwhile plumbers, architects and engineers had left fragmented lives for a new wholeness and totality which had no margins in which to hide.

Mr King graduated in engineering from London University in 1960 and worked for eight years in industry. He has been the rector of a highly industrialized parish for five years. In describing the change in his life he highlighted three circumstances: wider social involvement, the disappearance of any real distinction between his professional and private life, and the lack of precise criteria for estimating 'success' in his new career compared with engineering:

In what ways did your life change when you left engineering for the ministry?

The obvious change was the financial one. Clergy pay isn't wonderful. It made a difference in other ways. As a professional engineer you lived in a certain kind of neighbourhood and associated with certain people in various kinds of set patterns. You indulged in recreations and pastimes and clubs and so on which were narrow in the sense that they were confined to a fairly limited professional group of people. But the church is very much a neighbourhood thing and reflects that neighbourhood. So probably the biggest change is that one lives and works in areas that one wouldn't have dreamt of going to before. And one finds that, although it poses problems, it's a jolly sight more interesting than one would have thought.

I don't find that my life has been cramped at all. In most respects it has opened out tremendously to a lot of new possibilities. And certainly it seems to me that life is very much a matter of movement, that one has come from somewhere and one is going somewhere. And it does seem to me that life ought to be a continual process of development.

His family life has been submerged by professional work: 'My wife was quite disgusted, really, because she expected to be marrying an engineer. She's now a medical social worker and she's been an adoption worker for many years too. She was able to adjust fairly readily.' There are no longer separate segments in his life:

> I think before life was much more fragmented and you tended to see things in compartments. Perhaps this was inevitable — my work was in one compartment, my concern with social problems, politics and so on were in another, my social life and personal relationships were in yet another. But I would say that now I see things as much more of one piece and interrelated.

Former precise distinctions, categories and criteria have been softened. He no longer has precise criteria for measuring his achievement:

> I'm still sure that I did the right thing, although I've come to realize that I don't do anything constructive. I suppose that in this kind of work you can't look for results in the way that one used to in a technological discipline with measurable results. It's wrong to do so. But with my kind of training and background it's hard not to, and frustrating when you can't.

Mr King's experience of wider, more indeterminate, diffuse and open social categories seems to be mirrored in the changing conceptual framework within which he interprets the world. He still maintains that there is 'one moral absolute — in the Bible — which underlies the whole of the Christian faith'. But for him

> moral distinctions are much less clear-cut than they were. The interpretation of this moral absolute in practical terms becomes increasingly difficult and less clear-cut. It is almost impossible to set down on paper what is right and what is wrong. Circumstances are infinitely varied. You cannot say that abortion, for example, is always wrong — or always right. In this sense my moral judgements have become much less clear-cut than they would have been in my former way of life.

Mr King's concepts of temporal sequence and biographical stages have also been modified: time and human life are without sharply defined sequences and segments:

> Generally speaking it seems to me that life is a matter of continuous development at different levels — but underlying this is spiritual development. People who discover this and are able to prove it in their lives are very close to discovering what life is about. And maybe beyond this life, too, there's a tremendous amount of

growth and development that we still have to undergo in a different way. I don't know, but I would guess so. The thing about this life, and the thing that makes it so invigorating and exciting, is that you're always in a state of becoming. You've never got there. But we can't think beyond space and time — they're the limits of our earthly minds. It's pointless to talk in terms of 'becoming' when you're thinking in terms of eternity. But we have to use these kinds of images because they're the only ones we're able to grasp...

Mr Chapman, the ex-policeman, feels that he has now been admitted to the many-sidedness of human life when formerly he was limited to people who had transgressed. He is now a co-ordinator of diverse activites: 'I think you have to train your lay people to work: there are lots of jobs they can do to keep the machinery going.' He has been a vicar for nine years and lives in a large vicarage with a spacious hall with an ornate staircase and marble floor. There is a safe in his study and framed certificates on the walls. But he has a sense of involvement: 'You have to convince people that parsons are human. You have to take every opportunity to put across Christian teaching. You can do this even in a pub.' As a policeman, 'people came to your attention only when things went wrong. Here you're involved in everyday life'. But he now has no private life: 'I've let myself in for a lot more work. In the police force, when you'd finished your time, that was it. This is twenty-four hours a day here — always on the go. But I don't think I've lost anything.'

The former plumber, Mr Peters, also feels he has widened his social life. His rectory is a large house in the main street of an industrial town. His large study is dominated by a huge white plastic three-piece suite. He was a relaxed man, in his mid thirties, who talked easily and openly. He had enjoyed plumbing: 'I really enjoyed it. I used to go to work and whistle all day. I was happy because I got pleasure out of my work. I'm still happy doing bits of plumbing jobs.' He does not think he has lost anything by becoming a parson, but he spoke rather wistfully about his lack of any private life:

One thing I find is I haven't much time for any private, social life. We're supposed to have one day off a week — Saturday; but you sometimes get a funeral or a wedding or someone comes to the door. I can't say — 'Go away, it's my day off'. I wasn't called for the ministry for that. When I entered the ministry I found that we were supposed to get four Sundays a year off — some try to stretch it to six weeks. I thought, 'Eh, that's a lot is that: I'm only used to

a week's holiday'. Actually I got a fortnight and thought it was a
lot, but I realize now it's needed. With meetings almost every night
my wife and I don't get much time together.

Mr Ford, the former textile chemist who had reached a senior
managerial post in industry by his late thirties, no longer had a
segregated private life. He pointed to this as the major change that
had arisen from his change of career:

How has entering the ministry changed your life?

The main change is that I've had to spend more time on church
matters than before, which is to be expected. It does mean that
whereas before I could do a nine-to-five job, and then come home
and forget about it, now I can't. Now I'm on the job twenty-four
hours a day, if necessary. I think this is the aspect that my wife has
found more difficult than me — it's quite easy for me, because I
know I'm in the right job.

A former architect, Mr Peel, now in his mid forties finds that his
work as a vicar is many-sided and more responsible; his social life is
wider and more varied; and it is easier to get his present work accepted
by 'society at large'. As an architect working for a local authority he
was working on 'a fairly big scheme — the idea was to develop a new
method of construction'. But the work was monotonous: 'It entailed
lots of tedious detail, and in the middle of this — it seems most
strange — a phrase kept coming into my head: "What doest thou
here, Elijah?"'

Mr Peel's work as an architect for a local authority was actually less
responsible, and more difficult to 'sell to the public', than his work as
a parson:

An architect with a local authority has no responsibility with
money — that's the concern of the country council. You deal with
contracts worth several millions — and it's not your money. Now
I've got to be more money-conscious. Also, in architecture there's
a continual battle to be accepted by society at large: a lot of what
you do is aimed at creating an impression for others or to the
profession. I think in the ministry, by and large, you're here to
serve. You are accepted by the way you are concerned for people,
not by how you appear to them. You don't have actually to sell
anything to do your job, whereas in architecture you're continually
selling yourself. I think in the ministry you can be unconcerned
about yourself.

How has the ministry changed your life?

I think my social life has been vastly expanded. Not in terms of going to concerts and theatres — time doesn't allow. Whereas in architecture I moved within a professional group, my contact now is with many more people, from all walks of life. I found professional groups awful. It's like clergymen when they get together, too.

Mr Morris also worked for ten years as an architect, and has now been a parson for nine. He was formerly in a suburban, middle-class parish and is now in a working-class area. He, too, feels that he has been rescued from a restricted social and professional world: 'From my middle-class background I had a fear of this sort of area and the kind of people.' But he has found that he is no longer involved in the highly competitive social life that he experienced as an architect. The change was a greater problem for his wife:

My wife took a bit of time to adjust to the change, because when I married her I was an architect, and it took a bit of time for her to adjust. The main way my life has changed is lack of privacy. If you're doing your job properly you need to use your house an awful lot for meetings and classes and so on. There are people in and out all the time. We have so little time together. Occasionally we push off to our cottage in North Wales, but not very often. The things one has less of are privacy and spare time. But I don't think I feel debarred from doing anything I did before. I used to enjoy fishing — but now again it's a question of time.

None of the parsons interviewed had been 'bureaucratized', imprisoned within a narrow division of labour, and reduced to a liturgical specialist. The change they had all experienced had been in a precisely contrary direction.

It is the non-bureacratized, non-specialized character of their work that they prize most highly. A former engineer said he became a parson because 'I realized there are so many people dealing with bits of people and what most people want is somebody to deal with them as a whole.' He had been a lay preacher but wanted to be more than a liturgical specialist: 'As an ordained clergyman you have to be responsible for people's whole lives, not for just a few minutes on Sunday.'

A former engineering draughtsman finds his main justification and sense of worth in the non-bureacratized nature of his work:

You need a certain independence from the structures and the system, if you want to use words like that, in order to do your job. You can help people kind of independently, apart from the social service structures and the legal structures. As clergymen we're independent: we represent the Church, maybe, but the service I give to people is very much my own. I don't represent any official attitude. You've nothing to hide behind. A social worker always has his department and an official attitude. We clergymen haven't — we're just ourselves, responsible ultimately to God.

It is in funerals that the parsons find their deepest satisfaction and integration with the community. And it is current trends to bureaucratize death that they find most deeply offensive and strongly resist. One interviewee expressed a deep sense of outrage: 'It hurts very much to get a phone call from the crematorium saying they've fixed up a funeral for someone you've never heard of, and is that all right. This impersonal business — it hurts. You're like a plumber. I find it very difficult. I'm just saying a lot of words over a box.'

This was echoed (without any promoting) in other interviews. One parson was talking about the deep satisfaction of his work, but observed:

One thing that does frustrate me, is the number of funerals and cremations at which I officiate for people I can't and don't know anything about. Yet I feel it's incumbent on me to say something to these people. I cannot use the prayer-book service as it is. But I feel I must try to help these people. I don't think of it as a service for the dead. It's for those who are left behind. Funerals are a big part of my ministry.

But to bury people you know is deeply satisfying. When Mr Ford, the textile chemist, had moments of self-doubt in the early days of his ministry, they were allayed by his first funeral: 'We all like to feel we can help people, but I felt for the first time that I'd really done something. I came home from the funeral and said to my wife, "Yes, I'm in the right job".'

Rational life-planning and the hand of God

It has been argued that long life in a world of change, diversity and choice makes rational life-planning not only possible but necessary. Long life in a world of change and infinite variety may call for radical redefinitions of the self. These redefinitions may be quite fundamental, indeed 'transformations'. Berger says of modern man: 'Just as his identity is liable to fundamental transformations in the course of his career through society, so is his relation to the ultimate definitions of reality.'

The deliberate life-plan charts a course among possible alternatives. 'The life-plan becomes a primary source of identity.'[20] But it is constantly reviewed and revised, and life-planning takes place in a perspective that includes a succession of professional roles. The longer life expectancy of men in modern industrial societies encourages rationality and banishes the hand of God: 'We may speculate that the decline of fate and God's will as explanatory concepts is related both to the extended length of life and to concomitant changes in the timing of death.'[21]

The twelve parsons appeared to be modern men, established in 'straight', secular careers in the mainstream of industrial life, as engineers and architects, who had changed course relatively late in life after a period of very careful and deliberate planning. But what was remarkable about them in general was not 'transformation of identity', but continuity. And throughout their often protracted and anguished period of decision-making, they were listening intently for the voice of God. God invariably spoke to them through the ecclesiastical bureaucracy of selection committees.

Mr Eliot, the former engineering draughtsman, spent fifteen years, from the age of twenty to thirty-five, wondering whether he should enter the ministry, and whether he would be entering for the right reasons. He experienced no great revelation, but over these years there was a steady accumulation of signs and pointers:

I was a convinced churchman, you know, and a committed Christian, and I did lay work. And I just thought then, you know, it was a good thing (to enter the ministry), but I was never quite sure whether I wanted to do it for the right reasons. It took me fifteen years to sort out whether I was doing it for the right reasons. This feeling of eventually ending up in the ministry stayed with me throughout my time in the Air Force, and through all those various jobs in engineering. I got to the stage once when I said to my wife, 'We're either emigrating or I'm going into the ministry'. It had to come to that kind of crunch. It was quite a battle I was having with myself. I'd gone through the stage when I was sure I wanted to go in, and come to a phase when I didn't want to go in. And yet things were pushing me that way, events, you know. We call them the 'open' and 'shut' doors — various little leaders that were kind of pointing my life in different directions.

By now the 'pointers' were contrary to Mr Eliot's personal inclination; and he was, moreover, doing very well in his engineering career. Finally, he looked for a divine decision in the selection committee:

I was getting more and more money in my job. I'd a good future in front of me in many respects, and we'd now got a family, and a house. But there was a constant niggling in the mind, that would never go, regardless of what I did, you know. I mean, some phases you overcome, and they disappear. Well, this one never did, you see.

Eventually, not long after I'd become a lay reader, I went back to the vicar and asked him to recommend me for a selection conference. You go away for a few days, with a number of other people and five examiners. I decided then that this would be it for me. If the conference recommended me for training, that's it. If they didn't, I wouldn't try again. I thought that would make my mind up for me, which it did, of course. They recommended me for training — and I came out at the other end a clergyman.

Mr Porter, a former boiler engineer now in his mid forties, warned the interviewer that his progression to the ministry was a long story. It extended, in fact, over a period of eighteen years. During that time he was looking for a sign, for evidence of a 'call'. The unexpected, unplanned and irrational in his engineering career tended to be given divine status: bizarre events and changes in fortune were taken as evidence of the divine will.

Early in his career he was offered a job in Trinidad and cabled his acceptance, but the man who had made the offer was ill with food poisoning when his cable arrived. However, when the man in Trinidad recovered, he came to England, and offered Mr Porter a job in Gloucestershire. 'It was about this time that I'd first been considering whether or not I had a call to the ministry. This offer came at a time when I was looking for an answer. But with this coming out of the blue, I thought, "Well, this is it. You can't turn this down".' There was an increase in salary, in status and opportunity, and it was near his girl friend. Clearly he had not been called to the ministry.

But in the event he found he was really a foreman rather than the assistant engineer. Perhaps he had been called after all. 'I began to wonder about the way things had gone wrong in Gloucestershire. Was this not saying, "Well, what about it?"' In the meantime he had married and moved again, to the north of England, and his career was prospering: 'Promotion came, and I was having a marvellous time. I saw my plans on paper, the foundations laid, right up to the finished article.' But the events in Gloucestershire still seemed to point to the ministry:

> It would mean throwing away all my engineering training, and I did think, 'Is this right?'. So I decided to put it to the test, and went to a selection board for training for the ministry. I think you must make a decision to follow a course of action, and you will be shown whether you have made the right decision.

The selection board's acceptance showed him that he had. 'Having had the seeds sown, I was always aware that it would come up. And having, I suppose, rejected it because of career, I accepted it in spite of career. I suppose that sums it up. I told you it was a long story.'

Many years of self-examination and looking for the hand of God typified the changeover from a secular to a religious career. Mr Peel, one of the architects, spent eight years in his profession, but was constantly looking for evidence of a 'call'. He had no experience akin to conversion, but 'I first wondered whether God would call me to the ministry while I was still studying architecture'. He talked to his vicar who advised him to continue with architecture but, if he still felt he was being called, to take the lay reader's exams. This he did, and eight years later entered the ministry. 'It was for me a gradual process of moving from one to the other.'

Four of the twelve parsons had experienced something akin to conversion (although one was at pains to emphasize that there had been 'no blinding flash of light'). But these experiences were all in the context of pre-existing strong religious faith. In no instance was there inversion or reversal. Conversion was simply more of the same.

Mr Morris, the other former architect, was brought up in a prosperous middle-class home and his future was rationally planned: 'My father was very enlightened. When it was time to think of my future career, he sent me to a psychologist. I was put through various tests and the idea of architecture was mooted.' He duly proceeded to university and a degree in architecture, and practised his profession for ten years.

But at university he met deeply committed Christian students. His upbringing had been conventionally religious, but 'it became evident that what they meant when they said they were Christians was different from what I meant. To them Jesus was someone who was real and alive'. It was at this time that he himself became a deeply committed Christian, and felt that his personality was radically changed:

> I experienced an intense personal witness with Christ, and suddenly nothing else mattered. I used to be very introspective, and suddenly none of the things I'd worried about seemed to matter. This had the effect of turning me inside out. I became really happy for the first time. This was the turning point in my life. It didn't affect my career yet. I still had the idea that parsons were parasites.

Over a period of ten years, 'gradually the conviction that I ought to be in the ministry full-time came over me. I'd done quite a lot as a layman. I felt God was calling me'.

Mr Peters, the former plumber, had also experienced conversion by contagion. This led him eventually to enter the ministry, in spite of the great happiness he found in plumbing. He had always attended church regularly, and the vicar asked him to help with the youth club: 'Some of the young people in that club would speak about the Lord Jesus as someone they knew as a personal friend and saviour, whereas I couldn't. I didn't know what it meant to know God in such a close and intimate way. And so I began to seek a closer relationship with God.'

In his search, he had a long talk one night with a visiting parson: 'Something very strange happened to me tht night, because I really felt committed.' He knew then that Jesus had died for him:

> This parson asked me if I wanted to become a committed Christian and commit my life to Christ, and I did. I knelt down and asked the Lord Jesus Christ to be my saviour. And that changed my life. Because I loved plumbing, I do one or two jobs still. I was good at plumbing — I was top in the northern counties in the City and Guilds examinations, and I'd had some work on exhibition. So I was full of that kind of pride in my work. I got pleasure from it. But I suddenly felt that I wanted to do parish work and pass on the good news of Christ to other people.

Mr King worked in industry after graduating in engineering at London University. He was brought up in a middle-class home in which 'religious faith was taken for granted, really ... and I suppose church was always very much part of my life'. But he had no thought of entering the ministry; his turning point came through an old lady:

> The person who changed the direction of my life was an old lady
> who, through my association with the church, I'd taken to visiting.
> She lived alone and was remarkably bright and intelligent — a
> delightful person. She was an atheist, in fact, but one who was
> always looking for faith. And somehow it was she who changed my
> life — it wasn't a clergyman or someone of great religious faith.
> She was searching, and I suppose I was searching as well, although
> there was about sixty years difference in our ages. And I suddenly
> realized that what I had begun to find was tremendously import-
> ant ...
>
> If you try to put this into words you almost have to use the kind of
> imagery you find in the Bible when you read about St. Paul's
> conversion and the light on the Damascus road, being struck blind
> and that. Well, I can understand now how this language comes
> about, because when you try to put this experience in words, it's
> very difficult. It just so happened that one night when I was sitting
> nattering with her, drinking tea and watching television, it sort of
> came to me in a flash — that this is what I had to do. I had to
> become a clergyman. It's so absurd, really. It wasn't anything I
> seriously considered before.

His subsequent acceptance for training confirmed him in his new
identity: 'Everything seemed to happen quickly. Everything dropped
into place, which tended to confirm that what I was doing was right.
And this vision I had then, although it's been a bit clouded at times,
has never disappeared.'

Mr French had a more intense, protracted and complicated involvement with religion before he entered the ministry. For seven years,
from the age of thirty-three to forty, he was a full-time bishop in the
Mormon Church ('it all started as a doorstep conversion ... What
attracted us was the warmth and friendliness of the people'). At forty
he sold his house and was going to Salt Lake City but could not get an
exit visa. He went back to his old job as a clerk, and began attending
his boyhood church: 'When I came to the communion rail, I broke
down and wept. I knew I'd come home.' But he is emphatic that this
was not a 'conversion': 'It's not like a blinding flash of light. I realize
that can happen, but for most of us it's a slow process. It's important
for you to have all that background as to why I'm now in Orders.'

This stress on continuity, on change through steady accretion, was
more typical than sudden conversion. The change in the parsons over

the first one or two decades of adult life accords closely with Brim's notion of adult socialization (and resocialization) as 'personality drift': small but incremental shifts occur from time to time in what an individual asks of himself, and successive minor alterations may finally add up to a major transformation.[22]

Mr Ford, the textile chemist, provides the most explicit illustration of this process. It was over a period of eighteen years, while he was working in industry, that his involvement in religion deepened and his view of himself changed: 'It was only gradually over the years that the idea came that perhaps I ought to be a clergyman — and it wasn't a very pleasant idea in the first place.' He thought he should have a revelation:

I thought you had to have some mystic experience which would tell you beyond doubt what you ought to be doing. Well, I never did and never have. I've discovered since that God works through ordinary people and ordinary events, and it's only afterwards that you see the significance of them.

But he, too, found the will of God in the ecclesiastical bureaucracy:

I asked to go through a Selection Board. I would see what they said. If they said I ought to enter the ministry, I would take it as God's will through them ... because I've never had any of those remarkable experiences that some people claim to have had.

A marginal man

In general the parsons interviewed had been well satisfied with their previous careers but were still more satisfied in their present work. They had no sense of social isolation or loss of status. They were busy men with a sense of purpose and fulfilment. The had their problems, but they seemed to be assured and capable men, confident in handling the issues that faced them. Only one had the classical symptoms of the psychologically marginal man.[23] He was anxious, with a history of minor psychosomatic ailments and a deep preoccupation with social and professional status. But his psychological marginality had not developed after he entered the ministry. It had a long history, with roots deeply buried in his personal biography.

Mr Hudson was forty-four when he was interviewed. He had been ordained a year before and was now a curate living in a terraced home in an industrial town. He had first talked to his vicar about the possibility of entering the ministry when he was twenty-one. It was only after another twenty-three years — of which twelve were spent as a lay reader — that he finally made the change from draughtsman to parson.

Throughout his life he has been dissatisfied with whatever circumstances he was in, and is unhappy in his present job. He has been misled once again:

> This church isn't quite what we expected. I mean, the community, the fellowship, is not what we were led to believe. We expected to be working harder. We came from a church that we thought was rather dead to one that we thought would be full of life, but now we realize that it was livelier where we were before.

He was the only parson who complained of being underworked.

The war and his working-class origins prevented him from obtaining the education and career that he should have had. 'When the war came, in 1940, I didn't pass the eleven-plus. I was one of those marginal cases. The teachers told my parents that in normal times I would have passed and gone to the grammar school. I finished school at fourteen and became an apprentice machine tool fitter.' He had wanted to be a cartoonist, 'but work in industry was all you could get in those days, coming from a working-class background, with no background at all, as you might say. So I had to start at the rock bottom, on the shop floor'. And in industry his career was not as smooth as might have been, because 'The thing in industry is, it's not what you know, it's who you know'.

When he went to do his National Service, 'they changed the structure of the RAF' and so he could not be given the rank he was properly entitled to as a trained engineer. He has a strong sense that people do not generally get on in life through personal merit, but from being in the right place at the right time: 'Don't think I'm bearing any malice at all, but people not as good as me got promoted in the office merely by being there at the right time. But so often, if your face doesn't fit...'

When he first went before the selection board for the ministry, he was rejected. He was in despair. 'It made me ill. I had lots of little ailments: my eye closed up, and all sorts of other little things. That's when I took up making my model soldiers.' He wrote to the Bishop to complain about his rejection: 'I said that Christ hadn't let me down, but I felt his Church had. I had a long letter back...' Finally he was accepted by a selection board in another region, wrote for a place in a number of theological colleges, and was turned down by all of them. (He finally took a part-time course of training locally.)

> I didn't get in. I think they thought it would look better to have lots of graduates. Things have always happened to me like this — perhaps it's fate. When I was young there was the war and I couldn't go to a grammar school; then when I was joining up they changed the RAF; then I couldn't get in to Salisbury or Lincoln...

His religion is inextricably mixed with issues of social status: 'I've been a Christian all my life and I was a lay reader for twelve years. People in the office would come to me to have their passports signed.' He still goes back to his old work place, but stresses that this is 'not to show off, but to let them see I'm just the same person'. He insisted: 'I still regard myself as working-class, you know, not like someone who suddenly becomes middle-class when they've gone somewhere else, like the students, for instance.' But he insists too much. In fact he has a powerful sense of having crossed over from one world to one utterly different, and he marked his crossing ceremonially with a stag party: 'I had a stag night, just like before a wedding, before my ordination. Like a bachelor night out. All the boys went to the Red Lion in Bolton.'

Social unease and bitterness are mixed with a neurotic preoccupation with death. He was talking of inductions:

> You know, when a vicar's inducted to a parish, all the vicars and readers are there. And there's a sort of one-upmanship. I know I'm not very clever, but I think it's time a lot of other people started looking at themselves. It doesn't matter what you do — if you get more money, it'll only buy you a better coffin. My mother died when she was forty-five, and I'm forty-four. When I reached forty, things seemed to alter. Death is quite a real thing to me. Time is short. It may be sooner than we think.

Mr Hudson's study was crammed with his model soldiers and clocks of all shapes and sizes. The clocks chimed erratically, never in unison. They seemed to symbolize Mr Hudson's involved biography of fresh starts and setbacks, his fate never to be in the right place at the right time.

Conclusion

The parsons who had entered the ministry from mainstream secular careers appeared to have no sense that they had moved into a marginal world or were now in careers that were irrelevant to the contemporary world. On the contrary, they had a sense of escaping from restricted social and professional worlds within a highly developed form of the division of labour. Their social lives were wider than ever before, but they had to be cautious in making friends in case they appeared to have 'favourites'. This very fact was a testimony to the very special indeed 'central' status which they enjoyed.

There is some evidence that parsons today may have some difficulty in 'accounting' for themselves, and establishing the legitimacy and rationality of their occupation. The 'plausibility structure' of their world is weak. They may give significance and order to their world by placing themselves — and their congregations — in statistical categories. The world of religious observance has been reduced to manageable order if the percentage of overall church attendance can be cited, and one's own church be shown not to differ from the norm.[24] The twelve parsons interviewed in this study felt no need to justify themselves in terms of church attendance statistics (the blind people interviewed had made their world orderly and meaningful by placing themselves in statistical categories: see Chapter 6). Their plausibility structures were robust. It was sufficient that they had been 'called' and were doing the will of God. Their activities in this world were justified and made sense because of their special relationship with the sacred cosmos.

The parsons had previously followed scientific and technological careers and often referred to precise criteria of success and achievement which had afforded satisfaction and reassurance in their former careers. They were quite clear that such criteria were inapplicable now. Mr Morris, the former architect, who had once regarded parsons as parasites, was asked if he was still of that opinion: 'If the Church of England operated on productivity according to the number of converts, then perhaps parsons would be seen as parasites. I think you can do a lot of good work as a lay preacher, but if God calls you to the ministry, that's where you're meant to be.'

When they entered the ministry, formerly fragmented social spheres appeared to give way to an embracing unity of life. Hard distinctions between social spheres dissolved, and this was especially apparent (and not always welcomed) in private, domestic life: family life was overwhelmed by, and submerged in, professional work. The disappearance of internal boundaries between different segments of social life appeared to be mirrored in a more unitary conceptual order.

All the interviewees were asked how their ideas and priorities had changed since they entered the ministry, and what views they held of social changes taking place in the contemporary world. They tended to deny that their ideas and priorities had changed, but in answer to the second question most of them said they could no longer accept the tidy and comparatively rigid moral categories to which they had formerly subscribed.

Some pointed to their wide experience of life before ordination: 'I'm not as rigid as some clergymen. My experience of the world colours my views, though I do try to remain true to my faith.' Others ascribed change to their experience as parsons:

> Yes, I've had changes in what I regard as important and unimportant to me. Roman Catholicism was once heresy to me: I'd just no room for divergent patterns of any kind. Now they're no longer important, as long as you hold the basic creed. The things that have become more important are things like the principles of what belief is: the roots on which the superstructure is built.

Mr French thought it was 'senseless not to remarry divorcees', and Mr Ford said, 'I'm in favour of Gay Liberation, and abortion I'm generally in favour of', but neither thought their views had really changed much since ordination. Mr Peel thought his had: 'Yes, I think I've changed a lot in the distinctions that I make. Before I went into the ministry I would literally categorize people as those with it and those without it — heathens and pagans on the one hand and devout Christians on the other. Now I wouldn't make such clear distinctions.'

Mr Hudson, the 'marginal man', stands out from the rest in his unswerving adherence to views he has always held:

> I've always upheld the marriage vow, and I still cannot uphold extra-marital relations, never have done and never will do. It's a bit different now with all the contraception that's going on, Women's Lib., they're talking about sleeping around like men used to. But for me, love is holy. I've only ever been out with one girl, and that's my wife. I might be old-fashioned. Again, I find it very difficult to talk to anyone who's going towards a divorce.

He is still very moderate about drink: 'We do have a drink at Christmas — we've got some Cyprus sherry left now.' Mr Hudson's moral categories were as sharply and uncompromisingly defined and bounded as the sacred world into which he had moved over from the profane.

The parsons had not experienced 'conversion' if by that is meant both a sudden change of self-conception and orientation and a 'paradigm-shift',[25] the acceptance of a new world view. By contrast, for instance, with members of Alcoholics Anonymous, whose experience is akin to an atheist's joining a fundamentalist sect, the parsons had no sense of being reborn, but rather of 'coming home'. Alcoholics often count their 'birthdays' from the time of their initiation: they are new men.[26] The parsons had no such sense of personal discontinuity: on the contrary, they had a strong sense of personal continuity extending far back before ordination, which was a fulfilment and culmination, rather than a reversal or inversion of self.

It is true that they had been very busily life-planning, and they had consulted and talked to various people — in some cases fairly casual acquaintances — while doing so; but their families did not appear to have been the 'life-planning workshop'[27] which Berger sees as the new overriding structure of family life. What was remarkable was the extent to which decisions appeared to be taken without consulting highly significant others, so that wives, daughters and fiancées were faced with a *fait accompli*. And original life-plans — often constructed with painstaking rationality and even the aid of an occupational psychologist — were experienced not as a properly designed project which included personal identity, but as false consciousness. It was the very rationality of the plan that destroyed a sense of identity. The legitimacy of their action lay not in careful calculation and the harmonizing of relevant 'timetables', but in 'signs' which came from a separate reality.

4 | Artists: precarious identities in private worlds

Artists were chosen for study because they appeared to subscribe to values and embrace a way of life which placed them off-centre in a routinized, bureaucratic and industrialized world. When they gave up careers as teachers, clerks and mechanics they turned their back on society. Their lives, like the parsons', were not tidily and routinely divided into public and private spheres; but whereas the parson has no private life, the artist often has nothing else. The artist, it seemed, moved to a private base and so changed his relationship to society; perhaps, too, he changed his identity, for 'Identity ... stands in a dialectical relationship with society'.[1] The full-time, professional artist changed the terms of the dialectic from which identity is born.

The public and the private are not only separate compartments between which, increasingly since the seventeenth century, we have divided our lives;[2] they are also categories for ordering experience, contexts in which knowledge of society is organized in individual consciousness. The consciousness of modern man is formed by a tension between public and private spheres. All schools are 'public schools' and, from the age of five or before, public modes of experience alternate with private worlds. The private sphere is not only a workshop for constructing life-plans; it is a decoding room where personal experiences in the public sphere are reviewed, processed, given meaning, rendered acceptable, and turned into sense.

Industrial managers, no less than workers,[3] appear today to be 'privatized'. The Pahls concluded from their study of managers and their wives that neither the career nor family life, but the tension between the two, was the supreme social reality: 'it is the tension between the conflicting value systems of home and work, of family and career, which provides the dialectic of social reality for the middle class.'[4] Home was a very separate world, a heavily defended base, from which the demands of work were reviewed and their meaning and legitimacy assessed.

Berger sees the distinction between the public and the private as a particular but highly significant aspect of 'pluralization':

> Modern life is typically segmented to a very high degree, and it is important to understand that this segmentation (or, as we prefer to call it, pluralization) is not only manifest on the level of observable social conduct, but also has important manifestations on the level of consciousness. A fundamental aspect of this pluralization is the dichotomy of public and private spheres ... The individual in a modern society is typically conscious of a sharp dichotomization between the world of his private life and the world of large public institutions to which he relates in a variety of roles.[5]

The private world stands in contrast to the individual's 'bewildering involvements with the worlds of public institutions'; it is a carefully constructed centre which provides 'an order of integrative and sustained meanings'.

It is commonly claimed that before the Industrial Revolution, and certainly during the Renaissance and in the Middle Ages, art and the artist were 'integrated' with society. Artists were public no less than private men. (Recent studies of Renaissance art and society have laid bare the organization of artistic work as a public, workshop enterprise.[6]) Recently the 'anti-art' movement in France has tried to destroy art as a separate and private activity; but since the Industrial Revolution, throughout what Jacques Barzun calls the 'art epoch' of the past hundred and fifty years, art has been encapsulated in communities of artists.[7] The study of 'local' artists reported in this chapter was an attempt to explore some of the personal consequences of encapsulation.

Artists like parsons are pre-modern men. Parsons are made marginal by secularization, artists by industrialization. The marginality of both was experienced as freedom from structure: both artists and parsons were quite explicit and often eloquent about the overstructured condition of other men's lives. But there were very important differences between them. Both lost or surrendered a half of life: but the parsons 'went public', the artists 'went private'. The parsons insisted that they were still ordinary men; the artists had no doubt whatsoever that they were altogether extraordinary. The parsons resisted the attempts of significant others (parishioners) to define them as superior mortals; the artists needed no encouragement to claim superiority to the great mass of men who form society's centre. In spite of some shared characteristics as pre-modern men, the parsons were 'convergers', but the artists were 'separatists'.

However, the separate, encapsulated worlds of the artists were far from uniform. In every case the artist distances himself from the wider society by expressing contempt, disdain or pity for its inhabitants. But for some the public sphere was remote and anonymous (although signals of recognition from this anonymous world were eagerly looked for and highly prized); while for others it involved extensive personal contacts. But not one of the artists interviewed — even the most publicly involved — thought that he shared the same world as other mortals. In some cases the sense of personal detachment took them to the brink of personal dissolution.

A number of artists living in and around a northern industrial town were interviewed in 1974 and 1975.[8] Contacts were made through galleries and by one artist providing an introduction to another. Although they were therefore in some sense a network, they were not a close 'circle', and some had very little contact with or knowledge of the others. Altogether eleven were interviewed at length about their way of life, interests and personal involvements. Ten were men, one a woman. They were mostly in their twenties or thirties, but one man was in his early fifties and another in his late sixties. Some had paid employment apart from their art work, but all painted pictures for sale. All had been born and attended school in this part of northern England, and some had never lived (or even visited) anywhere else. They were all artists who were apparently living with their 'roots'.

Distancing oneself from the centre

The artists who were interviewed had a lively sense of being different, but it was a superior difference. The world of 'ordinary people' was comparatively debilitated and trivial. No artist doubted the importance that art gave to his life: there was at least sharpened visual perception, but more commonly a sense of involvement in activities which had a self-evident claim to override other commitments. Other people might be a little wary of you, but they also looked up to you and many envied you. Ordinary work 'in the system' produced 'cabbages' and pathetic subservience to hidebound convention.

Roy Preble is an art school teacher who has now decided to leave his job and become a full-time artist. He has been teaching for fifteen years, but he has wanted to be an artist, he says, from the age of six. But the move into full-time professional art is a major one: 'It's just like emigrating, really.' The marginality he is about to embrace has no connotation of inferiority: 'You've got to have people like this, offshoots from the mainstream. Think of Watt, for example: he could have been just an instrument maker all his life.' It is the routine of school life that has all the connotations of inferiority: 'You become a cabbage ... and then retire.' Art is an overriding imperative: 'It is probably linked somehow with the basic soul of a person. I have felt it like a bell ringing at the door, becoming more insistent all the time.' The alternative to embracing life as an artist is to be squashed: 'You see people who are squashed, and you see people who are not.' As an artist he will stand with the tiny band that has defied this fate.

Albert Fisher is also a teacher, but he has not yet taken this final step; and so he must feel contempt for himself as well as for all those who are for ever 'in the system'. He is in his late twenties and has so far had only modest success with his art ('the most I've sold anything for is thirty pounds'); he realizes he has to come to terms with the art world as a system of patronage, and is prepared to do so ('I used to think I was wrong, but there it is: the only way you can get somewhere is by doing a bit of creeping'); but he thinks of himself as an artist rather than a teacher, and will become a full-time self-employed artist as soon as possible: 'It's just a matter of getting contacts.'

He has a particular contempt for all headmasters ('I've had several scuffles with my own headmaster about wearing jeans'), but a more general contempt for all schoolteachers: 'I look at older members of staff and think, "Oh, God, you're going to get just like that. Stop yourself now".' He sees himself as somehow different from other people because he's an artist; but he does not feel socially excluded by other people: 'It's not artists who are odd, it's other people. I think other people are odd, people who work in factories are peculiar. But I think middle-class housewives who have to say the right kind of things and watch what the neighbours think, are peculiar. In fact I feel sorry for them.' But he's contemptuous, too, of himself because he's still one of 'them': 'I've been right through the system and turned into a little teacher.'

For Albert Fisher art is a moral imperative and his career as an artist must take precedence over all other personal commitments. He is married with children but separated. His domestic ties had prevented his further studies in London: 'There's the Slade, the Royal College or the Royal Academy, and that means you do another three years. Now by doing that, no matter what kind of work you produce, you get contacts. You make contact with galleries in London.' His marriage prevented his going to London:

> Everything kind of piled up like a great muck heap around me ... Anyway, I've got right away from it now. I was tied down to one place and that made me boil over. It was like putting a stopper in, creating this tension. And people start expecting you to wear a sports jacket. I thought: 'That's not for me. Piss off out of this...'

In utterly different circumstances the high claims of art are heard and heeded, and no-one feels diminished or excluded by becoming an artist. Joan Kerr is in her late twenties, unmarried, and has a job in textile design: the claims of her part-time art work have ended two engagements to marry. She is a very sociable, indeed gregarious, young woman who enjoys dancing and pubs. She is modest about her part-time art (although ideally she would like to turn professional), but would like to be famous ('people do know me, you know'). She would like to be married but senses a threat to her art, and at the last minute draws back. It is true that the vicar warned her and her fiancé that artists are strange people and difficult to get on with — he knew because his son was one; but this was not the reason for not going through with the marriage: 'This last bloke, I'was very fond of him, still am, really; but he didn't have any interests of his own. I felt I would never have time for my painting.'

A former bus driver, Mike Smith is forty and has been a professional artist for the last ten years. For him art is just a job and he calls spades spades. He just drifted into full-time art after discovering that he could paint pictures which would sell. He paints for the money and runs a Rolls Royce: 'People say, "If he can afford a bloody Rolls Royce, he must be a bloody good artist".' But lately 'this aesthetic principle' has unwittingly crept in ('You don't start with it but you could end up with it'), and in general he has a sense of personal enhancement. He has a greater awareness of the visual world than ten years before. And he has entered a wider universe: 'Before I was definitely provincial. I looked on myself as a northerner. But today I'm a universal citizen. I used to think that the world was a massive place. It's not all that big, really.'

For fifty-two years, from the age of thirteen to sixty-five, Jim Steel despised his job as a clerk in the tannery. He is a widower and has now retired; he lives in a small stone house in a busy road. He had always wanted to be an artist but his father was against it and found him an office job. 'I never escaped.' But he has always painted; it has been a compulsion: 'You have to do it, like some folk have to kill somebody.' He has had some modest success: galleries have bought work he has shown in local exhibitions. 'People take me seriously. I'm happy about that. And sometimes at some functions ladies come up to me and say, "I've got one of your paintings — a farm and some trees".' Painting has been the real centre of his life: 'It's the only thing that's really interested me.'

He delights in invisibility: 'I'm very good at playing the part of a perfectly obscure, wretched creature creeping around with a shopping bag.' But this is a pose, and he knows it. He has never really wanted a bohemian life as an artist: 'Miserable business, that, having to sit around drinking metal polish. I'm not very interested in what artists are supposed to do.'

The world of the tannery was a miserable business, too, and compared with artistic activity contemptible: 'You just did it for the money. I treated it contemptuously, the business of keeping a set of books, running an office staff, paying wages and things.' Eventually he was company secretary and saw the hollowness of life in the boardroom:

> Taking directors' meetings, these six funny, stodgy men, you know. Preparing the agenda, listening to them talk, taking notes, then write the minutes in such a way that they'd be satisfied. You have to be careful about procedure. But there's nothing difficult about it. Business is a poor business. Being an efficient business man is the easiest thing in the world. You learn the basic craft, and you're laughing.

For a half a century Jim Steele watched with contempt: reality lay elsewhere, and was stored up in abundance awaiting his retirement.

The ambiguity of local ties

Local artists appear at first sight to have turned inwards to their roots for meaning and significance which they cannot find in the wider world. They have distanced themselves from the 'centre' and found meaning and support in the traditional, stable and personal relationships of neighbourhood and kin. This is illusory. They hate their home town. The northern artists who are the subject of this study had generally rejected the dominant and central values (and constraints) of an industrial, bureaucratic society in which they were not 'at home'. But they were equally 'homeless' in the mill town of their birth. At best their relationship with their 'own' locality was uncertain and ambiguous. Their principal concern was to communicate their personal vision to the wider, outer world which they despised and, finely and sensitively tuned for the purpose, to receive back signals, however weak, of recognition and applause.

Tony Little and Theodore Baron are both local men of roughly the same age (late twenties) who are making their mark regionally and nationally as painters. They differ sharply in many respects, not least in their sense and actual degree of social isolation. But they are alike in two principal ways: both feel some sense of superiority because they are artists, and both reject the label 'northern artist'. They are reaching towards a far wider community than their mill town in the north of England, and are intensely concerned about the wider public's response to their paintings. The wider world is relatively anonymous: it is populated by highly generalized 'typifications' such as dealers and rich bourgeois buyers and unknown men and women who walk round exhibitions of art. It is among the generalized typifications that they seek significance and an abiding sense of reality.

Tony Little is a full-time artist who grew up in this northern mill town, graduated from a local college of art, is unmarried and still lives with his parents. He has never been to London. He is a surrealist painter, his inspiration has been Dali, and he likes metaphysical art. He paints rubble; and he hates the mill town.

He is utterly lonely. He knows two or three fellow artists in the area, but has no sense of 'belonging around here'. He concedes that to an artist 'the area itself is interesting. But I'd rather not live here. Manchester I hate even more.' But he has no wish to travel and would like to live in the country: 'I've never been that interested in travel, although I wouldn't mind visiting London some time. But it's not a burning ambition. I don't think I've had a holiday in eight or nine years. There doesn't seem to be enough time.' But through his painting he feels that he is 'trying to become one with the universe, to feel part of everything that goes on around you. You can feel your personality slipping away. It's interesting to walk on the brink.'

Tony was interviewed in the front room of his parents' stone terrace-house. This was the 'best room', papered in old-gold print, with heavy brocade full-length curtains, a gold carpet, three-piece suite, coffee table and ornaments. His mother came in and told him to take off his paint-stained coat. He spoke with a strong local accent. He explained that after art school he had worked briefly in advertising but for five years had devoted himself entirely to art. There had been no protracted period of testing out his commercial worth; his income was still fitful and uncertain and he needed his parents' support: 'I wouldn't have been able to do it if it weren't for them. They don't really understand what I'm doing, but they're willing to stand by me.' He has had considerable success in exhibitions and has good contacts with galleries. He aches for financial independence ('There's nothing makes you feel happier than a successful exhibition') and is confident that he will achieve it.

The demands of his art cut him off from the community and even limit his involvement with fellow artists. He feels lonely and sees few people but does not believe that a small group of artists can live and work together: 'I don't think an artist can live in a group and produce anything valid. You can never really be yourself. You've got to be able to be alone. I couldn't work with another person in the room.' He is contemptuous of attempts to promote co-operative art: 'This chap from the Arts Council ... I just couldn't take what he was saying. He wanted to start these communal art activities, you know. Called it "Art Labs". I couldn't stand that...'

Marriage would threaten his art:

It would be very pleasant. But I'd say that art stops you from forming any firm relationships, because if you get too involved, and feel like getting married, unless the other person is very, very sympathetic, you've got to get a job and drop the art. I don't want to come to the point of having to throw up one or the other. I know many artists that are married and just had to stop painting because it was messing up their lives.

He has a strong sense of the boundary which separates the world of art from 'outside'. And he is contemptuous of the outside: 'Outside — I mean, what can you talk about? Football, for instance. I mean, it has no interest for me. I've seen arguments flare up over the length of cricket pitches. I couldn't be like that.' The barrier is always there:

There always seems to be a sort of wall built up in front of you, you know, and you're looking through a window, rather than outside. Now John, another painter round here, has done some drawings with birds and things like that. He seems to be trying to free himself from this idea that he's behind a wall. But it only strengthens the idea that he really is behind a wall.

He despises the world which excludes him. There are artists and there are 'ordinary people': 'Their attitudes to life are totally different. Other people's lack of understanding separates you, you know.' He has no illusions: 'You're an outsider. You feel it yourself. You feel more of a spectator than a participant in what's going on around you.' But he has a strong sense of his superiority, and involvement in the world of work, at any level, could only diminish him: 'The jobs I've had in mills, in summer holidays ... you just feel your mind slipping away.' He does not regret abandoning his career in advertising: 'I'd rather do anything than that — you know, these chaps panicking because they've spelt one word wrong in a rough layout ... they spend months working their heads off and then have it thrown back in their face.' Most of his art school friends have stayed in advertising, but he has no sense of loss or of having been left behind: 'You feel superior, really.' He accepts that his years as a professional artist have probably made him unfit ever to re-enter the world of ordinary work:

> It does mess certain parts of your life up, being an artist. One artist I know he's working in a mill now, you see. Very intelligent lad, but being an artist for a certain length of time has messed him up. He just can't get on with anybody at work. He won't be happy ever again, probably.

Art, Tony feels, is confrontation: 'That's what it is about — confronting sombody with something you've produced.' And in this sense art ties him to the world. But the tie, he feels, is more indirect, and therefore more tolerable, than writing poetry: 'You know, I just couldn't write poetry. It's too personal. But painting ... I think it takes guts, a real tough chap, to write poetry.'

Tony's art is confrontation and may upset and disturb people: 'My paintings use reality, but they use reality in a rather strange sense.' But a positive response from the other world of anonymous consumers of art is vital to him — and incognito he follows viewers at art exhibitions around to hear what they say about his paintings:

> You get five people who just walk past the painting without hardly pausing, and then you'll get one who's really taken with it. And that's great. You follow them around, because they don't know who you are, and you're listening to what they say. I even had one woman who cried at one of my paintings. I was really happy, not because she cried, but because if affected her.

Tony's dialogue through art is anonymous and indirect, with a minimum of self-exposure. He is now painting a solitary figure in a landscape — a clown surrounded by very uniform objects, very balanced, symmetrical: 'It's a clown, but it's also virtually a spaceman. The landscape, it's supposed to be rubble, but it turns more and more into another world. A clown in an empty landscape. There's nothing more useless than an entertainer without an audience. Or more lonely.'

Theodore Baron has a full-time job in industrial design. It is this, he thinks, which enables him to be truly an artist. He has no need to meet dead-lines or paint 'pot-boilers': his industrial job does not detract from his art but, on the contrary, makes possible his artistic integrity. He is now in his late twenties, married with children: he hopes to be a full-time self-employed artist one day, when he is firmly established. He feels that his art is 'gradually taking over', and in five years or so 'it might take over completely'. But he has a shrewd appreciation of market conditions and the importance of dealers. He has had four successful one-man exhibitions in the north and will have one shortly in London. His work has appeared in the Royal Academy. He is confident about his art but feels uncertain in the network of contacts that promotes it and knows he must learn and come to terms with 'the system'.

He is a local man who has lived in the mill town all his life and has married a local girl. His art is no threat to his marriage: his wife is sympathetic and goes with him to look round the galleries. He is a prudential man who carefully keeps an eye on the wider world: 'I make a point of going round exhibitions. I pay regular visits to London because I'm interested in development in British art.'

He has no sense of being an outsider or suffering from any stigma because he's an artist; on the contrary, he has a sense of special status: 'It can get quite embarrassing. This sounds a little bit conceited and big-headed, but people come up to you and say, "Oh, are you so-and-so?" People tend to talk *up* to you.' He knows various artists in the region but says he doesn't consider himself a member of a circle or clique. And although he paints industrial wastelands, canals and iron railings, he rejects any suggestion that he is a 'northern artist'.

The society he addresses and whose acclaim he wants and needs extends far beyond a mill town in northern England. He says he's not 'alienated' from the modern industrial world, but claims 'detachment'. He greatly admired Lowry: 'He can stand outside the crowd and look in. I'm not quite as detached as that. He's had a very lonely life-style, never been married, and his parents died when he was fairly young.' He is intensely concerned about public reaction to his paintings: 'It would be nice to have a tape-recorder hidden behind each picture in an exhibition; then the artist could play it back. That would be great.'

Tendencies towards public or private faces

Robin Coleman embraces the technological world which he claims to despise. He delights in technology but proclaims victory for nature in the end. He is a public man who promotes large-scale public art. But he stands aside from his public performances, disclaims the title of 'local artist', and sees cosmic messages in his paintings of the neighbourhood's multi-storey blocks. He talks often of Leonardo da Vinci and sees himself as a Renaissance man.

He is a successful man. He is delighted to refer to reviews of his work in the *Telegraph*, the *Guardian* and the *Sunday Times:* 'I've become quite famous in England, and very famous in the north. I've been on the box lots of times.' He was born in the north and went as a day-boy to a local public school ('a real right-wing fascist establishment'). After university and a degree in Fine Art he taught for two years in a technological college and then decided to make a living as an artist 'and see how much integrity I could retain'. Now married and in his late thirties, he feels that he's reached 'quite a powerful position, really, which I always wanted to have. But the great power I've got, which really pleases me, is that I can do my own work and make my own statements. At the same time my art has nothing to do with any provincial, mill type of mentality.'

He drives fast motorbikes. His large studio has benches with heavy hammers and assorted tools, chains and block and tackle in one corner, vast unfinished pieces of sculpture and lengths of timber. His immense paintings are in intense colours and the shapes are sharp and clearly delineated from each other. He is dismissive of art schools and advocates a system of apprenticeship for artists: 'Foundries and engineering works have a lot to do with contemporary art, and so do building sites. Art students should be apprenticed to foundries and welding shops.'

He has been engaged for many years in works of public arts. Once he painted the two end-walls of a terrace of stone houses: 'We painted them in lovely colours and designs in a week. Fantastic, because on two days we were rained off.' And another year he erected an enormous board in the market square for everyone to paint: 'I split it into strips. And everybody in the town, not just the children, had a go. You get people really excited. At the end of the week I gave the painting to the town to be exhibited in a school.'

His art celebrates the technological society: 'I went to San Francisco and New York for the simple reason that America has the maddest technology of all.' But he's 'into organic gardening' and proclaims that 'The consumer society must go: we've got to slow down and live simply'. And the technological resources of his studio are mobilized to attack the technological age. He is experimenting with fibreglass and mixing in colours and metal powders; and his vast murals show repressed minorities struggling and waving with violent gestures against the technological society: 'It is crumbling, you know; and this mural, when I've finished it, will express what I feel about the failure of technology and the way it has downtrodden the man.'

He has no sense of being separated from the community because of his art: 'I suppose some people say, "Who's this scruffy bugger" because I always look pretty dirty.' But he feels he can go into anybody's house if he wishes to do so: 'I know everybody. Pakistanis and Italians, know them all, on friendly terms, and councillors and the local MPs — all these people, who are all people in the world.'

He sees no barrier between himself and the world, but claims exemption from some of its disciplines. He is scornful of the world that has to submit to the industrial system and 'straight' careers — like his university friends who went into advertising. 'And several guys even got jobs as salesmen with Gillette.' As an artist he is above the discipline of time-regulated work: he is proud of his freedom 'to just sort of take off for the day, you know, and walk over the hills'.

He is proud, too, of his detachment and essential loneliness, his lack of real personal involvements: 'I can go into a pub by myself and sit down and draw and drink a pint and talk to anybody. But I've no friends — friends like such. I like women very much ... But in most conversations, I really don't want to know.' He is untroubled by his detachment: 'I might just be born not to feel lonely. It's an enviable situation in some ways. I like all these things, aeroplanes and fast bikes, but at the same time I feel outside them all. I always keep myself outside ... like with friends.'

Like Coleman, Donald Elton is a man in his late thirties who was born and went to school in the area, went away for a few years (to London) and now lives and works in the mill town as a self-employed artist. He is an intensely private man. For him modern technology, and especially film, have virtually destroyed modern art: 'I think painting's almost dead, except for a few isolated individuals who have simplicity and love of painting.' Today art is the creation of publicity: 'It has little to do with the artist's inner vision.' But he himself sees art as religious and mystical, 'a thing rich and various, a vast network of dreams'. Although he rejects most modern painting he is sympathetic to contemporary sculpture: 'It is such a silent art. And it is more or less colourless. But there is a flame in the silence. It speaks of endurance. There is something deeply impersonal in the sculptor's art.'

Donald is unmarried and is now living with his parents again. His childhood was happy and he always liked art at school — 'the only thing I was any good at, really.' He has always liked music, 'perhaps Beethoven more than anyone'; for him music represents the youthful innocence from which art springs: 'I used to rush home to listen to Wagner when I was about fifteen. There was something heroic about this. And that was a state of innocence. This music helped me to grow as a person and as an artist.' He has always been drawn to 'dark poets', and increasingly so in recent years:

Maybe you can idealize the darkness. I think you can. The idea that heroes can only exist in a dangerous environment, a dark environment. There wouldn't be any heroes in paradise. Have you read Gerard de Nerval? He's a dark artist, a French poet of about 1850, one of the great romantics of French poetry ... before Baudelaire. T.S. Eliot quoted a line from him about the dark prince, in his quartets. He considered himself the last of the troubadours.

Donald reads Rimbaud and is enjoying reading Hesse, especially *Steppenwolf* and *The Glass Bead Game*. A copy of *The Prodigy* lay open on his studio floor.

In his mid twenties he moved down to London where he lived and painted for seven years. They were restless, nomadic years: 'I stayed at the police station the first night, then in a hostel. I used to change my address about every three months.' And they were intensely lonely years:

I was very lonely. Art can be a very isolating thing, when you put it before everything else. You see, it's commitment, a spiritual commitment; but innocence is a miracle, it's a matter of loving life. In one's ignorance and loneliness one loses innocence ... it needs a certain kind of endurance. I had a breakdown. I couldn't stop working. But that was nine years ago. Since then, I believe, I've made one or two masterpieces...

He is no longer the same person: he has lost his innocence and become very ambitious, 'wanting to produce something that is great'. But it is a very spiritual ambition: 'I don't like parting from my work. In fact I wouldn't sell some of my work.' His art remains deeply private, not for promiscuous public consumption.

His first breakdown was not the outcome of loneliness, but of a suffocating sociability:

> I had one person living with me, and then another came along. I wanted to get on with my art. I felt I had no privacy, I felt trapped. And then there was a sudden wrench in my mind and I thought I had completely destroyed myself. I went to the hospital in despair. Sometimes I've thought that I'd never wish to live my life over again, because some periods have been very bad, when I've lost faith and been in utter despair.

In London he had some experience of drugs: 'I've had some great feelings, you know, when you feel very happy; but you're too far into things, too close to things really, to make anything of them. You can't capture them, they're too vague, too spread out, if you know what I mean.'

Back in the north he has no cosy sense of belonging: 'Living up here where my roots are can be quite isolating: I don't know anyone here in the north who is of similar temperament to myself.' His father is pleased with the idea that he's an artist: 'He's very proud of this picture I did of his mother. But we're very much apart. Although I live with him, I see very little of him, really.'

But he fears the possibility of rootedness and the consolations of belonging. He feels more part of the community than he did in London:

> Though I think it can tie you down. You get consolation from returning to your roots, but I think you have to overcome this. One doesn't really want to be consoled. Up here, where I know people, what they do, work and play, it seems a closed life. I think you've got to open yourself up to the world.

He works in a studio with two fellow artists, but insists that they're not a movement of any kind, that they're all individuals and do very different work. But they argue about art: 'It lessens the isolation, because the isolation can be very severe living in the north, and being the only one that has this interest. If you're working entirely on your own you can get yourself into a right mess.'

The group's relationships are too loose to be experienced as restrictive, although they have been given a common identity in *Guardian* reviews. They have a somewhat disreputable bohemian image because they have attracted various hangers-on: 'Lots of hippies at one time, and all sorts of strange people. And then there was Henry, who had no money, so he used to bring in those big 12lb turkeys that he'd nicked from the supermarket.'

Donald has had four major breakdowns. He has moved out of society and into eternity where he met death as a friend. He has experienced death and rebirth:

Now in Huysmans and the decadents there is a kind of dark, sensual thing that can be self-destructive. But Rembrandt, he's a man before he's an artist. This has been my failing these last few years: I've become an artist before I have a man. I don't treasure people in my life now. I used to treasure people, but my isolation has taken this from me. I tended to destroy this. But in the last few years I think I've come back.

He has inhabited disparate worlds:

I've been in danger of different worlds. My own world became too intense. I've been in hospital four times. One's ideals can cause these. They're a mystery, really. I mean, the mind's a miracle. Everything, moving your hand, speaking, it's a miracle ... The last time I went into hospital I thought I was dying. I woke up in the middle of the night and a thought came to me, that the world was a dream. My mind kept moving out of focus, believing that it had entered a different region. It was terrifying. All my warmth left me. I felt cold all over. And a kind of ease, a tremendous ease, and I thought that was death. It was such a vivid experience, such a clear experience.

He has met death again and now tries not to regard him as a friend: 'A few months ago, I felt a relaxation, like turning off into death. And I've had to change my thoughts and try to feel the opposite, and to feel afraid of death. It's a terrifying thing, it's so strange, and yet death sometimes is not terrifying.' And he has walked out of his flat and turned out of time into eternity:

It's happened twice. I've got into situations, through loneliness probably, through having a naive conception of eternity. Time can be a very frightening thing, because it's an infinite thing ... I remember one morning I felt quite gay and I came out of my flat and in my ego I wanted to share this happiness with eternity. And I felt a kind of twist, a kind of rebound in my head. I couldn't do this, the instant was wrong. In my innocence I had thought that eternity could be contained...

Donald has been influenced by cubism and likes simplified forms and 'pure shapes' but his work is 'more subjective, really'; yet through the formality and simplicity recognizable figures emerge. 'The greatest art is religious-mystical, but it is also natural.' He is not a public artist addressing a northern mill town: 'I think an artist is a spokesman for everybody. He speaks for the world.'

A public man

Paul Rose is a celebrity with a sense of destiny. He is a highly successful portrait painter and painter of greyhounds. He is now in his early fifties. He was born in the north and has seldom been away except for his five years of war service in the Navy. He has rich and powerful sponsors and patrons. Since his first paintings went to Bond Street more than twenty years ago, he acquired an agent in America, 'things have gone well. It was destined, really, from the beginning. And I've never changed my style since the day I started. Not that I'm ever satisfied, mind. But my style's still the same.'

He lives in a village street which is flanked by green fields with stone walls; his house is in a row of stone houses with glass porches and small neat gardens in front and hills at the back. The sitting room is small and square with brownish wallpaper hung thickly with pictures in elaborate frames. They are mainly portraits in dark, fierce colours. The mantelpiece is deep in ornaments and there is a comfortable three-piece suite.

Paul Rose has always been involved in art and there is no point at which he could say he moved from a 'normal' life into the world of art. But he has a very strong sense of the difference between the life he has lived and the requirements of 'ordinary' careers. He is deeply contemptuous of the 'rat-race' and its values, which he has not had to embrace:

My life is involved in art, and that's the end of it. I'm not in the system. I wouldn't join the rat-race. I've had a career keeping out of the rat-race. That's been my sole intention. A simple life, you know ... I've no hankering for lots of money and what have you.

I'm comfortable. I manage. Never loaded, never broke, but comfortable, you know. And my wife's the same, probably because we both come from families that were steeped in convention. As for me, having lived with it in my youth and having dropped out of it, we prefer to stay dropped out. There's too much falsehood about the rat-race and convention.

He is apart but has no sense of being an outsider; on the contrary, his apartness confers power and status 'inside', while at the same time affording release from the bind of convention. He says he has few close friends outside the art world, but a wide range of acquaintances. He readily accepts that he's somewhat apart, and this delights him:

Oh, yes, I'm very pleased. Very pleased. You couldn't get me in. If you were to come along and say, 'Look Paul, here's a top design job, £40,000 a year with ICI' I'd tell you to stuff it ... And I don't have to put up with convention. I can do things you can't do and get away with it. They come to expect unconventional things with me. This is the privilege you get for being outside.

He is a licensed outsider and is never lonely (and with women 'you just can't go wrong'):

If you're an artist you need never be lonely. People just drop in and say 'I haven't seen you for a bit, Paul. I'll just come in and look at your paintings.' And the phone never stops ringing some days. I have to ring the operator and tell her I want it taking off the hook. The worst thing you can do is go to the phone when you're putting someone's eyelashes in, each one to be put on independent, you know.

He is a popular man and enjoys great occasions:

There's an exhibition coming up ... well, we have MPs attend, and one or two lords, councillors and so on. Now it's a collar and penguin suit night, really, but I turn up in my usual clobber. And they take me as I am. In fact they'd think there was something wrong with me if I ever dressed myself up. That is what the advantages are. And people speak to you you don't know. So you've always got this air of friendliness about you.

At Christmas he gets cards from civic dignitaries, and at other times 'you get invitations to the civic ball, civic Sundays, and that kind of thing. Well, sometimes I go and sometimes I don't. But when I go, I get introduced to the lot, you know.'

He is active in pressure group politics over issues which relate to art and the environment. In this way he has actual political power in the community, which he exercises with prudence and restraint. He hastens to point out that he's no revolutionary:

A few years ago we formed this group to work for the good of art. We're all eminent artists in the group. We like to involve ourselves in the environment, and if we can get any conservation orders on something we think shouldn't be torn down, we do. We've got a lot of political strength in the group: we've got two councillors as honorary vice presidents and we can swing about eighty-three votes behind any councillor. We're not a revolutionary group, but we seem to manage to get a say. But we don't press it if we know there aren't any funds to do anything about it...

Paul Rose has a shrewd sense of business and some contempt for his clients. He knows he does well in inflationary times, when even working-class people often feel that their money is better spent on an 'original' than placed in a bank. And he relishes the snobbery on housing estates where an original outranks a Constable print. His paintings sell well in America, and he holds on to his dollars until the exchange rate seems favourable.

He painted a beauty queen in a variety of poses: 'They were all bought by businessmen, idiots, who paid out good money for them just to see a bit of crumpet on the wall.' He specializes in painting animals: 'People bring their pets. They generally park round the corner and bring them out of the car. And I painted forty-seven dogs for the canine societies of America. That was $350 a time.'

His life is disciplined and carefully planned. He has been to London to make sketches of alcoholics, but 'it's a matter of planning. It's not dashing off on a whim.' He is proud of his 'wildness' but it never disturbs his routine. Above all, he maintains, an artist must be stable; but he must also be careful not to get into a rut.

Paul Rose has no quarrel with his locality and none with England. He refuses generous invitations to America: 'I told them I wouldn't go to America for a nugget a yard. There's no place better than Britain. You can call it what you want, but it's the finest country in the world.'

His break with convention is within strictly circumscribed limits. He has developed no 'counter-cultural' sympathies:

The hippies did artists a great deal of harm. We lost a lot of respect through them. People thought we were the same. Artists are very respectable people. There's very few of us leeching off the state. I've no time for hippies at all. Drop out by all means, but do something constructive. And another thing: there should be a lot more patriotism than there is. There should be a Union Jack in every classroom, and on every village green, tall and proud. We need more discipline, that's what we need...

Conclusion

It would be absurd to try to construct from these sketches a simple, composite picture of the artist as marginal man, utterly separate from the public side of life, essentially solipsistic, his identity poised on the brink of dissolution. Contact with the wider world varied considerably in ideological stance, extent and particularity. But two overriding general themes ran through the interviews: the artist's strong sense of his superior apartness, and the precariousness of personal identity in private worlds.

Of course these studies have no baseline in early personal histories from which to measure any subsequent change. There was a general emphasis on long standing commitment to art extending back into early childhood, 'a bell ringing at the door becoming more insistent all the time'. This was a powerful inner compulsion which could survive years of discouragement: 'You have to do it, like some folk have to kill somebody.' The sense of a separate identity as an artist could be kept intact for half a century, stored up for full flowering in retirement, maintained unimpaired while wearing a bureaucrat's mask for half a lifetime. A decisive sense of change might come not through taking up art but from turning professional: it was 'like emigrating', a major step into a new world.

'Emigrating' in this sense might involve social ambiguity and financial uncertainty, but no sense of stigma. To be called 'a scruffy bugger' was only a back-handed compliment. Far from feeling stigmatized, all felt superior, and they distinguished themselves unthinkingly in their talk from 'ordinary folk'. This sense of superiority was more than self-congratulation at escaping the constraints of routine employment and structured careers; it arose from a sense of involvement in activities which stand at the very summit of human values. They would agree with Jacques Barzun that art is now 'accepted as the highest product of the human spirit ... The Western World assumes without question that the works of the artistic mind are superior to all others.'[9]

But moving into an artist's world usually meant a drastically attenuated public side of life. Any invasion of his private world was feared and resisted. Marriage was a potential threat to the artist's private world and might be abandoned or avoided explicitly on these grounds. The new reality was sharply distinguished from the reality of everyday life which was sustained by endless talk about football matches and arguments about cricket pitches. Even the 'public artist' conceded that he had 'no friends', and though he visited pubs he often sat alone, because 'in most conversations I really don't want to know'. Being an artist made one unfit for re-entry into everyday reality: 'He just can't get on with anybody at work (in the mill). He won't be happy ever again...'

The public for most of the artists was remote, anonymous, intermittently experienced. One artist followed unknown people around art galleries to hear what they might say about his paintings; another would like microphones installed behind his exhibited works so that he could know the judgements of faceless viewers. The world of the artist seemed to have no particularized, public side which was concretely experienced.

Who were the immediate, contemporary 'significant others' who supported them in their conception of themselves? They were 'local artists' with no sense of community; and they appeared not to form their own alternative community to any significant extent. As local artists in a northern industrial town they might have been expected to huddle together in a modern version of the Pre-Raphaelite Brotherhood. They did not. Their association was very loose. They suspected the Arts Council's zeal for 'workshops'; and one attempt by three artists to share a studio had been disturbed, fragile and short-lived. The most spectacular personal breakdown occurred when an artist was joined by others. Different timetables for living had to be synchronized: 'I felt I had no privacy. I felt trapped.'

What changes in self-conception arose from taking up an artistic career? The former bus driver who 'drifted into art' almost by accident and now owns a Rolls Royce was clear that his earlier philistinism had been eroded by genuine aesthetic concerns, and that his social and intellectual horizons had greatly expanded since he became a professional artist. The artists usually pointed to a progression in visual acuity, a growing ability, even compulsion, to see things 'not as other people see them'. This was sometimes rather inarticulately expressed, perhaps in terms of going 'bog-eyed'. A general and theoretical conception of what art was about, rather than the support of others, sustained and encouraged them in their unfamiliar perceptions. They knew with the authority of history and theory, rather than the support and prompting of friends, that their job was to reformulate the reality of everyday life.

What were the consequences for personal identity of moving from a world with roughly 'equal' public and private sides to one in which the public side was severely attenuated? When the world was collapsed to a single dimension, was there a corresponding collapse of personal identity? The parsons appeared to become more robust and whole when they 'went public'; the artists seemed more fragile and vulnerable when they 'went private'.

Donald's experience of 'inverted' time (which was strikingly like the experiences of a lesbian described in Chapter 7) might suggest a Durkheimian interpretation, perhaps this is an illustration of the symbolic replication of the social state? Edmund Leach has discussed the relationship between temporal concepts and marginal states, defining the marginal situation as one in which 'ordinary social time has stopped'.[10] A simpler and perhaps more convincing explanation lies in the importance of time as the unexamined bedrock of everyday reality, and its emergence as a self-conscious problem when the reality of everyday life is undermined. Donald's intensely private world had no temporal co-ordinates or bearings in the public sphere — through career structures or more humble daily agendas — which would hold it firm when the private structure of everyday life was under threat.

But this study of artists must end with a paradox. When the social world lost one of its two sides, the sense of personal identity did not contract (though it probably became more precarious); it expanded to a sense of all-embracing humanity. These 'local artists' felt kinship with a wider universe. Whether they felt smugly at home or ill at ease in the local world, they were all anxious for wider acclaim, and most of them kept scrap books of reviews of their work. They think of themselves as outside men; their situation is marginal at least in the sense that it lacks the clear structure and agreed definitions of most modern employment. But they do not feel trapped and belittled in a marginal world; they have a sense of belonging to a wider, even transcendant universe of actions, meanings and values. Their home is neither a northern mill town nor a network of artists. It is the whole of humanity.

5 | A home for the disabled: a change of tense

Death, say Berger and Luckmann, threatens one's primary socialization as a man and a moral being.[1] In its presence we are stripped of our secondary socialization into occupational and other adult roles which become an absurd irrelevance. The imminence of death presents a sub-universe of meaning which threatens the routine reality of everyday life. Categories of thought and 'typifications' which formerly made sense of the world are emptied of meaning and significance. The sub-universe of imminent death is the marginal situation *par excellence*. Death must be 'legitimated' (through religious or other theoretical explanations) if the plausibility structures of everyday life are not to be wholly subverted and personal identity is to retain its shield against the onslaught of nightmare. Death threatens chaos and the dissolution of our fugitive identities.

A Cheshire Home for the incurably physically diseased seemed an appropriate place to investigate the consequences for personal identity of the omnipresence of death. Even long term prisoners expect eventually to be free and plan with careful deliberation to keep their identities unimpaired until the time of release; in a Cheshire Home keeping identities intact could have no such point: release will only come with death. As a 'total institution' a Home also afforded an opportunity to examine Goffman's contentions regarding resocialization as stages of an inmate's 'moral career'. Perhaps, in exemplification of interactionist socialization theory, Cheshire Home residents would receive the institution's definition of themselves and their situation, and would accept as entirely 'plausible' their terms of waiting in the anteroom of death.

Life-planning was hardly expected to be a source of personal identity for inmates of a Cheshire Home, but it was expected that time would be problematical and change it's meaning. Research into inmates' subjective 'timetables' in superficially similar institutions — TB hospitals[2] and high-security wings of prisons[3] — emphasizes the significance of constructing 'bench marks' to order the flow of time and structure its progress towards a final desirable end — release. In a Cheshire Home there is no release and time is not a commodity to be wasted or saved; it is simply an extended present experienced under sentence of death. The TB patient interprets the privileges he is granted as markers on the road to recovery (and he may even bargain and negotiate with staff regarding the precise timing of his discharge); long term prisoners, for whom time has become an abyss, 'an open landscape rather than a set of pigeon-holes', may measure, order and regulate the flow of time through progress in weight-lifting prowess; but the only 'progress' for the Cheshire Home resident is in the stages of his disease, which can have only one, non-negotiable end.

The inquiry

A Leonard Cheshire Home is a protected enclave in the margins of the world. Typically a large house in a rural setting, surrounded by its own (often densely overgrown) gardens and grounds, it provides a safe refuge for its residents from the intolerable and impossible demands of normal life.

The inmates or patients (they are invariably referred to simply as 'residents') have voluntarily entered the Home, usually with a great sense of relief and an even greater sense of privilege. Theirs is a 'sub-universe' with only attenuated links with the wider society. It seemed likely that a Cheshire Home would be the location of a counter-reality; a social base as described by Berger for the construction of a counter-world with its own institutionalized cluster of counter-identities.

There was, in fact, a quietly tenacious normality. It is true, there was none of the strident ambition and competitiveness that was apparent among the blind (see Chapter 6): the severely physically disabled persisted in a more muted version of normality. A Cheshire Home is an instance of 'quietist' marginality. But the three categories which give shape and meaning to the lives of normal people — sex, age, and occupation — were categories still used for interpreting their lives and the world (even though these categories were officially disregarded and discouraged). Only temporal categories were modified: 'distorted' time perspectives made the past very shallow and the present infinite.

In 1974 interviews were carried out with fifteen residents of a Cheshire Home. The Home had thirty-two residents (fifteen men and seventeen women) and its daily running was in the hands of a matron and three nurses with supporting domestic staff. The interviewees — who included two couples who had fairly recently married in the Home — were nine men and six women. (The men included two short-stay residents who had come to the Home for a few weeks to give their wives some relief). They were selected as far as possible from those who had had a period of normal, healthy life before becoming physically handicapped; but two men afflicted from birth were also interviewed, one a congenital spastic, the other suffering from muscular dystrophy.

The men ranged in age from twenty-one to fifty-three, the women from thirty-four to sixty-five. The most common disease was multiple sclerosis (four men, five women). The sixth woman to be interviewed suffered from degeneration of the spinal cord. All six women and five of the men had degenerative diseases which had progressed over a number of years, with a steady decline in mobility and general health, before they entered the Home. But four of the men who were interviewed had been cut down suddenly in the full vigour of manhood: three — a window cleaner, a slaughterman and a long distance lorry driver — had been paralyzed in road accidents at the age of twenty-nine, thirty and thirty-five respectively, and a ship's cook had been paralyzed by a stroke at the age of forty-three. All fifteen interviewees were confined to wheel chairs and had little control over their limbs. Their speech was slow and often slurred and indistinct.

On average the men were younger than the women but had been in the Home longer. The men had been in the Home for between two and thirteen years; excluding the two who were handicapped from birth, they had been seriously ill and unable to work for between four and thirty years; the average age of the onset of illness was thirty-two. Thus they had generally enjoyed a considerable period of normal, healthy, productive life before they fell ill and had spent some years as handicapped people — usually in their own homes — before entering a Cheshire Home. Although the women were older and had been handicapped for much longer, they had been in the Cheshire Home for a much shorter time — from a few weeks to six years. On average they had been handicapped for some twenty years before entering the Home, and two had been in hospital geriatric wards. But five of the six had worked for a considerable time until they fell ill (on average in their early thirties): one had been a war-time inspector of munitions and later worked in the potteries; one — a Cambridge English graduate — had been a schoolmistress; one had been a manageress of a Co-op shoe shop; one had been a factory worker, and one a nurse. Seven of the nine men had similarly been well established in work — a motor mechanic, a marine engineer, a ship's cook, a slaughterman, a window cleaner, a storekeeper, and a long distance lorry driver.

Three of the men were bachelors, three were formerly married but their marriages had broken up through the wife's adultery after their illness started. (One, aged fifty-two, had recently remarried, this time a fellow resident in the Home, aged sixty-five). Both the short-stay men were still married (one had five children, the other two). One male resident, aged twenty-one, had recently been married, for the first time, to a fellow resident aged thirty-four.

Three of the women were spinsters, two had recently married two of the male interviewees, and one fifty-year-old woman was still married and spent one weekend in four at home with her husband. (The husband never visited her in the Home).

The interviews were carried out in bedrooms or in the 'quiet room' set aside for visitors; they were tape-recorded and lasted for between one and two hours. The interviewees were encouraged to talk about their lives before entering the Home, to give an account of life in the Home, and especially to say in what way they felt cut off from the world or still in touch with it. They were asked about the different stages or phases of their lives and what they saw as 'turning points'; and they were asked about the way they felt they had changed in outlook and attitude, how their priorities had changed, and what they now regarded as important in life that formerly they had not. Within this very loose framework of questions about biographical stages, changes in outlook and social relationships, the interviewer allowed the subject to talk freely, gently probing issues which arose and seemed likely to throw light on the nature and consequences of a particularly harrowing form of marginality.

Marginality as sanctuary

Migrant southern negroes who work during the harvest months on isolated labour camps in the northern states of America have been studied as a marginal population which is stigmatized and in retreat behind 'the relatively impermeable boundaries established by the larger society'. Life in the camps is very low-key, competitive and aggressive behaviour is discouraged, individual differences are minimized, and interpersonal relationships are shallow. The workers are usually opting out of the strains of normal life, and 'the migrant labour stream seems to represent a respite from the demands of society, sometimes by choice, but usually through lack of alternatives. A camp is, in this sense, a sanctuary, marginal to society.'[4] The marginality of the Cheshire Home is not dissimilar. Residents insist that they are 'really normal', but for their physical handicap (but they know that 'A lot of people think that because you're physically disabled, you're also mentally disabled'); they have a secret pride in particular gifts or abilities — perhaps their willpower, their understanding of human nature, their tolerance, or even 'second sight'; but theirs is not a competitive world. They keep a 'low-profile'. The wheelchair is a great leveller. The residents are not without conflict and tension, but theirs is a wheelchair republic.

Residents are generally full of praise for the staff and deeply grateful for their patience, skill and unfussy helpfulness, and for the secure environment which they provide. They are grateful for the personal attention that they receive and for the fact that theirs is not a batch existence. (Four of the interviewees — two men and two women — had previously been in the geriatric wards of hospitals and knew the difference.) At first sight the Cheshire Home appears to be a good example of Goffman's 'total institution', but in reality it fits Goffman's picture only in a very superficial way. Residents do not 'march through the day's activities in the immediate company of a batch of similar others'; only if they all stayed in bed — as they would in a geriatric ward — would uniform treatment of their non-uniform disabilities be possible. Nor do inmates and staff conceive of each other 'in terms of narrow hostile stereotypes'.[5] The truth is more complex.

A woman in her sixties who has been in the Home for five years and before that spent a period in a geriatric ward, said:

> I really didn't know what to expect when I came here. But you see, when you've been like I was, some years in a geriatric ward, because you can't be cured, you're labelled, just one of a number — a place like that is shocking compared with this. And you're all packed together. This isn't a hospital, this is our home. The only thing wrong is you don't have a front-door key. You can go out when you like, so long as they know where you're going and when you'll be

back. And you can have visitors all day long. But most important, you have a great sense of security. You know that if you tumble you'll be missed and they'll come looking for you. I've settled down. I don't say, 'Oh, I wish I was away from here'. Of course in a small community you get mixed feelings. You may bring up a subject that treads on somebody's toes, and then the balloon goes up. But it breaks the monotony. The winter's the worst, when we're all hemmed in. In the summer you can go out on the patio. But life is more normal here because we can do things. We have our own shop in the dining room, and a telephone. But of course there have to be some rules. You couldn't manage without them.

You have a sense of community here?

That's right. Of course some people who are handicapped are very bitter. But only odd ones. You'll find there's more happiness in a room of thirty or forty people who are handicapped, than there is in a room of thirty or forty people who are well and strong. You see, when you're set aside from doing the big things in life, you see the beauty around you. We amuse ourselves watching the birds on the patio. Whereas you people, you'd walk past and ignore that. We see the beauty of small things. There are two sides to everything in life. I'm grateful for what's been done for me. It must have cost the state a lot of money, you know, not being able to work since I was thirty.

The sense that the future, whatever it may hold, is provided for, comes out strongly in the interviews. A spastic in his late forties, who was cared for by his mother until she died a year previously, feels privileged and secure:

I feel privileged in being accepted here. I actually came for a month at first — a trial period. It was a trial on both sides. But I'm privileged in the way the staff look after me, in giving me my meals, putting me to bed at night, and getting me up in the morning. Of course there are some things I don't like — I have to go to bed at 7.30, but some go at 8 o'clock or even 8.30. But I'm very tolerant, a placid person, very quiet and observant. Some people are quickly annoyed by things that happen, but I don't make any remarks about what people do.

Do you look forward to anything, apart from meals?

Yes, I look forward to the future, that there will be people that will be able to look after me in years to come. Oh yes, I'm always doing that.

Nevertheless there are 'moaners'. Both staff and fellow residents resent their 'troublemaking' and inability to appreciate what is done for them. One or two regularly complain about the food and even have items of food brought in by the orderlies. The staff, who eat the same food, feel that such moaners simply show a lack of understanding and a generally low level of mentality. They point, by contrast to others — who usually have educational qualifications and are known to have held fairly high-status jobs — as intelligent and understanding people who are 'worth talking to'.

Two bitter and unco-operative men are both fifty years of age and have multiple sclerosis. One has been in the Home for thirteen years, the other for nine. The staff say that the former refuses to bathe or change his underwear; he refuses to go on the holidays and excursions that are arranged, but resents the fact that Matron does not cajole him into going. He has no visitors: 'To tell you the truth, I've got a sister-in-law and her husband, and they've not been near the place in five years. They live just over there, first road on the left, first on the right. They never come near the place. Nobody's been in five years.' He feels that the Home is less selective in its intake than it used to be, and he resents his fellow residents: 'They're all strangers, now. I've never seen people like this before. It wasn't like this when I first came. They were fussy then who they took. It's not right that you have to live with them all.' And the staff are now inadequate: 'They haven't got enough staff. They can't get us up in the morning. You have to wait. There's no one to shave me.'

The second man is socially isolated and refuses either to go out or do anything constructive in the Home: 'I don't do anything now. I used to make stools at one time, but I got fed up with it. I used to have a pint, but now I just watch television. I never go outside. I don't go on outings. If you don't go out you don't have to come back. I just watch television day and night.'

It would be wrong to conclude that these two men, similar in age, in the nature and duration of their handicap, and their period of residence in the Home, represent a 'stage' in the 'career' of a Cheshire Home resident. They stand out as exceptions even in this small population of interviewees. Indeed, this study gives little support to any tidy notion of stages of institutional socialization like those that have been suggested for prisoners[6] or inmates of mental institutions.[7]

Goffman maintained that a patient in a mental institution, stripped of his previous identity, often failed to find a new one:[8] he reached a stage of 'moral loosening' or 'moral fatigue'.[9] Of course unlike prisoners and the mental home patients on whom Goffman focused his attention, Cheshire Home residents are voluntary: they have even entered into and passed a kind of competitive test for entry. But what is striking is the apparent persistence of the biographical self and, in general, the absence of moral fatigue. (It is true that the staff suggested that some interviewees might be 'unreliable', but the consistency of their accounts of themselves and the Home made their testimony entirely convincing.)

A third middle-aged man (aged fifty-four) with multiple sclerosis, who has been in the Home for eight years, was strikingly different from the two described above. Like them he is confined to a wheel-chair, and now his sight is rapidly deteriorating. He is outgoing and highly gregarious: he has 'colonized' an area of corridor, at a main intersection of passageways, which gives him a strategic position in the Home's communication network. He dislikes the official sitting rooms which, he feels, are dominated by television and discourage conversation. He is usually in conversation with two or three people, residents or staff. Communication is his main activity which he explains by saying that he is 'bone idle really'.

He appreciates the advantages of the Home and the difficulties of running it: 'To be in a place like this is marvellous, but it must be an awful job to make everyone feel contented — everyone's different.' He does not feel one of a batch: 'I like it here, there's just enough people. You don't just become a name or a number. You retain your individuality. You can stay as you are, which you can't if you become one of dozens or hundreds.' But he knows that the handicapped are mildly stigmatized and marked off from the wider society, and recognizes that inside the Home there must be a process of levelling down.

Do you have many visitors?

My mother, when she was alive, came every month. Now my sister comes once a month. I used to go every month to the Masonic meetings in the town, and I was invited to a lot of other places. I seldom go on organized day trips. You get used to living with all handicapped people. You've got to live with it. It's more difficult with strangers, for them to adjust to you, rather than you to them. They show sympathy, they make allowances, and that rankles a bit.

I think they talk down to you. The point is, they think you're barmy. Well, I'm not. It's difficult for them to know what to do.

Have you made friends with people here?

Oh, yes. Of course some people are full of woe, 'Oh look what's happened to me'. But what difference does it make? You've got to live with it and above it. All this moaning is wrong. You've got to get people to realize what they are and not try to be a big shot. But some people say, I used to be this and that. Well, that's just too bad. You're this and that now, so forget what you used to be. You live for the present, and not for the past or future. The future is in the lap of the gods. You just hope. It could be a damn sight worse.

The Cheshire Home is a sanctuary. Individual differences and competitive achievements and statuses are played down; life is low-key, muted. And yet for most residents it is a less 'marginal' world than the one they knew immediately prior to entry. As their illnesses have progressed they have become more and more socially isolated; they have realized they have become 'just a nuisance'. The Cheshire Home builds new if limited links with the world.

The Cheshire Homes themselves constitute a nationwide network: residents often go to another Home for a 'holiday'. Some prefer this to temporary re-entry into the normal world: 'I look forward to going on holiday — I go on exchange to other Homes. I like that, but not everyone does. It's a change of scene and different people to talk to, a different atmosphere and way of working.' But most look forward to contacts outside the enlcosed network of Cheshire Homes:

When a group's coming to entertain, we look forward to that. And then there are the day-trips — we're going to Blackpool one day, Southport another. And then there's the races. And there's a dance on Saturday for the helpers, and residents can attend that if they want ... We had a Garden Party in June, which a lot of people attended. And on May Day we had a little celebration. People came to the Home — played games on the lawn. It was all very exciting.

By contrast illness in their own homes was socially isolating:

You don't get the company that you get here. You don't see as many people — you can't go out to see people. You get visitors now and then, but I spent hours and hours alone in that room. I saw the opportunity when I came here, I saw the opening — I saw the space in the house.

Another resident observed: 'There's more to do here. At home, when my husband was at work, I just used to sit and smoke. You've got to be strong and well to run a home.' A former merchant seaman is quite emphatic that he is less 'cut-off' than during his time at sea — a Cheshire Home is not at all like a ship: 'You're less lonely than in the Navy. People gather round you more. There's always someone coming in or going out. You're never left alone for ten minutes. Perhaps that's because I run the shop.'

But relationships within the Home are kept shallow, relatively uninvolved. Residents resist being totally engulfed by the institution: relatives and friends who come as visitors are of major importance. These are the people with whom one can talk about intimate and personal matters. A married woman of fifty who has been in the Home for a year talks over important matters with her husband: 'You don't talk to comparative strangers about your affairs, private affairs. The people here, you can't say they're friends. They're people you're with, they're quite nice really. You're friendly with them. There's some you're more friendly with than others.' A single woman of fifty-three who has also been in the Home a year said: 'I have quite a few friends who live near here, fortunately. I've made friends with the two people I share my mealtable with, but I haven't any best friends here, not in the sense I used to have. I know most people and their names, and I know the ones who are always complaining.' Even after three years in the Home another fifty-year-old woman draws a sharp distinction between her real friends outside, and fellow residents with whom she only exchanges pleasantries:

> I don't have a lot of friends here. I'm very lucky I have one or two friends who come to see me. I know them better. They knew me before I was ill. They've always come over the years. I get on well with people here, just speaking to them, but I never get into deep conversation. I prefer it like that.

When someone dies, the pattern of life and relationships is not deeply disturbed.

Death and personal identity

In a Cheshire Home death is always at hand. Residents have often seen members of their own families die from the same illness as their own. One woman in her fifties who is suffering from multiple sclerosis has seen her three brothers die from the same disease. She is an expert on its stages and consequences and knows she will live for only two or three years. The young man of twenty-one who recently married has muscular dystrophy. Four years ago he entered the Home with his brother who was suffering from the same disease. The brother died a year ago. The young man knows that he is unlikely to live beyond his mid twenties. The man of fifty who has been thirteen years in the Home has seen many people die and is preoccupied with death. His mother died some years ago in the local hospital and he still counts up the weekly deaths that occur there: 'I don't know what they did to her, but if you read the local paper you see what a lot of deaths there are. Last week there were nine deaths, the week before that seven. Since Christmas 102 people have died there.' He measures his time in the Home by the deaths that have occurred around him: 'When I first came here, there were only three of us. There was Jock and Tom and me. Tom died soon after, then Jock died five years ago. There have been thirty-two deaths since I came here. It's very depressing. Four of them have died in my room.'

This, for Berger, is marginality in its extreme and 'purest' form. Death, and the prospect of death, constitute crises which involve the risk of a breakdown of reality.[10] And while one's 'primary socialization' is deeply threatened, one's 'secondary socialization' is simply trivialized. In fact, marginal life and the prospect of death in a Cheshire Home leaves primary socialization largely unaffected. It is the loss of one's identity as a lorry driver or window cleaner that is the paramount affront.

Berger asserts:

> The experience of the death of others and, subsequently the antici-pation of one's own death posit the marginal situation par excel-lence for the individual. Needless to elaborate, death also posits the most terrifying threat to the taken-for-granted realities of everyday life.[11]

For Berger the high drama of marginality calls for nothing less than a fundamental revaluation of the self:

> The reality of secondary internalizations is less threatened by marginal situations, because it is usually irrelevant to them. What may happen is that such reality is apprehended as trivial precisely because its irrelevance to the marginal situation is revealed. Thus it may be said that the imminence of death profoundly threatens one's previous self-identification as a man, a moral being, or a

Christian. One's self-identification as an assistant manager in the ladies' hosiery department is not so much threatened as trivialized in the same situation.[12]

All the residents insisted on the continuity between their present and former selves, even over perhaps thirty years of illness; and all pinpointed the break in their working lives as the real move into marginality. They looked back on their working lives with fondness and pride. None mentioned any revaluation of their Christian selves, except to disclaim any current strong interest in religion. Their deepest problem before entering the Home was that they had indeed become trivialized, had become 'nuisances'. 'I didn't want to live with any of my relations. I felt I had just become a nuisance.' The Home provides some reassurance: 'Even if I want a hair moved from my face, I have to ask someone to do it. You're so dependent. I said to one of the nurses, "I feel such a nuisance". She said, "You mustn't talk like that, Betty", and that helped a lot.'

They insist that they were normal once and are normal now. 'If it wasn't for not being able to get about', said a paralyzed middle-aged man, 'I'm as normal as anyone. I haven't changed my outlook in the ten years I've been paralyzed. Life is much the same in or out of a chair. The only thing is, you can't do what you want when you want.' Another looked back over more than twenty years of incapacity: 'At first you plan to try to do things, but eventually realize you can't. But I don't think your personality is altered.'

Two of the men conceded that in the early stages of their illness, as they became more dependent on others, they had become very irritable; but claimed they had since become placid and tolerant. 'I used to be bad-tempered. Now I never lose my temper. There's not much point, it gets you nowhere. I'm more placid. Nothing floors me now.' Some see themselves as always having been strong-willed and still being 'fighters':

In the war, in the army, I was an amateur fly-weight boxer. I had twenty-five fights and won twenty-three. I can defend myself even now — with words. When the doctor told me seventeen years ago that I'd got disseminated sclerosis, I knew I'd never get better. I'm not a fool. I took it on the chin, like a man. I've still got fight in me, and will have for the rest of my life.

No-one looking back even from prolonged and extreme marginality finds his former occupation 'irrelevant' or trivial. It is precisely 'secondary socialization' into an occupation that gains in significance. The former schoolmistress now in her fifties who has been confined to a wheelchair for eight years was asked (like everyone else): 'How has your life changed by coming to this Home?'

> Well, the big change, really, was nearly twelve years ago, when I had to give up my job as a teacher. Of course life has changed a lot since I came here a year ago, but I've adjusted to the routine — getting up and eating. I'm very grateful to the folk who run this place. But the biggest change was when I stopped work. I miss my job most of all. I really enjoyed the pupils and what happened to them after they left. I hear occasionally now, but it's not the same. I went to a play production at my school a week ago. I go sometimes. I'm still more occupied with outside interests than inside.

The former ship's cook would go back to sea if he could — and he is still very interested in food. He looks back on his twenty-six years at sea 'very often. I think about it with admiration. They were a grand lot of men and lads. I like the ship and I like the life. I'd go back tomorrow if I could.' And the former slaughterman, now fifteen years away from his work, said 'I do miss my job. I can still, like, bone a piece of beef or shoulder of lamb, and do when I get the chance. I couldn't kill one now, but I can still bone.'

Questions about change led invariably to an insistence on continuity and normality. At fifty-one a former motor mechanic recalls giving up work thirty years ago:

> I was very fit till I was twenty-one. I was a good mechanic. But I've got no future, to tell you the truth. I don't know why I go on. I've lost everything. I would have been a very good motor mechanic. That was all I wanted, I was so good with cars. But you don't really change. I'm just like I was then, except my eyes are worse now I'm older. I had an old car in the back garden which I used to take apart and put back again. I ought to be a motor mechanic now.

From the receding margin of the world modest occupations relinquished decades ago provide a reference for the whole of life and seem to grow rather than diminish in significance.

Categories of age and sex

Goffman maintains that in mental hospitals the patient capitulates to the official, psychiatric version of himself: 'The patient must ''insightfully'' come take, or affect to take, the hospital's view of himself.'[13] Psychiatric doctrine and the routines of the hospital instil the lesson of deep-seated incapacity:

> In the mental hospital, the setting and the house rules press home to the patient that he is, after all, a mental case who has suffered some kind of social collapse on the outside, having failed in some overall way, and that here he is of little weight, being hardly capable of acting like a fully fledged person at all.[14]

The Cheshire Home likewise offers the inmate a new version of himself, but the inmate quietly, obstinately, and successfully rejects it. The official version of the inmate is that he is now neuter.[15] Although the Home contains roughly equal numbers of men and women, who spend the day together and share the daily round of activities, they are treated as essentially sexless. Differences in age are also disregarded. And the residents tenaciously maintain age-sex categories to structure their relationships and interpret their lives. The residents have signally breached their officially neuter classification by marrying one another.

Cheshire Homes admit people between the age of sixteen and fifty, but exceptions are made, and some who are admitted at fifty are still alive many years later. The age range is therefore wide. Age differences are certainly less important than in the outside world, but their significance is now wholly obliterated. Older women wish to look younger ('Well, actually I'm fifty-seven, but I hope I look younger than that'), and older residents feel that the young should be in a separate establishment. One man in his fifties said: 'When people are in wheelchairs, age doesn't make much difference', but later went on to express some impatience with the young:

> Some of the residents are young, about twenty. I think the young should be kept with the young, the old with the old. Of course very old people aren't allowed in. But once you're in you can stay as long as you live. But the young should have their own place. I don't like their pop music.

Sexual identities are more persistent and important. A former merchant seaman, a life-long and unrepentant bachelor, has discovered women for the first time: 'All the women seem to have a kind disposition, and are more soft to the touch than men. I get on with the men, but I think I'd sooner have the women. The women are kinder, more understanding. At sea I was with all men. They were rough. This is gentler.'

The Home levels all residents to the status of 'single' and gives no special consideration to residents' husbands and wives, who are simply categorized as relatives. It is true that when a husband or wife is physically handicapped the marriage is placed under great strain and is likely to end in divorce. One married woman still sees herself as being married and having a husband, and regards her fellow residents as sexually negative: 'I have made friends here, but ladies or men can't make much difference. They're all the same here.' Staff would agree with her, but most of her fellow residents would not.

An unmarried woman in her fifties, who is unable to walk, can now scarcely grip with her hands, and is rapidly losing her sight, was very carefully dressed when, without prior notice, she was interviewed. One of her pleasures in life was having her hair set. She wore a careful combination of colours, jewellery, and a scarf, fixed by a gold clasp that needed constant attention. She wore a bracelet and a ring. During the course of the interview a male orderly entered with a pile of laundry, mainly knickers. He dropped them on the bed. The resident was clearly upset and embarrassed by the public handling of women's underclothes by a male. She gave an account of her life in the Home. She regrets that she can no longer knit, but her pleasure now is that 'some days they do your hair. I like that.'

Another single woman of fifty who now has little control over her facial muscles but occasionally manages to smile, had her hair carefully styled and was wearing some jewellery she had made. She would have liked to watch more television, but accepted as the way of life the male dominance of programme choice: 'I can't read like I used to, so I watch television. There's one colour set and one black and white, but they sometimes have the same channels on. My choice would usually be different, but it's the men who decide, and certainly when it's football.'

The men are quite clear about their masculine identity in spite of sexual impotence and broken marriages. Three of the seven permanently resident men who were interviewed had been married, and all three were now divorced. Their wives had left them for other men after they fell ill, and the marriages had ended in divorce. One man who has been divorced for twenty years looks back with understanding on his wife's behaviour: 'She left me, she was perfectly justified. I can see her point. I had become very bad-tempered. What got me down was being so dependent on my wife. We'd always got on very well, but I became a perfect oaf to live with.' He has come to terms with his incapacity ('You just go along knowing what you can do, and that's it') but still claims to have sexual ambitions: 'Of course, you don't come to a place like this expecting to find dancing girls in every room; but I've still got one ambition, but I don't think I dare mention it...'

The other two divorced men were bitter about their former wives. One said: 'I was coping quite well — I was issued with a car — but when I found she was messing about, I lost interest. As long as I don't ever meet her again, that will suit me.' He has been in the Home for nine years and is still totally preoccupied with other-sex relationships and prides himself on his attractiveness to women:

> I don't talk to the men. I've got two ladies who take up most of my time. And a nurse who was at the hospital where I was before comes to see me. She took a fancy to me, and that was that. I don't bother with the men. Talking to these women is all right. It would be awful, all men. If there were no women here, you'd get fellows who go mad when they do see a woman. But I don't think it's any good getting married like this. What future have you got? No house, and you can't have a life like you should when you're marrried.

He believes there is a cure that the Home is keeping from him ('It's Eastern syrup — with arsenic, and strychnine and a drop of quinine'). This would make him sexually potent and able to dominate women. 'Why can't I get it? I'd be walking around and crushing women now.'

The third divorced man has remarried in the Home. He has been confined to a wheelchair for fourteen years. Of his former wife he says: 'She didn't do her best. And then she found a young man and committed adultery. That was very bad. I think so, anyway. Later she met a wealthy old man and got married to him. She was a beautiful girl. I don't know why she should do such a thing.' He regards his recent marriage to a fellow resident in her sixties as an unqualified success, and he proudly wears a wedding ring: 'We had the wedding at the Congregational Church. It was a wonderful wedding — not top hats, but I had my best clothes, which are worn out now. We had a hundred guests at the reception. I was very popular then.' He is rather less popular since his marriage:

> Some people don't like my wife: I really don't know why. Some of the residents thought I was stupid to get married. But I knew what I was doing. That's all that matters. I'm a lucky man. That a woman should accept me. When I got engaged I'd only got four pounds ten. And I proposed to get married on four pounds ten. But money isn't everything.

His wife is equally satisfied. She recalled their courtship with pleasure:

> My husband came here from another Cheshire Home for a fort-night's holiday. That was three years' ago. Now, I have the gift of what they call 'reading'. When I look at a person for a few minutes I can tell what sort of person they are. I could see that he was after me. At that time I was decorating postcards and selling them. He wanted some to send back to the other Cheshire Home. I said, 'I won't take the money', and he said, 'I'll give you a kiss for them'. Anyway by the time the fortnight was up he'd asked me to marry him. He said, 'All I can give you is my name and my love'. So I said I would. The Matron tried to stop it — said it was just a holiday flirtation, but I said, 'No, we intend to get married'. The Chairman of the Management Committee said we could get married, but there was no married accommodation for us. We got married the following August, and eventually we were given our own room.

Marriage has made a great difference to her life:

> We enjoy married life. And there are things we can talk over in private which we couldn't talk about with others. Of course, we've both got the same disability. I do think that if one of a married couple becomes disabled, and the other is healthy, the healthy one gets tired of it. We don't have that problem.

The younger married couple (she is thirty-four and he is twenty-one) are also delighted with their marriage and would recommend other people in Cheshire Homes to marry: 'It has worked out so well for us.' On the other hand, they do not feel that marriage has made a great deal of difference to their lives: 'It's just the same really. We'd prefer somewhere of our own. A living room would be good. We would prefer to be more separate.' Both staff and residents play down their married status:

> We have our own bedroom and it was all decorated for us. But it's small. It doesn't have much room for our things. We've got such a lot of stuff now. We've got two single beds, but we've pushed them together. We would have liked a double bed. They said the room wasn't big enough. But we pushed our two single beds together. We chose new wallpaper and curtains and things.

They realize that their no longer neuter status faces the staff with problems:

I think it was hard for the staff to get used to — especially with the buzzers at night. They didn't know if it was a man or woman wanted. When they come, some knock on the door and some don't. We'd like it if they all did. It's different when you're married. When someone comes we just stay while the other is attended to. The staff don't bother now. We need them. We really can't help each other.

Permission to marry had to be fought through the Management Committee but, once granted, the wedding went ahead in style: 'We had 120 people at the church and the reception. We had a kind of salad and things. It was nice and we enjoyed it. We had lots of photographs.' They sit closely together throughout the day, and he looks fondly and protectively at his wife. She speaks only with great difficulty and often falls asleep.

Life in the pluperfect tense

For Alfred Schutz the meaning of social action was essentially retrospective: we apply meaning to lived experiences only after the event.[16] This is a very doubtful proposition in respect of normal people leading normal lives.[17] But it seemed to be true of the severely handicapped people interviewed in this study. The far-distant experiences before the onset of illness were the ones on which they focused their minds, and which were frozen in the gaze of their attention.

In their marginal world occupational identities stood firm in the presence of death and age-sex categories retained their significance in a world which was officially neuter. But temporal perspectives lost their linearity and a circular present sat precariously on a deep past which contained everything of real importance.

The deep past was clear while the recent past was shallow and cloudy, less sharply etched, more distant. But this unreal recent past, the period of ill-health, might extend over thrity years and have lasted two or three times as long as the early years of normality. The present emerged from the past in slow motion. It was lived on a truncated time-scale but was infinitely extended. A future leading out of an eternal present did not exist. Personal futures were the most taboo subject in the Home.

Interviewees talked about their experience of time in answer to the specific question: 'How do you get through time here? Is it a problem?' and often in answer to the more general question: 'How did your life change when you became ill and came to live in a Cheshire Home?' The problem of time in the Home has three aspects: the taboo on talk about the future; the duration of quite simple physical actions which formerly took minutes and now may take hours or even days; and the remorseless recurrence of events which makes life cyclical, constantly turning back on itself. All the interviewees mentioned their heightened awareness of the seasons and appreciation of summer, and the massive and protracted operation of getting more than thirty people up in the morning, and putting them back to bed.

The day is more crowded and interesting in the Cheshire Home than it was, as a rule, during the period of illness prior to entry, a former housewife said:

> There's more to do here, and it it's a nice day I sit outside. Time goes quicker in the summer, but it sometimes drags in the winter. It used to get more boring at home. I don't look to the past or the future. I look forward to coming down in the morning and smoking a cigarette. When I think about the past, it was when I was well. That was a happy time. Just the time before I was ill. No-one can look to the future, able-bodied or not. You just don't think about it. You just get on with now.

The time to which she looks, when she was well, is ten years ago.

A man of fifty finds security in recurrent events:

> You see, there are four things: there's Christmas, then there's Easter, then there's the summer holiday, and then you're looking forward to Christmas again. They come round, and round, and round. They are very important to me. I think you notice the seasons more. I notice the leaves coming off, and when the trees are in full bloom. But there's one day that's very important, and that's the Garden Party that we have the first week in June. I do look forward to that. And I watch football on television every Sunday. But I don't look many months ahead. You see that many come and go, you can't afford to look too far ahead.

In an eternal present, time is always returning to where it began.

Life is lived in slow motion but time passes quickly: 'Time passes very quickly here, because there's something going on all the time.' The marine engineer who developed multiple sclerosis twenty-four years ago and has been in the Home for eight said: 'It's amazing so many years have gone by. You get contented, just going along knowing what you can do and what you can't.' He recalls his life at sea more than twenty years ago with enthusiasm: 'I really liked my work. Looking back it was a beautiful life.' Now simple tasks require close attention and take up time. A middle-aged woman says she hasn't the time to do all that she wants to do: 'Writing letters or something like that takes me ages. I write a line and then I can't go on so I have to leave it for another day. Then it's nearly dinner-time and I've done nothing I wanted to do.' A man in his mid forties, who has been paralyzed for fifteen years, recalled the time-stress of his working life: 'I used to worry a lot about getting ahead with my work, you know, doing a bit of work each day for the day after. Well, that's daft. You meet yourself coming back.' Now he tries to walk from his bedroom to the sitting room: 'It's just fifteen yards. I set off at two o'clock and at four I may be half-way there. But if they offer to push me, I say "Oh, leave it. If I don't get there today I'll get there tomorrow. There's no rush".'

The time when they were well is vivid and immediate and contains sharply differentiated events; the present and recent past lack the same quality of sharpness. A woman in her fifties said: 'I think I'm beginning to look back on things more', but her mind skips the last twelve years of illness: 'I used to like going up mountains. And I think of things connected with my mother, the things she used to cook, and how she made jams.' For the former manageress of a Co-op shoe shop, reality is more than twenty years in the past but is still vividly present. She is now unable to move any of her limbs and her arms are permanently supported by a pillow. She cannot turn her head and needs to be fed. She worked until her illness incapacitated her at the age of twenty-nine:

> I was in charge of the shoe shop. It really was a full-time job, from 8.30 in the morning to 6 at night. It was busy. I made it my God. I really enjoyed it. When I had to give up I was very upset. And I'd been so active, such a big walker. I used to set out every morning at about 7.0 o'clock and have this long walk to work, because I really enjoyed it. I keep thinking really, when I look at the past, why should this happen to me? But I think more of when I was well and working. I just think a lot. My mind is very clear, but I remember walking most. I daren't think about the future. I don't allow myself. I quite realize I've nothing to look forward to. I don't do anything now. I can't read, and I don't like television because it bothers my eyes.

The former lorry driver aged fifty-two has been paralyzed for seventeen years. When asked what he still misses most, he said, 'The road. I loved the road — I loved driving. The police were very strict: I got pinched in Derby for doing twenty-four miles an hour. But in those days we were called "knights of the road".'

Conclusion

Occupational and sexual identities survive the onslaught of grievous illness and long years of residence in a Cheshire Home. Only time is seriously distorted, differently phased and emphasized. Nevertheless, the temporal structure is crucial for conferring a sense of reality: it is the deep past, sharply etched, that gives meaning to an amorphous present. Berger and Luckman place great stress on the importance of temporality in the social construction of reality:

> The temporal structure of everyday life not only imposes prearranged sequences upon the 'agenda' of any single day but also imposes itself upon my biography as a whole. Within the co-ordinates set by this temporal structure I apprehend both daily 'agenda' and overall biography ... Only within this temporal structure does every-day life retain for me its accent of reality. [18]

The severely physically handicapped have their special temporal structure within which they take their bearings and from which they extract personal significance.

Their socialization into illness and institutional life has no clearly marked stages or any obvious progression: after initial despair on learning the gravity of their illness, and a relatively short period of frustration and irritability (especially in the case of the men), they appear to reach a plateau of development. They themselves empha-sized continuity, that they hadn't really changed. Certainly there was no evidence of the 'moral loosening' which Goffman says leads mental home patients to 'practice before all groups the amoral arts of shame-lessness'.[19] On the contrary, there were many indications of heroic attempts to be as self-sufficient as possible and to help fellow residents to the greatest possible degree of personal-physical independence: 'You have to help one another. Like I can't fasten my braces, but he can lean over and clip them on for me.' One man whose hands are still nimble said: 'I get great pleasure if I can make someone a little apparatus which they can fit on their hand to light a cigarette.' In spite of the tensions of institutional life, there was a much stronger sense of solidarity and loyalty among the physically handicapped than was apparent among the blind, and a much strong sense of their separateness from normal society.

In the light of 'interactionist' accounts of marginality in general and institutional life in particular, it seemed likely that the residents in a Cheshire Home would make a fundamental revaluation of self and of life: that they would develop new perspectives, priorities, and categories for making sense of the world. In the event, there was a stubborn but unobtrusive normality. Only 'moaners' emerged as a rather special (and deprecated) category of typification, and this fact in itself emphasized the general insistence on normality. An inclination to typify themselves as 'just nuisances' appeared to be effectively counteracted by the staff of the Home.

Even religious beliefs appeared to be little influenced by their experiences: death was not legitimated and integrated with the rest of life through religious belief, but remained the final outrage, the paramount affront. One woman mentioned that she had been to communion that morning, but hastened to add: 'I must sound very religious, don't think that, I'm not. I don't think about religion. I just like to go to the services. I don't see the chaplain or talk to him. I just like to go.' The purpose of regular religious observance seemed to be to provide her with a vague time-scale which helped her to get through each week. Others similarly disclaimed any special interest in religion: 'When I was in the army I started to be religious and in a way I am now. I still believe in God, but there are many things I do not believe. But that's not because of my illness.' One resident was asked about Lourdes: 'I've heard about it, but I've never wanted to go myself. I don't believe in miracles.' They did not find in either theories of an impersonal fate or of a personal religion an over-arching symbolic system which made their lot intelligible or death acceptable.

Only the woman of sixty-five who had recently married showed any interest in the supernatural. She claimed to have 'the gift of dreams' and 'the gift of telepathy', and illustrated these gifts at length. She claimed to have had foreknowledge of the death of relatives, and of crises in her own life. 'But I'm no fortune-teller. I just have these gifts and make use of them. Sometimes they're a nuisance.' But they are not gifts which have developed since she became ill or entered the Home: 'I've always had them. You see, my mother was a little bit that way, and a sister, but I have more of the gift than they had.' It is perhaps this degree of 'abnormality' and claim to special status (as a seer) that make her the most unpopular person in the Home.

Goffman has emphasized the malleability of adult identity in asylums, Cohen and Taylor have emphasized its resilience in long-term prisons. There are obvious similarities in the positions of long-term prisoners, inmates of asylums, and residents in a Cheshire Home not only with regard to the boundary with the world and problems of privacy, autonomy and time, but especially with regard to the custodial role of staff who occupy an apparently strategic position as 'significant others' with power to redefine the inmate's sense of reality and conception of himself.

Long-term prisoners in the high-security wing of Durham goal were sustained by a deep and unabated contempt for the 'screws'; but Cohen and Taylor recognize that these immediate, contemporary circumstances are insufficient to account for the maintenance of personal identity under prolonged and massive assault. Explanation must be sought in personal histories:

> We have asserted that the men in E-Wing hardly lost their identities as a result of being processed through the prison system. Being processed did not seem to have significantly changed them. They frequently joked about the labels which others had attempted to fix upon them, they asserted their superiority over their guards, and developed ways of dealing with attacks upon their self-conceptions. The inmate culture of E-Wing cannot be fully understood if we regard it as a simple product of life in the wing. It is not just the history of the wing that is important to the inmate culture; we must also take account of the history of the men who make up its population.[20]

However, it was not only the past, but the future, that sustained them: at least the men in E-Wing could fight personal deterioration because they expected eventual release. In the Cheshire Home support for identity was predominantly retrospective, in identities with no present or future utility, but always vividly remembered (though seldom mentioned) and available for recall.

6 | The world of the blind: a supernormality

Alfred Schutz wrote about the importance of preconstituted 'recipe knowledge' as a constituent of everyday reality. A major break or discontinuity in social life would render the recipes unworkable, interrupt the flow of habit and give rise to changed conditions of consciousness.[1] People who have gone blind in adult life might be expected to experience such a major discontinuity, find well tried practical and social recipes unworkable, and undergo a significant change of consciousness.

Recipe knowledge provides both precept for action and a scheme of interpretation for situations and procedures which are so typical as to be virtually invisible, unremarked, anonymous. Marginality is the breakdown of typicality. Berger and Luckmann have extended Schutz's discussion of recipe knowledge in their account of the social construction of reality. They write of a pre-theoretical 'social stock of knowledge' which makes the reality of everyday life a 'zone of lucidity'. But recipe knowledge stops short at the margins of everyday life: it does not embrace the darkness of marginal worlds beyond. The reality of everyday life is 'overcast by the penumbra of our dreams'.[2]

Schutz also writes of enchanters — and Berger of over-arching symbols — which reconcile the everyday world (where well-tried recipes suffice) and enclaves of alternative reality (in which the recipes are useless). Schutz sees the enchanters in *Don Quixote* as guarantors of the co-existence and compatibility of discrepant universes of meaning. Enchanters translate realms of fantasy into realms of commonsense experience. 'Nothing remains unexplained, paradoxical or contradictory, as soon as the enchanter's activities are recognized as a constitutive element of the world.'[3] The study reported in this chapter was carried out with an alertness to the possible existence of 'enchanters' — or at least of over-arching symbols — in the world of the blind.

This chapter first examines the nature of the boundary between the sighted and the blind and the way in which it is kept open or closed; it then describes the way in which the blind give their world the 'accent of reality' through a remarkable array of 'achievements' which legitimate their claim to normality and a place in the world of the sighted; it then illustrates the uselessness of old recipe knowledge and the way new recipes are used not to subserve an alternative reality but to reaffirm the old. And finally it describes a sub-universe or enclave within the paramount reality, for which spiritualism provides a meaning and brackets a world of extraordinary sensation, nightmare and pain with the ordinary relationships and predicaments of everyday life.

The inquiry

The archetypal blind man is Tiresias, the Theban seer: marked off from the world not only by blindness, but by his supernatural perception and access to forbidden regions of the mind. Homer was in his mould. It seemed likely that a study of the blind would show a strong sense of apartness and community based on their common affliction and social experience.

In fact theirs was a highly 'convergent' marginality which resolutely turned towards society's 'centre'. What emerged from this study was an impressive supernormality. Blindness did indeed promote personal change, not in the form of deterioration, but of 'improvement'. New physical and social skills were acquired, the young perhaps developed rapidly in social maturity, and all in social awareness. Sometimes new musical and literary interests developed. But change was more of the same: the blind augmented their former selves and became larger than life.

There were exceptions to this 'linear' development: a sub-universe of alternative reality was sometimes close at hand. But the overwhelming picture is of their determined orientation to the sighted world; their insistence and often cunning in maintaining access to it; and their sense of essential continuity with their former, sighted selves. The normal world is sharply marked off from theirs, uncomprehending, embarrassed, over-solicitous or condescending; and acceptance within it must be worked at unremittingly. The personal abnormality of blindness was minimized by placing it in a statistical category, and the inadequate in handling the social situations of blindness were not the blind but the sighted. It was the normal who were gauche and inept in negotiating the barrier between the sighted and the blind. For the blind the supreme aim was 'achievement' according to the standards of normal society. Formerly modest and unassertive men had found a new resolution and self-confidence.

In 1975 seventeen blind persons who had been sighted at least until their early teens were interviewed for between three and four hours. (All the interviews were tape-recorded.) Eight were adults (six men and two women) who were selected from the register of the Northern Blind Aid Society: four were selected from council house estates, four from areas of owner-occupied housing. Nine were boys at a boarding school for the blind — selected on the basis that they were at least sixteen years of age and had been sighted at least till the age of twelve. The adults ranged in age from twenty-seven to sixty-six; they had been blind for between one and twenty-seven years. They had gone blind, on average, at age thirty-four; they had all been gainfully employed; but none of them at this time was in a full-time job. Their previous occupations had included barber, upholsterer, factory worker, roundsman, salesman and clerk. The boys at the school for the blind ranged in age from sixteen to nineteen; they had been blind for between one year and six; two had been blinded suddenly in accidents, but the other seven had a history of deteriorating sight and often other illnesses which had involved periods in hospital. But all subjects had a 'before' and an 'after' and were able to talk about the change that blindness had made in their lives.

The adults were interviewed in their homes and the boys in their school. The interviewer invited each subject to talk about himself, and the way his life had been changed by blindness. They were asked about their experience of sighted people and their relationships with others who are blind. They were asked what they felt they had lost through blindness, and also what they might have gained. But the main thrust of the interview related to changes in values, attitudes, interests and aptitudes that they had experienced and felt were attributable, either directly or indirectly, to blindness. Questions in this area were answered at length and with great care. Interviewees were at pains to distinguish between changes that would probably have occurred in any case from growing older, and changes that seemed to arise from the state and experience of blindness.

Modes of integration

All the interviewees wanted 'integration' with the sighted world and most were remarkably successful in attaining it. But the blind seemed to have little sense of solidarity among themselves. They divide the world into the 'sighted' (normal) and the 'blind', and this distinction has important practical consequences and implications; but the category 'blind' does not correspond to a social group with a community of interests and purposes. They showed very little 'we-feeling': in fact, the blind did not appear to think very highly of the blind. Other blind people were neither 'significant others' nor their 'reference group'. They achieve a measure of integration with the sighted by excusing their objectionable behaviour, by acquiring skills which qualify them for admission to normal society, by working hard at communication and remaining as mobile as possible, and by cunningly exploiting their deficiencies. And their dogs are effective intermediaries, unfailing passports to the sighted world.

Goffman has pointed to the varying degrees of 'we-feeling' that exist in stigmatized groups:

> (there are) those whose differentness provides them very little of a new 'we', and those, such as minority group members, who find themselves part of a well-organized community with long-standing traditions — a community that makes appreciable claims on loyalty and income, defining the member as someone who should take pride in his illness and not seek to get well.[4]

Goffman maintains that the 'moral career' of the stigmatized person may include 'affiliation cycles' (and own-group identification may be especially weak during adolescence), but eventually leads to the recognition that the fully-fledged members of the group are quite like ordinary human beings and so worthy of loyalty. In fact, Goffman's examples from the world of the blind point to no such conclusion, and neither did the interviews reported below. It is true that the adolescent boys in a boarding school for the blind were highly critical of the characteristics of blind people as well as of the school; but men and women in their fifties and sixties, who had been blind for years, showed no sense of loyalty to or solidarity with 'their own kind'.

Goffman quotes an account given by a newly-blind girl of her introduction to a workshop for the blind:

> Here was the safe segregated world of the sightless ... I was expected to join this world. To give up my profession and to earn my living

making mops ... I was to spend the rest of my life making mops with other blind people, eating with other blind people, dancing with other blind people. I became nauseated with fear, as the picture grew in my mind. Never had I come upon such destructive segregation.[5]

Goffman claims that the stigmatized eventually accept their own kind ('What may end up as a freemasonry may begin with a shudder') but does not illustrate this process with examples from the blind. The material presented below suggests that they keep their faces turned resolutely towards the sighted.

Mr Wilson, who is forty-nine and has been blind for nine years, was not particularly critical of the blind, but felt they had nothing of importance in common:

I do most things that most people do. I'll have a drink and I go to clubs. And I try to run things as normally as I can. I don't believe in cutting myself off into a world or into an atmosphere where there's only blind people. I think that is bad. It's all right to mix with other blind people from time to time; but in truth, the only thing you've got in common with one another is your blindness. Nothing else. Whereas if you go with the people I used to go with, well, we've got general interests that are the same. I mix more with sighted people than I do with blind people.

Mr Wilson has mixed feelings about social centres for the blind, but supports them because of their value in extreme cases:

You must remember that the vast majority of blind people are over the age of sixty-five. A lot of them are widows, widowers, spinsters and bachelors. These afternoon centres that they go to, even if it's only for two hours a week, are wonderful things for them. They're really marvellous. They're waiting at home for the minibus to pick them up, and they're ready an hour and a half too early, because it means so much to them. And if the minibus for some reason either breaks down or doesn't come, it upsets them for a week. It knocks them out for a week.

It is important to get about, to maintain mobility, not in order to meet other blind people, but to escape them. Mr Price is in his sixties and very aware of the way in which blindness limits communication:

Blindness is not the same, say, as a fellow who has an accident and has one leg shorter than the other. I mean, that's nothing. His communication remains the same. But not with blind people. And of course the idea is to get amongst sighted people and not just stay behind with the blind. And in any case, they're not all my cup of tea. So I try to mix with sighted people. There are very few blind people that you bother with.

In the boarding school there was a similar denial of any special bond among the blind. A nineteen-year-old now recognizes that the blind are human, but has no particular taste for their company:

I'd never met a blind person before I had my accident, so I didn't understand the problem: a blind person was just something completely different, not just a human being who'd lost his sight. You don't know how to approach them. Most of all I miss normality, having normal relationships with friends, going round as a normal person, instead of being stuck in a blind society.

One boy had a lively sense of the mannerisms of the blind and was deeply concerned that he should not develop them himself: 'There are blind habits. I wonder if I'm leaning forward too much when I'm talking like this, or keeping my head down. A lot of blind people put their fingers in their eyes. Some spin round or flap their hands over their mouths when they yawn.' He has certainly no inclination to identify himself with the blind community or to take pride in his affliction.

The boys in the school for the blind maintain their links with the normal world they have left and look forward to rejoining it when they take up careers in the professions or in business. A seventeen-year-old complained: 'The activities around this place are so limited. Before I'd go out to youth clubs and dances and such like. Freedom here is very restricted. I go home as much as possible, and I still go back to my old school. They accept me as I was before.'

Berger and Luckmann have pointed to 'legitimation' as an important mode of integration: 'Legitimation produces new meanings that serve to integrate the meanings already attached to disparate institutional processes.'[6] The blind reinterpret the objectionable behaviour of the sighted and so are able to live with it. As Berger and Luckmann claim: '... "integration", in one form or another, is also the typical purpose motivating the legitimators.' The blind excuse the sighted, point to the legitimacy of their attitudes, and so refuse to be deterred in their strenuous attempts to achieve co-existence.

Like all the interviewees, Mr Wilson has suffered from the behaviour of sighted people but readily excuses it:

At first, when I lost my sight nine years ago, there were certain of my friends who kept away. But it was embarrassment on their part, really. They've come back since. They've got over their shyness. They didn't know what to say to me. This is the trouble with most sighted people. They just don't know what to say. They're just not up to it. It's no use condemning them or running them down. It's no fault of their own. Very often they're frightened of saying things like 'Do you see what I mean' or using certain words like 'blind drunk'. They think they may say something and want to bite their tongue out. And they just don't know. They think you've become a different person because you can't see. But I think the people I know have got over it nowadays. I've been to parties and all sorts of things with them, since I went blind, so my relationships probably haven't changed. They've probably broadened. I've got more friends.

Mr Wilson is fortunate in having been a barber in the neighbourhood for more than twenty years before he went blind: he knew many people and was skilled in opening up conversation ('As a barber you think, "Well, does he want a conversation? I can't start talking to him about horses"'). But he accepts that the responsibility for establishing relationships with the sighted is his, and that he must have a real contribution to make to social relationships:

I find the easiest place to talk to anybody is in a pub or on a bus. It's easy, and having a dog makes it so much easier. Yes, I've found that since I had a dog that people talk to me. You see, they'll talk to the dog first of all. If I'm, say, at the bus-stop, or getting on the bus, or even on the streets, somebody'll come along, and say, 'Oh, you're gorgeous, you're beautiful', and I'll say, 'Yes, and what do you think of my dog?' It's corny, but it puts the person at ease immediately. They've sort of got to carry on the conversation then, they can't help themselves, and they probably feel a lot better for doing it. This way it becomes a lot easier for the sighted person, who's never met a blind person, to go up and talk to him. You see, I think the onus is on the blind person to make the sighted person feel at home with him. If you sit at home waiting for people to come and visit you, you'll be very lonely. Even if you see half a dozen people in a week, what is it? A week's a long time. And people won't keep coming and coming, because you've got nothing to offer them. If you go out, you learn things, you've got something to offer people. You tell them something and they tell you something. You've got to work at being blind. If you just stay still, you go backwards. You've got to keep working on it.

A number of interviewees, both young and old, spoke of the horrified aversion which the sighted often show towards them. A man of thirty said:

They tend to ignore you. If you're with someone else they'll ask them how you are. You become the village idiot. Children shy away from you. People of my own age — their attitude is disbelief and horror. They more or less say to themselves, 'That could be me'. They must keep away from a blind man — they mustn't get in his way or say anything. It's as if they might be contaminated.

An eighteen-year-old boy commented on his encounters when out shopping: 'They say, "Oh God, I never realized you were blind", and they treat you as if you'd come from outer space. They don't realize that you live in the same world as them. They regard you as another form of human life.'

But they find excuses: 'I knew blind people when I could see. I can appreciate that some people have funny attitudes towards the blind.' One man in his twenties had been attending a college where he was the only blind student: 'The other students didn't know how to take a blind person. They either shied away or just said "hello". Sometimes they shout at you. After a while I took a guide dog along with me, and they'd tend to talk to the dog. Especially the girls. It's a way of getting over their shyness, helps them to communicate.' He excuses the failure of sighted people to make contact: 'You're not sure whether they're talking to you. But otherwise, unless they know your name, it's very difficult for them.' A schoolboy excuses the defection of his former friends:

They were caught very much off balance when I went blind. I wouldn't say they weren't true friends, or anything. Perhaps they just weren't sure of what was going on. Basically, when it comes down to it, you've got to make the effort yourself to talk to people. It's not really their fault. Having been sighted, I try to think how I would have reacted.

Neighbours can be over-solicitous, especially, perhaps, on old-established council estates, and their concern can amount to 'interference'. One wife observed of her blind husband: 'He does all sorts of things. He goes all over the place. And the neighbours say, "Fancy letting your husband do the shopping". He does all the shopping, and often people bring him back, thinking he's strayed out.' Her husband intervened:

> Let me explain that, my dear. A blind person who refuses help is a very lonely person. Now, I've always been a chatterbox and willing to talk to people. If I'm at the bottom of the street, and someone wants to walk me up the street, which I know perfectly well, I let them — just for the sake of a good natter.

Another man living in a suburban road is less fortunate in his neighbourhood encounters:

> When I'm down at the shops, some people will come up and ask how I am, but others I used to know just sheer away. I've noticed that with a number of people. But one doesn't know why. I mean, I don't know whether they think I'm not only blind, but stupid as well. I don't know. I don't blame them much: they just don't know what to do. It's a sort of lack of education, if you like. They just don't understand that blind people have lost their sight, and that's their problem, and otherwise they're as normal as anyone else.

Integration is both 'horizontal' and 'vertical'. Horizontal integration involves the current relatedness of social roles, vertical integration involves keeping up with the successive biographical stages of life.[7] The mature adults were primarily concerned with the former: keeping the current roles of the blind and the sighted in relationship; the schoolboys were much more concerned with the latter: ensuring that they kept their place in the forward march of their generation, and did not slip back from their place among coevals.

Blindness meant the slowing up of life; the older men and women found solace in this, time to think and reflect. A sixty-year-old man has abandoned the electric razor which his brother gave him: 'It doesn't give you a really close shave. Of course it takes a long time, now, using an ordinary razor, but I've got plenty of time now ... Being blind gives you time to think. I find that I can turn things over in my mind.' The schoolboys experienced it as a threat, a danger that they would be left behind. One sixteen-year-old boy expressed his impatience: 'I had my life planned out and on a smooth course, but now it's all jumbled up, sort of.' A seventeen-year-old boy who was blinded a year previously in a car accident explained that one of the biggest changes was realizing that 'it just takes much longer to do things. It's a question of learning to take time, and waiting.' He had hoped to be a police officer but has now decided to be a physiotherapist and has worked out the timing: 'I've got it worked out that if I pass the exams I'll work in a hospital for a couple of years, build up a reputation, then branch out on my own.'

The schoolboys claim that they have moved ahead of their contemporaries in terms of personal maturity, but fear that they will fall behind in their education and careers. They are annoyed with the school for not forcing the pace. Often it is the experience of hospitals that has thrown them into close contact with adults and dislodged them from their age grade. One sixteen-year-old boy explained that he couldn't really be bothered with his former school friends: 'I've grown up a lot since I went blind two years ago. I've come across a lot more people in hospital, and social workers and so on. It's widened the number of people I know, really. Perhaps that's because I lost my sight very quickly, and I went through a lot of different people's hands.' The normal, programmed progression through biographical stages has been threatened: in one sense he feels propelled forward, but in other senses he feels held back. He finds braille very frustrating: 'When a sighted person is reading and wants to refer back to something up the page, he just glances up and has the information immediately. In braille, you've got to feel along all the lines, which takes quite a while. It really drags.' He is pacing his academic progress carefully: 'I had a very tight academic schedule before I went blind, so I had to slot back in very quickly or I'd have really fallen behind. I still hope to go to a university.'

A twenty-seven-year-old man, married at twenty-one and registered blind at twenty-two, is fighting to maintain the phases of a normal biography. His eyesight deteriorated in his teens, he was frequently in hospital and his schooling was disrupted: 'I had been up to O-level standard. After a couple of years in hospital I went back to school and went in for typing, shorthand and commerce. I did one O-level in commerce.' In hospital he became more adult ('I learned a lot — how to adapt to older men, especially at fourteen') but fell behind in his studies. At twenty he was still seeking qualifications, and in fact obtained four O-level and three A-level passes in the next four years at a college of further education. 'But the education people had said I'd have to go to a school for the blind and spend four years just taking O-levels. Although I was almost twenty I'd have to go to school with sixteen-year-olds. I just couldn't accept that.' He now feels that he is doing quite well for his age and expects to get a good job.

Ambition: the accent of reality

The blind work hard to diminish their marginality and to achieve integration with the sighted world. And they stress personal continuity, that they haven't 'really' changed although they may have developed new interests and skills and, above all, an understanding of people (without the distraction and misleading cues of physical appearance). Their principal claim to a place in the world of the sighted is an array of determined 'achievements'.

Blindness for most of the interviewees appeared to have increased rather than diminished self-assurance and ambition. Of course recall of pre-blindness attitudes, sentiments and even aptitudes is a notoriously ticklish business;[8] but it did appear that at least some subjects were now prepared to attempt tasks which previously they would have felt were beyond them. Thus Mr Douglas, a man in his fifties who went blind at thirty-eight said: 'When I was a young man I had a decent voice, but I was always too shy to sing in public. But not long after I went blind I entered a public competition for whistling and singing. And I won it. I would never have done it before.' A sixteen-year-old schoolboy, blind for nearly two years, reflected on the change: 'I'm not self-conscious, in many ways, any more. I was very shy before, but not now. It can be a disadvantage — sometimes I say things I shouldn't.' Another sixteen-year-old schoolboy working for A-levels was asked whether he was less ambitious now: 'Oh, no. I'm more ambitious. I think the fact of going blind makes you feel you must compete more. Yes, I think it drives you to a great extent.'

Mr Douglas is now a successful writer. He left school at fourteen and became a tailor's cutter. For the next twenty-four years he had an undistinguished career: he was discharged from the Army in 1942 and then did a series of semi-skilled jobs. He is now a widower living with his daughter. He was interviewed in his house on a council estate, and constantly brought the conversation back to his achievements as a writer:

> I do all kinds of writing, anything you can think of — fiction and non-fiction. I went blind in 1954. I was working in the hospital service at the time. And before that I'd had all sorts of jobs — insurance work, work in a dairy, breadround, you name it...
>
> After the first shock of going blind I cried for nearly a month. And then my family rallied round me. I was thirty-eight when it happened. My wife, God rest her soul, was very helpful to me. I think it would have been much more difficult to go blind later in

life, say over sixty. Going blind up to the age of fifty is not as bad, but any older you're too old to start a new life. I consider I was just young enough to start a new life. I learned how to type, and now I write a lot of articles for magazines. I won't say I'm a prolific writer — it's not enough to earn my living. I took it up more as a hobby than anything else. The very first article I wrote was with the help of my daughter for the TV Times.

That started my little bit of writing. But one of the main ideas was to create a hobby, because the particular job that I worked at — press operating in an engineering works — was a very monotonous, tedious job. It was so automatic that I could sit at my machine with my thoughts wandering round, and that was really behind all my writing. I used to come home at night and get on to my braille typewriter and start putting my ideas on paper. And to my surprise, some of them seem to have caught on. I've been twice highly recommended in a world-wide competition — I got fourth prize in each case, which didn't mean any cash value, but gave me a bit of ego. And I've never been behindhand at boasting about what I've done as a blind person, for one reason: to show sighted people that we're just as normal as they are.

I never think of myself as a blind person, or as a helpless person. I think I'm as capable as the next man. In fact I think I've gained a lot through blindness. I've a better sense of touch. I can tell any coin of the realm just by feeling, and I won't say it's always hygienic, but I can tell a lot by smell. I think my stroke was much more limiting than blindness. Much more. Like many sighted people, among blind people you get all types. There's the type who'll sit down and wait for everyone to bring things to him. It depends on your state of mind. Me, I'm obstinate. I'd hate to be helpless. Now my grandson was born after I went blind and he's always accepted me as I am, as normal. I must admit, since my wife died he's been my life and soul.

I wouldn't have started writing if I hadn't gone blind. At the moment I'm engaged in writing my life story. I've written about a hundred pages so far. I think that as a blind person, if I can get it down properly, my experience could be a good example to others, whatever disability they have. The thing that I want to bring out about disability is that it can bring out a fighting challenge in the right sort of person. After that first month of misery that I went through in my own mind, I've never looked back.

Mr Douglas is a cheerful man with extensive social contacts and many neighbourhood friends. He is intent on proving to them all that he is as normal as they are. He insisted on making the interviewer a cup of tea and, as he did so, explained how he had developed tricks to overcome his disability — always using tea-bags, counting to thirty, etc. He was a man of infinite resourcefulness who commonly takes a pound for a pound's worth of goods and returns with seventy-five pence. He is not affronted when shopkeepers undercharge him because he is blind. And he knows that they are doing so.

Mr Mills has a staggering range of disabilities, apart from his blindness. He is thirty years of age and married to a schoolteacher. He has been blind for three years. He is a diabetic and has recently had meningitis. He has just had an operation for an ulcer on his foot. He has had a minor stroke, hepatitis and renal colic; he has to take cortisone tablets and have monthly injections, otherwise 'in a few years I would turn into a female'. Like other interviewees he reduces his singularity by placing himself in the categories of medical statistics, in which he seemed well versed:

Somebody's got to have these illnesses, why not me? You see, diabetes is a strange thing. One in ten people has it, and of them one in five will go blind. Twenty-three people go blind every day in Britain. It's a lot when you stop to think about it. But there's lots worse off than me. Why shouldn't I keep up the statistics?

He was formerly a salesman and now intends to do either milling or capstan work in an (open) engineering workshop.

He talked quietly and philosophically, but with calm assurance, about his past misfortunes and future prospects:

When I was first told that I was going blind, I sat down and cried for two weeks. And then I just sort of said, 'Well, so what? Am I going to sit here all day and cry about it, or get up and do something about it?' The first thing that hit me was, how am I going to cope? I have a wife and two children. The first thing was money, so we started looking for retraining courses ... Luckily my wife is a teacher at a local school — the two kiddies are there as well. We could sort of switch our roles. At the moment this is what we're doing. I do the shopping and the housework, the cleaning, washing and ironing. It's two-fold: I stand up for myself and help the family, and I keep myself physically occupied. Our roles have turned full circle. It's working, but I don't think I could take this

for long. The work isn't hard, but I need different work. When I
left school I went into a dental company, starting in the packing
room. But after a couple of years I became an assistant salesman,
selling to students in the Dental Hospital. Then we came here and
I went into industry. I liked both jobs. And the need to work has
made me push other people to see just what my capabilities are.

Now I'm doing a job that has to be done, right here in the home.
Nevertheless, I want to get back to open employment. You're just
marking time in a sheltered workshop. I need to compete — get
back to as nearly a normal life as I can. I know I won't do it over-
night, but I feel the need of something to strive for.

New recipes for old tasks

A blind man in his sixties, Mr Price, has invented a wide array of
recipes for practical tasks and social encounters. He is nevertheless, a
supreme illustration of 'supernormality', for his repertoire of ingen-
ious recipes have not created a new reality but reaffirmed the old.

Mr Price was sixty-six years of age, and had been blind for two years.
He had worked all his life as an upholsterer and lives with his wife in
an old but comfortable semi-detached house — a glass porch over the
front door, the front room with a white-tiled hearth and china
ornaments on the mantlepiece, plants on the window ledge, a three-
piece suite, a coffee table, record-player, glass-fronted bookcase and
pale pink anaglypta on the walls. But what might have been a tranquil
requirement has become a resolute struggle for 'achievement',
principally in coping with practical situations. Mr Price stressed his
normality and the essential continuity of his personality; he fights to
re-enter the normal world, but accepts various limitations — when in
company he cannot read facial expressions and has to wait for verbal
cues, and apart from more intimate family and friendship situations,
there was 'a line of demarcation'. It is 'not the same' at his political
association, and he felt 'in the way' at public meetings; but it is still
sighted people, and not the blind, who are his 'reference group'.

Mr Price was very neatly dressed. His hair was immaculately cut and
smoothed, his face freshly shaved. He wore dark glasses with thick
black frames. His manner and phrasing were rather formal and
precise, like a bureaucratic official's, but he was quite fluent. He
became animated when his wife joined in:

*How would you say that the experience of going blind has changed
your life?*

I went blind suddenly more than a year ago, soon after I retired. Of course it was a great shock. But when I'd got over the initial shock of blindness I said to my wife, 'Well, don't worry, I'll continue doing the things I did before. Almost, at any rate ... as far as possible.' And in fact I do most of the things I did before.

I used to got out shopping with my wife. I still do that. But the problem of tending the garden ... well, I can't weed it, or anything like that, but the main thing is cutting the lawn.

Eventually I found that, though I couldn't cut the lawn like a normal person, I could cut it a different way. I couldn't cut the lawn straight, like sighted people do, in nice straight lines; but I cut it anyway, in a sort of system, a couple of yards at a time. And as I'd covered the whole lawn, all my wife had to do was to come and perhaps touch a corner here and there, where I may have missed. I did that quite successfully, so that's no problem to me either.

You see, this is a victory. One might have thought, 'Oh — you'll never cut the lawn again'. I do cut the lawn, so that is again one of the things I did before.

Losing your sight is a terrible thing. It's devastating. But I don't think my temperament's changed. I don't think it has changed my views. I believe in God, but I'm not what you call a religious man. I've not changed. Whether I will later on I don't know. The only thing ... I've always liked to dress neatly. I'm particular about cleanliness. I'm probably a little more keen about it than before.

Of course I realize something I didn't realize before. You can lose contact with your friends, or people that you know, very easily. Being blind is something you've got to put up with. Communication between people isn't quite the same. If you're sighted, in a crowd you can see people's faces, their attitudes — smiling or sad or whatever, and you can talk to them. If you're blind you've sort of got to wait. Sometimes I can't remember the voices of the people I know, and you've got to wait until either they say something or my wife tells me who it is.

So you feel more isolated than you did?

One's bound to feel isolated, more isolated. I used to be very active in a political club. In fact I was the secretary. I had to give it up, of course. I'm still a member. They call for me when they have a committee meeting. But it's not quite the same. Once I get among them it's not too bad. I know their voices. I know them well. But I went to a public meeting. I won't go again.

You don't go out on your own much?

No. I'm waiting for the mobility officer. I could go out if my wife had a cold or anything. But in any case, it's a question of achievement. I find that since I was blind, I've always wanted to achieve things. Now, you can see there's a record-player in this corner. I bought that when I retired, because I was interested in classical music. Of course I wasn't blind then. I used it when I liked. But when I went blind it made no difference. I walked in here and put the whole thing on myself. The only thing was, I had to ask my wife what records I'd got hold of. I put it on myself, got the whole thing going, and so on. But I will improve; there's more progress I could make. I could eventually get all the records written on. I'll use a braille typewriter sometime in the near future and put on what kind of record it is. Once I've got it on the top of my sleeve, I'll be able to get my own records without asking anyone to get them for me.

Are you more interested in music since you went blind?

No, I don't think so. Music's always been a hobby. I don't think it's made any difference...

People who are stone deaf are worse off than people who are completely blind.

Do you think you've sort of gained anything from going blind?

Well, I don't really know. It gives you time to think.

Do you think you judge people differently now?

You get a sense of people. For instance, a chap I knew, I've known him for a long time. He saw me for the first time when I was blind, walking up the road. He said, 'hello', and we chatted a minute, and then I said, 'Well, come in one evening'. And he said, 'All right, I'll come down and see you'. He never did, and I didn't expect that he would. I could tell. But with other people it's been different. They've come. But I think with sighted people there's a barrier which it's very difficult for them to step over. Sometimes they come down, but it's not quite the same. There's a barrier there.

Wife: He's done very, very well, really, at coping with situations ... at times I've really been astounded. Right from scratch. Even in the hospital he decided he could manage without the barber. He shaved himself with a bowl of water. And he found a way of picking his suits, different suits, right from the beginning. He put a ball of paper in the navy suit, in the jacket, and a straight piece in the grey suit, so he knows which one to get. And the same with his trousers. He has something else in the pocket, and he knows that's a green one, and that's an olive one ... And he puts all the cutlery away, the knives in this section and the forks in that, and so on.

Mr Price: I've even taken a tray of tea upstairs, haven't I?

Wife: Yes. First time I had a migraine — I'm a migraine sufferer — I thought, half an hour on the bed with the curtains drawn. Twenty minutes later he comes up with a cup of tea. I don't know whether to laugh of cry. And as for his Braille, well, he's on his grand finale. I'm very happy about this. And when we go for a walk, people are amazed. I don't know what they expect. People think that because a person's gone blind ... but the mental state is just there. They're the same person.

Mr Price: But I think that underlying all my experiences is this sense of achievement.

Interviewer: Both before and after you went blind?

Mr Price: No, since. When I went blind I felt perhaps naturally that I must achieve something. I said, 'I'm not going to stay like this. I can't expect other people to help me. I've got to help myself.' So I mean anything in the future that arises, any problem, if I could grasp it or solve it myself, if it's something physical or whatever, I'll do it. If I can, that is. Where there's a possibility of me achieving something, I go for it. Now the handle came off the door, and I didn't want to get someone to put it back on. I went to the village and got some screws and put the handle back on. That is the sort of thing. I don't just sit back and say, 'I can't do it'. But naturally I can't do painting and wallpapering like I used to. I'd say that my best achievement is the Braille. It's hard. It's not easy, it's like learning another language. I don't know if you know, but only about 10 per cent of the blind people in this country can read Braille.

'Enchanters' and the reality of everyday life

Belief in a supernatural order enabled a few (but by no means all) of the blind to account for their affliction and make it 'legitimate'. In the case of one grievously afflicted middle-aged man a belief in spiritualism seemed at first to reinforce his detachment from everyday reality; but on closer analysis his spiritualism appeared to be a major source of 'integration'. Largely cut off from society by the severity of his disabilities, he remained tightly tied to the web of relationships of deceased kinsfolk, taking an active part in the 'everyday' problems and quarrels which had pursued them beyond the grave. In consequence, this very lonely man 'was never alone': he was still involved in everyday problems of family loyalty, illness and neglect. He appeared to illustrate Berger and Luckmann's argument that the symbolic universe encompasses marginal realms of madness and terror: it brings 'within bounds' the 'night-side' of life which lurks ominously on the periphery of everyday consciousness: 'Experiences belonging to different spheres of reality are integrated by incorporation in the same, overarching universe of meaning.'[9]

Certainly in the case of one sixteen-year-old schoolboy the symbolic universe of religion afforded an explanation and legitimation of his blindness and restored him to the normal world:

> About a year ago I became a Christian, which changed my attitude to life a lot. It gave me the Christian faith. Another thing, it gave me comfort in that I could see that perhaps there was some reason in my blindness. I don't think I'd ever have become a Christian if I hadn't gone blind, so I can see the purpose in my going blind.

Another sixteen-year-old spoke in a similar vein:

> It has made me more religious. At the moment I'm going to a faith healer, and she's been doing quite a lot for me. She's convinced that I'm going to get my sight back, and so am I. Obviously I want to believe it, but I do believe in God. She does it through God. She's got certain contacts in the spiritual world — she's in contact with a dead surgeon. She gets certain impulses in her hands as to which parts to work on, and through that she gives me treatment.

Religion makes his affliction explicable and manageable.

But by no means all subjects found an 'explanation' in these terms. Many explicitly disclaimed any increase in religious interest. One sixteen-year-old boy said: 'I've never been religious. I don't feel religious and don't think I ever will'; another said: 'I was brought up a Catholic and I've rebelled against that, but I think I might have done anyway.'

A third schoolboy has successfully resisted the determined attention of the Church:

Two vicars used to come and see me in hospital, and one of them decided it was a good time to have an onslaught on me. I made out I was receptive to see what it was all about, and quite frankly it didn't add up at all. It all boiled down to making this thing called a leap of faith. Every time you get a sticky question you sit thinking for a while and then come out with one of those terrible clichés.

(The 'symbolic universe' that integrated his marginality was that of biographical stages, in which he was determined to keep his place: his progression through life was still in the proper nature of things.)

Pain, dreams and disoriented time often characterize the world of the blind. Even the solidly normal Mr Price commented on the disturbing consequences of unending darkness:

At night my wife could switch off the lights. They're no use to me anyhow. I don't sleep as well as I did when I could see. I used to be a very good sleeper. I find that I go to sleep and then get up in the middle of the night. I'm conscious, and then later on I may sleep for an hour or two and get up about half past nine.

Even within the impressively normal world of Mr Douglas one glimpses a sub-universe of alternative reality. In half-mocking tones he recalled the recent period in hospital after he had had a stroke:

When I knocked on the door up above, St. Peter's, they said 'Clear off, we're not ready for you yet'. Now the first fortnight of this stroke, I was sort of in another world. I was conscious but I wasn't there. And I had a very vivid dream. It's rather remarkable. I dreamt that my brother-in-law and his son were at the side of my bed, and I knew it was my bed. They were looking down at somebody. Don't forget, I'd seen these people when I was sighted, so I knew who they were. And I'm looking down, and then ... I seemed to be on a different plane looking at them looking at me. I think I'd left my astral plane, if you believe in such things. It's quite feasible. When I became properly conscious, I explained it to my daughter and asked if Uncle David and Walter had been to see me, and she said, 'Yes, how did you know?'.

Mr Mills has been to Lourdes but is cautious in interpreting his experience. He referred to it when he was asked whether he had changed his religious beliefs:

No. I'm still the same practising Catholic. But something more — I feel indebted to them. Two years ago they sent me to Lourdes. I don't know whether they wanted a miracle, or what, but I went there purely to enjoy myself. And yet I came back with something much more than I'd bargained for. It's hard to explain to people who haven't been to Lourdes. There's a spirit of peace. It's difficult to put into words; it's an understanding and a coming to terms with yourself ... Possibly that's it. The thing is that the individual doesn't matter so much. There are so many people at Lourdes who are worse off than you are. So many young people. It just doesn't seem to matter. Everybody's happy, there's no sadness at all. It's a strange feeling altogether. You can't sort of parcel it all up and hand it to someone: it's an experience you have to feel for yourself.

He claims to have a heightened sensitivity to other people and even to know when his wife is approaching the house and what mood she is in, but he offers a naturalistic explanation:

Sometimes I can almost reach out and touch signals from people. I don't know what it is, whether it's the atmosphere, or tone of voice, or what. I can tell when my wife's been to see her mother and there's been an upset even before she gets to the house. With blindness I think you possibly gain more than you lose. I think you gain a better understanding of people. I certainly did.

In one notable case, mentioned above, the world of dreams, pain and disoriented time was tied to the paramount reality of everyday life through 'enchanters'. Spirits led Mr Clark from loneliness and pain to a tight-knit social web of departed kin. He has plastic shells instead of eyes; he is in constant pain; he sees 'horrid colours' all the time; and he has a constant high-pitched ringing in his ears.

Mr Clark is a married man with three children. He is now fifty-five years of age, went blind at thirty-four and has never worked since. He was formerly a machinist making shopping bags. Throughout the interview he rubbed his eyes and never strayed far from his concern with spiritualism:

Can you remember what it was like to be sighted?

Oh, yes, It started with the left eye and soon spread to the right. It began with conjunctivitis. It was a mystery why I shouldn't have got better. Eventually they found that it was a certain virus. It went through various stages, and I had ulcers all over my body. I was in terrible pain. I nearly lost my left leg through it.

I kept having treatment which never worked, then a friend gave me a bottle of holy water from Lourdes. This is the truth, so you might as well hear it. I rubbed the water on the ulcers and the pain just went. It all cleared up. It was the holy water. I'm convinced of that. I really believe in it and I'm not a Catholic. It hasn't converted me to Catholicism, by the way. It's just that I believe there are great forces at work outside our sphere, and not necessarily in the sense that people call 'God'. But there is a great something. I believe in healing, like absent healing, sending healing to other people. I believe it. I believe in all this and my wife and I have certain reasons for it. Shall I explain?

When the doctors gave me up, we contacted Henry Jones — he's a faith healer. And one morning my wife, Faye, said to me: 'I saw something at the foot of the bed last night. I just lay on my elbow and watched it.' She said she saw a figure at the foot of the bed, with a short beard and a top hat and a long frock coat with a fur collar — a Victorian doctor. And he seemed to be in consultation with someone at the head of the bed, behind us. The next night she was awakened by a noise, and she looked over to me and she saw a diamond-shaped blue light flashing over my side of the bed.

The next night I lay awake waiting for it. It made a short of 'whooshing' noise, coming towards me, louder. I dived under the covers and it started poking under them, and I could not accept it. I told it to go away — and it went away. Our youngest child said next morning that he had heard a hair-dryer in the night. That was the sound it had conveyed to him. It didn't really help me at all then, but there's since been help in other ways, through healing ... a little more tranquillity ... you could say psychological help. More acceptance...

I was thirty-four when all this happened, when it attacked me. Among other things that happened, I suddenly developed a great love of music — classical music. This is some good that has come out of my blindness. Before, it was like a cacophony of sound — it made no sense to me. I listened and it became beautiful and peaceful. Another thing that happened — I gave up smoking. I could smoke a hundred cigarettes in one day if I had them: a real chain-smoker. I have terrible insomnia, so I was smoking night and day. The next stage after that was suddenly the realization of the difference in technique of orchestral conductors. I came to appreciate the subtle differences. Those are some of the things that have happened to me...

Have your ideas changed in any way?

Well, my reading has taken a turn. I used to be fond of historical romances, now I'm keen on Victorian authors. As well as Jane Austen and the Brontës, Mrs Gaskell and Mrs Henry Wood, I'm reading Charlotte M. Younge — her books. These are the kinds of books I've become interested in now, as opposed to the ugly violence of today's writing. I'm looking for tranquillity, because I haven't got it in my life. Even though I've had my eyes removed and I now wear plastic shells, I've still got constant throbbing in the eyes, and I've got this oscillation with the most horrid colours in my eyes all the time. There's no turning my head away from all this ugliness and this constant high-pitched ringing in my ears. It never ceases. There's no peace. I can never find peace in my life except what I make for myself — music and reading. I don't have a lot of sleep.

And added to that, from the moment I went blind I lost my virility also. That's a great loss. It makes me realize how important it is and how much it's abused on television and so on — sullied by people using it loosely. That is a great tragedy ... I believe in sincerity when people speak.

Apart from your love of music and literature, have you gained anything' else?

I have a certain intuition. I think I notice some things more than other people. There is something else. I don't really like to talk about it with most people because, well, soon after my brother Eric died, I had these sensations of my head being stroked, and coldness around me, and also this heat on my face like a very powerful sunray lamp. And I had been saying for some time to my wife and my daughter that I was sure Eric wanted to contact me. Well, my daughter had been visiting friends in Virginia and they had been talking 'on the glass'. That made me decide to do the same, and we were immediately contacted by my dead brother. My father also died two Novembers ago, and I hadn't said certain prayers that in the Jewish faith you're supposed to say for the dead. Nor had my younger brother in Ontario. Suddenly, while we were on the glass, a message spelled out: 'Max is not resting in his grave. Tell Julian to say the prayers.' It was a message from Toby, my mother's name. I started saying the prayers, and my brother too, in Canada.

Another thing: my Aunt Rose passed away. Earlier, she'd done something against us. I was blind, the children were young, and my wife was having to go out once or twice a week on the markets to help out — the pension was so low. My grandfather, who was in his nineties, was living with his son and daughter-in-law, Rose. And one day my cousin came and asked me to take grandfather for a little time, and it turned out they were trying to push him on to us. Well now, after Aunt Rose had died, we were on the glass, and suddenly my daughter said: 'There's a most delicious perfume'. This was in the room where we were using the glass. Well, we said, 'Who's there?' and it spelled out 'Rose'. It was Aunt Rose. I asked her what she wanted, and she spelt out 'Forgive'. I said, 'We forgive' and asked her if she were at peace. She said 'Yes', and she's never been back since.

Then suddenly another thing happened. Last year we received a message, 'Contact Mary'. We said, 'Who are you?' and it was Sid — he'd died suddenly of a heart attack. He was very worried about Mary, his wife, who was ill with cancer. My wife phoned the hospital. Anyway, this year Mary died, but we were speaking on the glass a couple of nights later, and she was very unhappy and wouldn't settle. And my (dead) brother Eric came and said that Mary was terribly unhappy and wouldn't accept it: she was crying all the time. Something happened: one Saturday morning I got up and felt a great sadness in me, I couldn't stop sobbing. My heart was breaking. Now, it wasn't me — it was Mary in me. I was cold through and through. And I couldn't stop sobbing. And I said to my wife: 'It's not me, I'm taken over.' My wife got hold of me and soothed me and told Mary to leave me and be at peace. It subsided...

These are some of my experiences. I have that little touch: I have been given ... What I'm trying to say is, that is why I believe there is a Great Being. God as such does not exist. Jesus Christ is the Great Master. There's been a lot of mumbo jumbo talked about him. One day He came and said to my wife: 'Faye, the things that are being done in my name!' He was heart-broken.

The dead speak about him ... As for other things, it's not as we have been told by the Rabbis and the priests. We've been told on the glass that Jesus came from the planet Venus, and the Three Wise Men came on spaceships. And the so-called Ark was floating on these waters. Why we can never find it, because it was a spaceship that took off with the remnants of people after a great holocaust. There's proof of it, too. There are cave dwellings with paintings of spaceships.

We've had our own proof ... We've had friends around. There

are certain ones who the glass will accept and will speak to, there are others it won't speak to when it senses scoffing. I don't know whether you'd be accepted ... We can try, if you like. Next time I speak to Eric he'll mention some of the things we've been talking about ... Through blindness I've been given that slight touch of healing. I've got power coming in from outside. I'm never alone. I can feel forces all around me.

Faye, set the table up. There's no need to be afraid. There's more than we know of ... there's more than we know of outside our sphere. The dead don't die; they're with us all the time. There's no such thing as heaven and hell, that create so much fear. The dead are here all the time on a fourth dimension. They haven't gone away. You'll see when you speak on the glass. There's nothing to be frightened of at all.

Do you feel bitter about losing your sight?

No, not at all. I've fought a great battle. I went on a big drug scene. It started through being given sleeping pills in Torquay. In the end I was a terrible drug addict. I gave my wife and children a very bad time. And then I stopped. And now I won't even touch an aspirin. It's all nonsense. There's absolutely no reason why people should fight for sleep. You can find things to pass the night away. Sleep will come eventually for what your body needs. You mustn't worry about things. I've had a lot of time to reflect on things. Anyway, come on — we've made contact already.

Conclusion

The men and women interviewed in this study had clearly changed significantly after they went blind in adult life. After the initial shock of blindness, and perhaps a week or a month of crying and despair, they turned resolutely towards society's 'centre' and ingeniously maintained a social footing in the sighted world. Change was not transformation but development, built on the existing self. In some cases there were signs of bitterness, but in no case were there any illusions, about the attitudes of the sighted. Of course the categories of 'sighted' and 'blind' assumed an entirely new significance: these were the two basic categories in terms of which they ordered their lives. But life was now framed on long-term strategies and short-term tactics for keeping the two categories in alignment and denying any 'essential' difference between them.

The blind claimed a place in the sighted world on the basis of 'achievements'; and their achievements, measured from the baseline of their former, sighted selves, were substantial, and without any apparent limitation through age. It is true that one interviewee thought that the necessary achievements might be difficult if one went blind after fifty, but a man who went blind in his sixties (Mr Price) had learned braille and was remarkable for his repertoire of newly acquired practical skills.

Change and development lay not only in acquiring new physical skills but in organizing social relationships so they were not set apart. Musical and literary tastes often deepened and changed, and some of the schoolboys thought that far from being socially retarded, they had gained in maturity. Middle-aged men with an undistinguished life behind them found a new self-confidence and in one case success as a playwright. Even the will seemed to be strengthened and a life-long chain-smoker gave up smoking.

The 'significant others' who sustained their sense of normal reality were not others who were similarly afflicted. Even in the boarding school for the blind, blindness did not promote a sense of community: the blind did not join together to construct a new social reality or even to sustain one another in their grip on the old. Significant others were mainly the sighted members of the blind person's family. It was from a secure private base that the blind turned outwards to make their assault on the world of the sighted.

Many aspects of everyday life which were formerly routine and 'invisible' were now the subject of reflection — from dressing and shaving to mowing the lawn and identifying a person who was talking. New recipes were invented for the performance of routine tasks; but they served to sustain the old reality rather than subvert it.

The blind maintained their relationship with the sighted not only through social skills but through a shared symbolic order. The young accepted the schedules of ordinary personal, educational and occupational development and strove to adhere to these timetables. Statistical categories were similar to timetables in providing an over-arching symbolic order in which one could 'place' oneself. One in ten people has diabetes, and of these one in five will go blind: 'Why shouldn't I keep up the statistics?' Statistical categories enable the afflicted not only to place themselves, but to account for their affliction and give it legitimacy.

The blind spiritualist, Mr Clark, appears at first sight to be the odd-man-out in this analysis: in his pain and torment he has apparently cut himself off from the paramount reality of everyday life. But in fact his separate reality is constituted of entirely 'normal' problems of personal relationships which have simply 'carried over' from the everyday social world that he knew.

One of the most perceptive and subtle accounts of the social context of spiritualism has been given by Vieda Skultans, who investigated a spiritualist circle in a town in South Wales. The circle was composed of middle-aged, working-class women who were apparently reconciled to pain and the inescapable humiliation of traditional marital roles. The focus of the study is relationships and roles within the group, which convert pain (private and divisive) into suffering (public and socially cohesive). And in healing rituals traditional male and female roles are reaffirmed and made legitimate.[10]

Mr Clark's turning to spiritualism is also clearly related to his private anguish and pain; but he is not a member of a circle which might promote a sense of solidarity and sympathy in a context of relative anonymity. And yet his spiritualism appears to support rather than subvert the reality of everyday life. Mr Clark inhabits a universe of multiple realities; but Jesus Christ, the Great Master, embraces them all. The Three Wise Men who came on spaceships are verified by paintings in cave dwellings: it is evidence of everyday life which provides the accent of reality for the sub-universe which is now his primary home.

7 | The homosexual as stranger

This chapter reports a study of adult homosexuals and focuses on two aspects of change: role learning and the experience of 'liminality'. The transit of these young men and women from the 'straight' world to homosexual society was a status passage without institutionalized guidelines and rituals or socially defined and unambiguous roles. Subjects were phenomenological strangers in their 'own' homosexual world.

Role-taking is the central process in interactionist interpretations of adult socialization, resocialization and change. It is often predictable and accounts for conformity, continuity, and personal and social stability. It faithfully reflects the well-known expectations of significant others and members of the 'role-set'. But roles exist in varying degrees of concreteness and consistency, and symbolic interactionists have emphasized the range of role prescriptions from the tight definitions and even rule-regulated requirements of military, ecclesiastical and bureaucratic organizations to more fluid situations in which there may be as much role-making as role-taking.

An emphasis on role-making rather than role-taking underpins the symbolic interactionist's conception of the openness of adult personality. Fundamental transformations of identity are possible if we make as well as take our roles. In the interactionist perspective attention shifts from enacting prescribed roles to devising unscripted performances. Roles are actually constructed (says Cicourel) in the course of social interaction, through learning based on selective scanning of behavioural displays.[1] The stress is on spontaneity, creativity and choice.

Ralph Turner gave us one of the most important and influential formulations of the interactionists' conception of role as the outcome of exploration, testing what others want and expect: we settle, provisionally, on our role definition from an almost infinite array which would meet the logical requirements of the role. In his account of role-making he stressed change rather than stability and conformity:

> Interaction is always a *tentative* process, a process of continuously testing the conception one has of the role of the other. The response of the other serves to reinforce or to challenge this conception. The product of the testing process is the stabilization or the modification of one's own role.[2]

Testing inferences about the roles of others is a never-ending process: 'Hence the tentative character of the individual's own role definition and performance is never wholly suspended.'

This study began with the assumption that 'becoming a homosexual' would illustrate the open-ended extreme of role-taking and role-making; and this assumption was amply supported by the inquiry. Two features of the role-making process were more surprising: one was the limbo of doubt and uncertainty that preceded acceptance of oneself as a homosexual; the other was the extent to which homosexuals appeared to remain 'strangers', never comfortably and anonymously at home, in their own homosexual world.

Alfred Schutz sees the bedrock of social reality as 'the stock of preconstituted knowledge which includes a network of typifications'. The typifications are of people, motivations, goals and actions. The preconstituted stock of knowledge 'also includes knowledge of expressive and interpretive schemes, of objective sign-systems and, in particular, the vernacular language'.[3] Thus equipped we confront our fellow men in the concrete situations of everyday life. It was precisely such a stock of preconstituted knowledge and network of typifications that the homosexual appeared to lack when he confronted his fellow homosexuals. But no neatly packaged, standard stocks of social knowledge were in any case available. Roles seemed to remain always precarious, tentative, ambiguous. Here, indeed, identities seemed to be 'open' and constantly revised.

The homosexual entering the gay world was like Schutz's 'stranger' who finds his new world not a shelter but 'a labyrinth in which he has lost all sense of bearings'. The culture of the approached group is not a shield but a field of adventure, it is 'not a matter of course but a questionable topic of investigation, not an instrument for disentangling problematical situations but a problematical situation itself and one hard to master'. The stranger lacks routine and unreflecting recipe knowledge: he has left a world in which the performers of typical functions are unremarkable and remain comfortably anonymous, unnamed and undifferentiated like the legion of submerged servants in a Jane Austen novel. And he, too, is denied the comfort and solace of anonymity and typicality. He is always on show. It was the 'straight' world that the homosexual had left that was relatively unproblematical — the world in which he had grown up (often with vague intimations of his differentness), but requiring no 'attentional modifications' to apprehend its meaning. All the homosexuals who were interviewed in this study had felt totally alone when they came to a full realization and acceptance of their sexual nature. Discovering that a whole world of homosexuals existed was an emotional relief; negotiating admittance and acceptance was socially perilous. And like Saul on the road to Damascus many changed their names as they transformed their identities.

The inquiry

A study of homosexuals was carried out 1974-5 through observation and conversation in the gay bars of a northern city, and through extended, tape-recorded interviews with ten homosexuals (eight men and two women) who were seen, by arrangement, in their own homes. They ranged in age from twenty-three to thirty-eight. Three (two men and one woman) were very active in the Campaign for Homosexual Equality; the rest had no connection with any activist movement. Three of the men live in London: Ken, a London University graduate, is thirty and a social worker; Harold, who is an art school graduate, is thirty-six and very successful as a self-employed artist; George has a prison record, is thirty-four and works as a railway porter. In the northern city Jane, who is twenty-five and active in the Campaign for Homosexual Equality, has a job in social research; Tom (also in CHE) is a social science research student; Peter is also in CHE, thirty, and employed as a clerk. Raymond is thirty-eight and a window-dresser; Malcolm is twenty-four, comes from a poor working-class background and has just completed a university degree course in modern history; Jacob is twenty-six, a social science graduate and an executive in industry; Petula is twenty-five, an art school graduate who has a job at a centre for mentally-handicaped children.

They were all asked to look back over their lives and relate any stages or turning points in their social-sexual development; to give some account of their relationships with homosexuals on the one hand and with 'straights' on the other; and to say whether they felt in any way stigmatized. The three involved in CHE tended to talk at length about the movement, its organization and numerical strength. Peter especially came back repeatedly to the aims and success of the organization:

> We're the biggest gay organization in the country. Four thousand members. And we got four hundred new members from the publicity of the Malvern conference. Four hundred in one week — fantastic. And Malvern was a great experience. You should have been there. Eight hundred really together people. It was fantastic. Unbelievable.

Jane talked at length about the politically radical attitudes that hitherto withdrawn and docile women developed when they joined CHE:

> People said you couldn't get gay women into groups. But we've got a women's group up here that's got 130 members, and there isn't a bigger women's group in the country apart from Sappho in London. They become more militant than the men. There's a broader thing when people come out. They come out as something else as well as gay. Once you've come out about one thing, and are capable of dealing with it, you can say things like, 'I pick my nose'. Once a gay woman reaches any kind of awareness, she realizes how crushing the oppression of women is. And it just makes them very radical.

CHE has become an important means of bringing homosexuals — and not only the politically radical and militant — into contact with one another. They move into the 'gay world' from a position of extreme isolation. It is the gay world which the homosexual 'joins' and explores as a stranger.

Role-taking: strangers scanning the scene

The *Goya* is a 'gay pub' in a northern city and on a Saturday night in the Spring of 1975 its three bars were packed by 9 o'clock. The benches round the walls were covered with torn black plastic, there were no carpets on the floor, most people drank beer, but at the bar they sold Dunhill International. There were middle-aged men in cheap lounge suits and nylon shirts smoking panatellas; there were younger men well dressed in Aquascutum suits with beards and side-burns; a few, still younger, wore black, studded leather, winkle-picker shoes and knuckle-duster rings. A few men wore tight-fitting trousers and discreet jewelry and answered to women's names. There were comparatively few women; a few beautifully dressed girls in '20s-style outfits, and four or five middle-aged fag-hags with permed hair. Most of the men wore make-up. Two small slim negroes in tight-fitting bell-bottomed trousers and suede waistcoats framed the doorway to a rear bar.

A regular at the *Goya* who had been told about the research project had agreed to help with introductions. He was an accountant in his early thirties, dark, with well-groomed hair, wearing a black suit and black collarless shirt, smoking long, tipped cigarettes and drinking dry sherry. He answered to the name of Miranda. Everyone seemed to know something about everyone else. 'What do you expect?' said Miranda, 'all we ever do is gossip about each other'. In the rear bar a youngish man in a long transparent white dress and flowered under-clothes sang to the accompaniment of a piano and drums. The drummer was a man of fifty, with a soft, powdered face, a short blond wig and a sequined waistcoat. The pianist was also a man of fifty in a cheap tweed suit.

Miranda had found a Cambridge sociologist lurking in the lavatories. He wasn't even a good sociologist. 'He can't tell the difference between a gay man who behaves in a camp way because he's joking', complained Miranda, 'and when it's full-time behaviour. He thinks that all gay men behave like that all the time.' But Miranda has had wide experience of sociologists: 'The gay bars are crawling with them, dancing with each other with their tape-recorders switched on, thinking they've got a real one here.'

Later, at the *Pleiades* a tall, strongly-built bouncer wearing a wig and eye make-up stood by the door. The bar was much plusher than the one in the *Goya*. There were red velvet seats and curtains, William Morris wallpaper, rose-coloured lighting, and old theatrical posters on the walls. Customers were not drinking beer, but cocktails and sherry. They congregated in small groups of three or four, whispering to each other. The air was heavy with perfume.

Only a minority was overtly homosexual, and they presented themselves ostentatiously as either 'butch' or 'femme'. 'They send the CHE people mad', said Miranda, 'you're not supposed to be butch or femme. It's not nice in CHE. But people here enjoy it. They come to show off. And why not?' Again, everybody seemed to know something about everybody else. 'The butch guy by the juke box is a roller (prostitute)', said Miranda. 'Bill and I tried to pick him up once. Thank Christ he was already booked. We didn't know then that he was a roller. It could have been really nasty.' But although everybody seemed to know something — usually scandalous — about everybody else, eyes were searching, restless, scanning. Behavioural displays were under close scrutiny. Everyone was familiar and no-one was taken for granted. There was no routinely typical behaviour and no comfortable anonymity.

The problems and process of role-learning and role-taking in unfamiliar circumstances for which he had no preconstituted stock of recipe knowledge is well illustrated by George, the railway porter. He spent three years in borstal for house-breaking, and is now proud of the south London suburban semi-detached house which he bought twelve years ago. It is comfortably if rather ornately furnished, and the small garden is carefully tended: 'I slowly built it up to what I've got now, which is all my own. Which I think is quite good, considering how I started. You know it can be done.' His main problem with straight society — and especially the world of employment — is not his homosexuality but his police record.

He grew up in Wolverhampton and had his first homosexual experience at sixteen.

> It just seemed natural. There was no choice involved. Mind you, I did feel I was the only one. It was only when I came down to London ... I was sixteen and picked up by this old bloke in Wolverhampton. I was very naive. I just thought I was the only person like that. It was great, really, to come down to London and find that I wasn't. I was really relieved to find there were other people like me. I'd never spoken to anybody about it, because there was nobody I could talk to. I had to think it out for myself. It surprised me when I came down here to find that I wasn't the only one. The only one I ever met in Wolverhampton was the forty-year-old man.

But he lacked the 'recipe knowledge' which would give him an easy entry into homosexual society:

> I never used to do the 'cottages' (public lavatories) and so on, because I didn't know it went on. I didn't know anything about the pubs or anything. When I came down here I was much surprised.

I heard about the *Eagle* in the West End, so I went there. I was standing at the bar drinking half a pint of brown ale, and this bloke kept walking past me. And eventually he said, 'Do you want a drink?' so I said, 'I don't mind'. I hadn't got any money. Anyway, he bought me several drinks, and it came to closing time, so I said, 'Well, thanks. I've got to go now'. And he said, 'What do you mean, you've got to go now. What have I been buying you drinks all night for?' I said, 'Well, I don't know. You offered, and I hadn't got any money'. And he said, 'Aren't you coming home with me?' and I said, 'I'm not'. And he got really annoyed, you know. He started abusing me and everything. I said, 'I don't know what you mean'. And he said, 'Well, I've bought you'. And I said, 'No, you haven't, and I'm not coming home with you'. And he got really aggressive. I was really frightened. Well, anyway, another guy came up and asked what the trouble was and I explained to him. He had a word with this guy and he left me alone. And it suddenly clicked what the situation was. So for the next three or four months I just played it like that. If I fancied them I just went to bed with them, and if not I didn't. As for the gay pubs now, I think they're pathetic. Half the people there are so effeminate. I can't stand people like that.

George knows that the novice often learns his homosexual behaviour in gay bars, but he isn't 'really like that':

They're just copying people. Just because they're gay they feel they have to behave in a certain way. Whereas, you know, they should be themselves. The trouble is, we all get tarred with the same brush — that we all walk around like that and carry handbags, which a lot of them do and are really outrageously effeminate. But me and the friend that I live with are just everyday people. But a lot of people don't think this. They think we go chasing little boys and things like that.

George has comparatively few difficulties in his relationship with straight society:

Do you feel any stigma because you're homosexual?

No. I'm not embarrassed. And I've got no hang-ups. I'm gay and that's that. If people don't like it, that's just too bad. But it's not something I feel is an issue. A lot of people know about me at work. Some have asked me if I'm gay and I've said 'Yes'. Often they don't believe it because I don't look effeminate. If anyone came up to me and said, 'Are you gay?' I should say 'Yes' without hesitation, because I don't think there's anything to be ashamed of.

Have you ever found yourself discriminated against?

No, not really. No. But there is a stigma in my police record. I've lost two or three jobs over it, when I haven't declared it and they've found out. I'd get the sack from my present job immediately if they found out. Luckily I've got two good jobs behind me now. Normally they just ask for two jobs and you're OK.

The straight world is not invariably tolerant (but women usually are):

I really get on much better with women. There was this man at work one day who said in the course of conversation, 'Bloody queers, they ought to be castrated. I wouldn't be seen talking to one'. So I said, 'You know, I'm queer as you call it', and he said, 'You're not'. I said, 'I am, I've never been with a girl'. He was taken aback ... he wouldn't speak to me after that. And yet we'd got along perfectly well until this subject came up. And he just cut me dead. I can't understand it. Whether he thought it was contagious or not I just don't know.

The homosexual world really presents George with more problems than the straight:

I haven't felt the desire to go into gay pubs for a long time. I'd much rather go to a normal pub and drink there. I don't mind going into gay pubs, but they're so pathetic, really, standing there looking at one another. They're there for one reason, yet they won't speak to anybody. People I've been with, picked up in the pub or a club — I either go back to their place or they come back here. And we've gone to bed and had sex. And that's it. If you see them in the street the next day, they walk right past you. They won't speak to you. You've been in bed and you've had, what, two hours when you've really been together and enjoyed each other's company. To be snubbed by the same person the next day ... I just don't understand it. I got to the stage when I didn't want to go and pick somebody up just for sex. I wanted more than that. Because, all right, you can do that as long as your looks last, you can get away with it. Well, what do you do then? You're just left. Cast off. And they wonder why they end up lonely and nobody wants them.

Ken is a thirty-year-old London University graduate, a social worker in London, who accepted his homosexuality in his mid twenties, shortly after leaving university, and was deeply puzzled about how to behave, realizing the ideas he had always had of homosexuals were wrong, but uncertain about what was facade and what was 'real' when he scanned the homosexual scene:

> It's really frightfully dramatic, learning how totally wrong the world is: when you know that things aren't true, like I know that I don't fancy pre-pubescent children. I know all sorts of things now about gays — what we do and what we don't do. And I know more than a random sample. And then you measure this against rumours and assumptions, and you see how wrong society is and how silly in the way it distorts and stereotypes. And so you can be contemptuous about the whole straight thing. At least, that's the way it affected me. I think I was quite lucky because I came out in a dramatic way. I went to the Gay Liberation Front and my opinions were formed there.

Ken is still closely observing homosexual behaviour, trying to see what is essential and what is pretence. He has carefully scanned the gay bars:

> There are very few areas for you to learn about reactions and the way to behave. One is the gay bars and the other would be something like the Gay Liberation Front. In the gay bars you'd learn to be furtive and not to accept yourself, searching for Mr Right all the time, adopting all the norms of society but in a strange, parodied way — just wanting the same trip as if you were heterosexual. Like it could be a man at home doing the housework, but there wouldn't be any children. And it's seen to be a parody by the gays themselves.
>
> Luckily, that wasn't my first scene, though I've always been to the gay bars. I adore them. I worked in the *Coal House*, the biggest gay bar in London. I saw the absolute apologists for the commercial gay scene — all the mincing fairies and the leather queens. But I'm very glad that I didn't go there to learn how to behave. If I had done that, I should now be saying how horrible they all are, like they do — trying to mind that they're doing what they're doing, which is rather sick. I was taught to be angry. I'm sure now that the only healthy response is one of anger — I mean they only stopped putting people in prison for making it five or six years ago.
>
> And yet my first reaction was one of gratitude that my straight friends still accepted me. The Gay Liberation Front poured scorn on me for this — they said, 'Let them prove that they're militantly against this oppression before *you* accept *them*. Don't wait gratefully

for people to tolerate you: *you* may choose to tolerate *them.*' That makes sense on an ethical level. I suppose I'm really quite political, except that it's now on a more personal level — talking to gays and saying, 'Don't be so stupid. Why are you saying that?' Then they start sending each other up, and it's all part of this whole guilt thing. It comes out as people trying to be more camp than their friends. The whole thing's riddled with this self-hatred. I like to be able to reveal myself as gay to some straight people — the ones who expect the stereotypes. They try to cope with it by pretending they haven't heard or that I'm joking — because they know me and like me and the two things don't add up. I'm very much aware of women's rights and their oppression to the extent that I'm emotionally affronted by chauvinistic heterosexual morals, and sex-object women treated like cripples having doors held open for them. I'm really the most militant feminist at heart.

Then there's the whole question of black power. I'm very excited by it. These three — gays, blacks, and women — they're not wholly alike, of course, there are different circumstances attached to each — but emotionally I feel strongly about all of them. And so by extension to the whole working class — silly, fucked-up society that can't cope with most things. So it's all been a very good and liberating thing. I spent a time mentally in the ghetto, just obsessed with gay things, and from that I've come out to other things. I went through a very important process, very necessary for gays — the usual way is to talk about 'integrating'. But the only way is for gays to take real pride in their own identity. And you need all kinds of crude propaganda tricks to achieve that. 'Sending up' straights is a healthy thing to do for a time, as long as there's enough truth in it. You can talk about their boring lives, boring jobs, boring family set-ups. Most gays respond to being stereotyped by doing one of these things: becoming super-butch leather queens, saying 'Yes, I am a mincing fairy', or becoming *extremely* normal.

The thing I like about my friend Edward is that he's eccentric. He's so together about being gay that he's able to be — it's a sign of supreme self-confidence. He's eccentric in terms of the gay scene — he doesn't fit into any of these slots. Most gays are seen as eccentric by straights, but to themselves they're being fairly conformist.

I'm still trying to make sense of things, to put things together. I've got tons of impressionistic evidence that certainly a very high proportion of Catholic converts are gay, a very high proportion of caring people, and a high proportion of artists, for some reason. It's nice to try to make sense of these things that I know to be true. At one time I couldn't believe any blacks were gay — I had this idea of the happy savage, and the other of a gay being broken down, twisted and perverted. The two didn't mix. I was amazed to find the *Catacombs*, this gay club, full of beautiful West Indians...

The homosexual runs the same danger as Schutz's stranger, on the verge of two different patterns of group life, but often unable to feel loyalty to either. There are models in neither world which he can adopt. He desperately explores his new world beyond the gay bars, looking for models which he can admire. Jane, who is active in CHE, expressed the loneliness of this dilemma:

It doesn't do much for your self-respect if you've got to identify with people who are pitiful — the people who go in the gay pubs, and clubs, or people who dress in drag, or people who act out sexual roles like gay women who wear suits. Obviously that does you a lot of harm in your development. Not because there's anything wrong with a gay woman wearing a suit, but, if you don't want to, you think, 'Christ, everyone's like that. I'm the only person who isn't like that'. So not only do you have the problem of considering yourself to be a member of a group which is despised, but you also have the problem of dealing with the fact that you're the only gay person who's like you. An awful lot of gay people feel like that.

In the search for role models, reference groups and self-respect, the gay world may be scanned from a distance and devious learning strategies adopted. Tom, the young social science research student, observed:

You know, it's amazing the things people think about gay people, even when they know that they're one. They think that gay people are all very odd-looking, or very bizarre, and that they're totally promiscuous ... Some of us play this game which is called 'Leonardo da Vinci'. You need no pieces but merely some gay people, and you sit around and mention a certain famous name, and someone else replies that they're gay or bisexual and you get points. That's the essence. There are more rules ... Obviously a lot of the time when gay people say, 'Oh, So-and-So's gay', what's happening is that gay people need figures to identify with, people who are famous or important or well-known on television ... I find it very boring now when you sit around and say who is gay. It's pretty obvious why they do it. It's like if you're black, for example, or if you're a woman, if you're searching for honesty and security for yourself you need people who're honourable that you can identify with. If you're black you've got a few people, if you're a woman you've got less, and if you're homosexual, well, who declares himself openly as homosexual? Very few people. I mean, there are some famous people who've 'come out' as gay, but not many. Gay people have a continual fight to find and keep their self-respect.

Tom deplores the gay bar as a learning environment for the lonely stranger, but realizes that there are few alternatives:

> The clubs and the gay pubs are a world of their own, with their own values and standards of behaviour. If you could imagine what it would be like to be a heterosexual in a world where you don't know how to meet other heterosexuals, where you know vaguely about clubs you can go to, and that is the only place where you'll be totally accepted ... if you go along there and find people behaving in a certain way, even though it might be strange to you, you have a choice between behaving like that and fitting in and being accepted, or not and being rejected. If you are isolated and you need acceptance, love and sex, you choose to behave in the way that people do there.

The effect of occupation, age and social class

It is, of course, a misleading oversimplification to represent the homosexual as a stranger who leaves behind one society to be totally embraced by another. He lives in two worlds, but he seems often to have especially acute problems in relating to his 'own', homosexual world. If his job is low status, or high status but in the sphere of the arts, he may have little difficulty in his relationships with straight society. (On the other hand, he will almost invariable have difficulty with his parents and other family members.) It is the homosexual world that presents difficulties, notably in the changed and heightened significance given to age and social class.

The homosexual is in a position between two sharply contrasted worlds, one of which is in some respects the inverse of the other. This is not necessarily uncomfortable or distressing. He experiences society not as a fixed structure, but as a dialectical process. This is an experience — discussed further below — which may be profoundly regenerative. In the gay world there is less 'structure' and more 'communitas'.[4] The dialectic of structure and communitas, the alternation of phases of routinized living and spontaneous abandon, enables a man to stand outside the taken-for-granted realities of everyday life and enjoy experiences which are literally 'ecstatic'.

Raymond is thirty-eight years of age, a window-dresser who lives with his mother. He had his first homosexual experience at eighteen, but 'I always knew I was different — I didn't have girl friends and things like that'. He finds relationships with straight society easy and says he feels no sense of stigma: 'Of course, I've lived through this stage. When I was young I wouldn't have told anyone I was gay, unless they asked me. Now, of course, I couldn't care less.'

He has a sense of wasted time because it was a few years after his first homosexual experience that he successfully negotiated entry into homosexual society:

> For a few years after I left school, I was in a sort of limbo. I wasted a lot of time, because I didn't know ... I don't really resent that, but it would have been nice to have had it. Of course the gay pubs and clubs are totally false, but once you get together, you go beserk. When you get in a crowd of like-minded people, you're out of the limbo. And of course the gin flows, you let off steam, make silly jokes, let your hair down. But I have always had a lot of straight friends. I get on well with them. Being a homosexual has nothing to do with it. I like people, or dislike them, for what they are. When I go into a room and meet people for the first time, if you feel you're going to have a good relationship with anyone, you almost feel obliged, at least I do, to state that you're a homosexual. I do, and then that's it: you're on an honest footing, you've got it out of the way. On the whole it's ignored. Obviously if people have objections, they're not friends. It doesn't happen often. I think only one has ostentatiously spat at me. A majority, in fact my best friends, are all straight.

The homosexual world is more problematical, especially in relation to age:

What about homosexual relationships. Do you find them easy?

No. Of course in any big city centre you can find someone fairly easily. I don't personally because I'm thirty-eight and physically ... What matters is this slim figure. You find with male homosexuals everything is the youth cult. Now, it isn't so much with the lesbians. But with the male, it's the instant physical impact. Lesbians aren't the same. Maybe the physical isn't so important there. It's sad, all the males in the gay clubs, dolled up to the nines, competing with each other like mad ... But let's face it, I'm getting old. I'm thirty-eight. I've never been the gorgeous young dolly thing. Things are getting hard. Apart from the initial release thing — 'cottages' and things like that. But you have to do it. When you are attractive and the type who can walk into a bar and walk up to people, you don't need to.

Raymond is pleased with the social-class mix in the homosexual world and finds it presents no problems:

The gay world cuts across class barriers. You meet people and mix with them for what they are, not who they are. For example, I've a friend who is a lord, and yet Robert, who's a porter, is a very good friend. I suppose being gay does lead to meeting unusual people — people from the underworld I suppose would be included. I don't really think of myself as odd. But then, I don't really think about it. An awful lot of straight people are attracted to gays because they find them interesting and unusual.

Harold, a very successful artist, has a quite contrary view of the social-class mix: homosexuality 'cuts across barriers for sex, full-stop ... otherwise it reinforces the class system tremendously.' He is thirty-six, an art school graduate working as a self-employed artist in London, who spent five very profitable and sexually exciting years in the art world in Italy. He feels no stigma from his homosexuality (except when he is with his brother), and maintains that his occupation marks him off from mainline society more than his sexuality. At thirty-six he is deeply preoccupied with age and inclined to pass as thirty.

Harold's flat contained an expensive stereo set and piles of records — mostly Italian opera, a bed-settee, coffee tables, an elaborate fireplace decorated with postcards, peacock feathers, small framed drawings, and shells. There were two beautifully hand-painted men's shirts on the settee, decorated with flowers and exotic birds and finished off with Harold's signature. 'I love all flowers, especially irises', explained Harold, 'I've been drawing them for years'.

He had his first homosexual experience, and formed a relationship which lasted for a number of years, when he was sixteen; but already, at school, he delighted in extravagant behaviour: 'I used to wear green eyeshadow and dyed my hair platinum and wore beauty spots to cover my pimples.' But at eighteen he still found the homosexual world incomprehensible and at thirty-six still feels he's a stranger. Yet when he went to art school, 'I used to wear red satin trousers, and I used to get very upset by lorry drivers whistling'.

Then why did you do it?

Because I wanted to. Like when I have too much to drink I take my trousers off. At parties, I just feel like it. But I never met gay people much till after the age of eighteen when I went to my first gay clubs. I think it was just a kind of inborn exhibitionism. When I met the very first camp person I'd ever seen — I was about eighteen — I thought he was ... not mentally deficient, but a kind of spastic, because of the way he behaved. He was a very camp queen. I'd never seen anyone like that before.

For twenty years he has lived a full homosexual life, but is still hesitant and tentative in his approach to the homosexual world:

Most of my friends have always been heterosexual. It's only in the last couple of years that I've got to know a lot of gay people. In the gay world they have fantastically strict lines between butch and bitch, and queens and chickens. But I'm turned on by a great number of things, like tough little cockneys. I actually don't know much about the gay world, because I've never really mixed in it.

All the interviewees referred to an early period of 'limbo' — usually in their late teens or early twenties — when they realized they were out of step with straight society but had only a vague and shadowy knowledge of the gay world. The limbo or state of transition is what Turner (following van Gennep) calls 'liminality'[5]: it is a feature of normal social experience, for 'each individual's life experience contains alternating exposure to structure and communitas, and to states and transitions.'[6] In the biographies of homosexuals we see this process in an exaggerated form. For Harold these alternating exposures occur rapidly: he swings between two social modalities and finds it difficult to settle for long in either:

During my five years in Italy, two or three times each week I'd wear a suit, a shirt and a tie, and go out and have Swiss dinners and things. But I'd find after about two hours I'd go out for a walk; or if people came to dinner, I'd go out and do the washing up because I couldn't bear them any longer. I don't know what it is. I've tried hard to conform. I can't. It makes life difficult.

I thought as an artist you wouldn't have to conform?

Oh, yes, I do. Well, you don't absolutely have to. I'm just about managing without conforming. If I did conform and was nice to

people, like the people I've done those shirts for — they're two very
camp queens — I could probably get several more commissions. And
certainly if I'd gone to a couple of parties they've invited me to,
people would have said, 'Oh, you can do me a shirt'. I don't know,
it's silly, but I can't manage it. I have an agent who goes to New York
a couple of times a year, and she does quite well for me. It saves all
the hassling. I mean, the servile grin you have to assume, whether you
feel like it or not, when you take your drawings round...

Do you feel any stigma about being gay?

No, not at all. The only time I ever feel uncomfortable about it is
when I go out with my brother and his friends. I find myself acting
and talking in the most masculine way I possibly can, just in case
anyone makes a remark. My brother knows I'm gay, but I've never
been able to talk to him about it. I've never felt I was in a minority
group, actually never felt conscious of it. But I suppose that dealing
in fine arts, and being an artist, you attract the kind of people who
don't have inbuilt hang-ups about what you are, because their lives
are so ecstatic anyway. I mean, as an artist, I know I'm set aside. As a
gay person I've never felt this. I've been to a couple of CHE meetings.
I had a slight affair with the secretary. They were terribly militant,
terribly conscious. They get their politics and their sexuality in
terrible muddles. I don't think you should force what you are on
people. People in general aren't interested. It's like being militant
about wearing dentures. I've never felt that I needed a pressure
group to convince me that being gay's all right, because I always
thought it was. And it's given me a great deal of pleasure being gay.

Harold distances himself from the gay scene in England, but for five
years in Italy he enjoyed a seemingly uncomplicated involvement:

It was fabulous in Italy, because Italians come on so easily. I had a very
unpromiscuous relationship with Peter, who I went with to Italy. But
when I left him I had an incredibly promiscuous period. Somebody
told me that my approach was all wrong in London: that you don't
go up to somebody and smile at them, offer them a cigarette and
invite them home to bed. Which never occurred to me, because in
Italy that works — you smile at an Italian, you're friendly towards
him, and he immediately reacts in a friendly way. In England, if you
go 'cruising', people look at you in an incredibly furtive way which I
don't understand at all.

Are the police liberal in Italy?

Well, yes. I was picked up by the police once in Rome. That was about three o'clock in the morning. They wanted to see my passport and so on. I had sex with one of the policemen in the back of the police car. They were very nice. I mean, they were nice before one of them made a pass, and just as nice afterwards. They told me to be very careful going round the areas I was going round.

It's exciting to go out, pull someone, and have sex in the open air. There's a lovely park in Rome, and I sometimes used to go there all night with someone I'd picked up. And it was warm and nice and we used to lie on the grass and smoke and things. Sort of very civilized, which again you can't do in England that much, because it never gets warm. Which is perhaps why we're sexually so hung up, generally. It's funny, a lot of the Italians I went with were married men. That wasn't by my inclination, they just seemed to be, you know. Young, not too middle-aged, anyway. I don't mind if they're a little fat and hairy. A paunchy, thirty-five-year-old Englishman would definitely turn me off. But the Italian, the same man in Italy, is all sort of happy and nice. Completely different. No, I really think the English gay scene is very sad.

Although Harold distances himself from the gay scene in England, he shares its values regarding age:

How old are you now? I've been trying to work it out

Thirty. No, I told a terrible lie. Thirty-six. I had to go to Fortnum and Mason's publicity people for these fabrics they're doing. And there was this terribly sweet girl who kept saying how lovely it was for Fortnum's to have a young designer at last. And she asked me when I was born and I said 1945. And she wanted my father to be a bus driver. I told her he was a stoker. She didn't know what a stoker was.

His homosexual friends are well versed in the niceties of occupational rank and status:

If you're working-class gay you move in completely different circles from anyone else. I can't stand that. I noticed it in the dealing world. It's run, some of it is, anyway, by gays. In fact it's almost entirely run by gays, with just one or two exceptions. And they're the most incredibly nasty snobs that you could possibly meet. Incredible snobs. I loathe them, because they could really make me feel unhappy. They'd come to dinner and notice that one of the wine glasses was chipped, or something like that. Or that we only had one maid in Italy, and you should have a cook as well. And they could be so patronizingly offensive about it. It's incredibly destructive.

But the gay world often claims to cut across class?

That's rubbish. It does for a sex meeting. I think it cuts across barriers
for sex, full-stop. There's less of the class rubbish in Italy. I found
less, anyway. But in England I'd say it reinforces the class system
tremendously. The immediate thing people ask you after you've had
your first orgasm is, you know, where do you live, what do you do?
Do you have a car, do you have records, colour television, things like
that. It's a kind of stock-taking: how important or influential you are,
are you worth ringing up again? Actually I do know a very few people
who have taken a young, a very young attractive working-class person
and lived with them. But usually they keep them as far away as they
can from their social life. As far away as possible. Keep them for their
sexual life, but that's it. People I know quite well are surprised when
I say that I'm living with someone who works as a labourer. You
know, as though I've come down in the world. Which is pathetic. I
think people are naturally snobs, but it's very much exaggerated in
the gay world. Gay people don't really like to admit that they've
been 'cruising'. If you bump into someone you know who's
obviously cruising, they're embarrassed. Which again is different
from Italy. I think maybe the whole Mediterranean ... No, actually
Greece is different. In Greece people are incredibly aggressive, and
not very nice. Homosexuals there were very furtive. Except I was
lucky — everyone said I was incredibly lucky — I met this lovely
soldier. We spent a whole afternoon and evening making love...

Jacob, a twenty-six year-old social science graduate, who is now an
executive in industry, was the only interviewee who, in the normal
course of his daily life, feels a strong sense of estrangement, a need to be
constantly on guard in a hostile world. He is an ambitious man who
wants to go far in a responsible and rewarding career. He is keenly aware
that homosexuality is more acceptable in some field of employment
than others:

The thing is that you can only be overtly gay in a routine, poorly-paid
job, where it doesn't matter, like being a waiter or a hairdresser. Then
there's the theatre, or fashion. Not in the world of business. And I
work in industry. I have to pretend to be a heterosexual. When I went
for my first job after graduating I told them I was engaged. There
must be quite a few people where I work who are gay, but I only know
about one of them, an operator. I see him in gay clubs and pubs, but

I don't speak to him, because I'm terrified in case he starts speaking to me at work. I mean, in his kind of work it doesn't matter, if he's known to be a homosexual. He's just a process operator, whereas in my kind of job it could do me an awful lot of damage. I'm assistant personnel manager.

Jacob has very few heterosexual friends: the straight world is a threatening and hostile environment. He has learned systematically the customs, values and behaviour of the gay world — in his period of teenage ignorance and uncertainty, 'I went to the public library and read books about it'. Now, in the company of homosexuals, his behaviour is effectively flexible and adaptive — he has become a chameleon:

I have several facades. I probably have three: I have my facade at work, my facade at home — I still have a facade at home — and in the clubs where I camp it up with other gay people.

My friend says that when I'm attracted to someone and want to get him, I act as butch as possible; but when I'm with other queens — I call myself a queen — the mask drops. At work I have to be very careful — don't say 'Ooh' and 'lovely' too much.

The straight world is full of danger, and he has a strong sense of belonging to a threatened and stigmatized outsider group:

Do you feel that you suffer from any stigma because you are gay?

Yes, I do. I've been caught by the police three times. Three times. Which shows how stupid some of us can be. And my name has been in the local papers. I'm learning a bit more sense now, and meeting people in less dangerous surroundings.

But yes, I do feel that I suffer from a stigma in the eyes of society. I know in the university hall of residence where I was, some people wouldn't speak to me because I was homosexual. I was told by a friend that some of the students were actually scared of talking to me, in case they'd be thought queer. I wish it were possible to be accepted as homosexual. I enjoy my work in industrial management, but I know that the attitudes of my colleagues would change at once if they knew. I have to control the way I move my hands, the way I use words, everything. To try to keep up this seemingly heterosexual image that I have. At university it didn't matter — I'd wear Gay Lib badges to lectures, things like that.

In all circumstances of life Jacob puts on a studied performance. But his performances are not flawless:

We're not always as cautious as we should be. We do sometimes ask for trouble. But we're forced into such situations. People go down Hampstead Heath or Wimbledon Common looking for sex hoping it'll develop into a lasting relationship. Because they can't do it by smiling at a bloke in the street. In this way you're open to blackmail and mugging. I've been beaten up by youths. We're just regarded as suitable passive prey for any aggressive young man. The teenagers who express themselves in vandalism also go in for queer-bashing. I'm definitely aware of being in an oppressed minority. We wouldn't have sex in the open air if we could bring them home, introduce them to the parents. That kind of thing. We are the victims of circumstances. It sounds like a sob story, but it's true.

The gay world is not a perfect shelter ('There are people in the homosexual world who take a delight in breaking up relationships'), but Jacob feels more at home in it, less exposed and vulnerable, than in the straight world. But he knows that age may make him an outcast. Already, at twenty-six, he is preoccupied with growing old:

I do fear growing old. Sociology books say we lose our social usefulness. We, kind of, become pathetic remnants of human beings when we get older. And to some extent that's true. You don't see many elderly homosexuals in the pubs. Once the bloom of youth has gone, and you don't have somebody with whom you can have a Darby-and-Joan sort of relationship, there's not much left. There aren't the social pressures to keep a homosexual relationship together. I think probably homosexual men don't live all that long. We've got nobody to ourselves. We smoke more, drink more; we live more debauched lives. Comparatively. And a lot don't want to live all that long...

Role without status: structure and communitas

These interview data leave two overriding impressions of the homosexual as stranger entering a new world: the first is his freedom in choosing among available homosexual roles (or even creating his own), the ease with which he can 'shop around' among possible styles of behaviour; the second is the sense of joy and liberation that normally attends his (or her) passage from straight society. The movement from the straight world to the gay scene is strikingly like Durkheim's account of the movement (of Australian aborigines) from the profane to the sacred. The profane is boredom, the sacred is effervescence, delerium. 'One is that where his daily life drags wearily along; but he cannot penetrate into the other without at once entering into relations with extraordinary powers that excite him to the point of frenzy. The first is the profane world, the second, that of sacred things.'[7] Marginality is sacred and ecstatic.

Linton tied roles firmly to statuses; recently both anthropologists and sociologists have weakened or even severed the link as they have conceptualized societies not as systems of positions, but as processes. 'Every status is linked with a particular role', said Linton, and 'a role is the dynamic aspect of a status'.[8] The tidiness of this formulation, the neatness of the distinction, has been queried by those who see roles as less finished, more innovative, not as givens, but as processes developing in the course of social interaction. The homosexual has roles without statuses.

Symbolic interactionists deny any neat set of rules for a role. Goffman talks of a 'working consensus' of people in a given situation, an interactional *modus vivendi* which involves the temporary suspension of disbelief about the roles that people claim.[9] In the gay clubs and bars the conspiratorial and provisional agreement to honour claims to be butch or femme or chicken or queen was pure theatre. Gossippy backbiting covertly queried the claim even while it was staged.

Sarbin tied roles and statuses as tightly together as Linton: 'roles are linked with positions and not with the person who is temporarily occupying the position.'[10] Merton at least suggested that 'an array of roles' was associated with every social status;[11] and others — notably Levinson — gave the individual more latitude in solving the 'adaptive dilemmas' with which social structure confronted him.[12] Goode finally severed the link by defining status as 'the class of roles which has been institutionalized.' Status does not differ in kind from role: it is a matter of degree.[13] In the gay scene roles are relatively uninstitutionalized. They are fluid and precarious: relationships lack 'third-party backing', they are without support outside the immediate situation, in community-wide relationships.[14]

The gay world seems to correspond to what anthropologist Victor Turner calls 'communitas' in contrast with 'structure'. Social life for everyone is a dialextical process that involves successive experiences of both. But the difference between the two modalities of social life is deep, even 'abysmal'; life within structure swiftly becomes 'arid and mechanical if those involved in it are not periodically immersed in the regenerative abyss of communitas.'[15] And the essential characteristic of communitas is a relationship between concrete, idiosyncratic individuals stripped of both status and role.[16]

In communitas there is an ambiguity and instability of categories and classifications — precisely as in the homosexual world. And, as Mary Douglas has argued, ambiguous categories are at the root of our ideas of pollution.[17] Ambiguous categories (as in the classification of forbidden meats in Leviticus) spell defilement. The homosexual suffers from his categorical uncertainty: he eludes our customary socio-sexual categories; and he has difficulty in holding firm to his own.

And yet, as Turner maintains, communitas has something magical about it. He resists any simple equation of communitas and the sacred,[18] but his account of communitas is strikingly like Durkheim's account of excitable sacred gatherings,[19] which in turn is strongly reminiscent of the 'gay scene'.

As he talked about his explorations of the new-found homosexual world, Ken, the thirty-year-old London social worker expressed intense excitement, and in a sense of wide-ranging choice of behaviour. He described his transfiguration:

The first time someone said I had a beautiful stomach I was knocked out. People had always told me what a mind I had, but to be loved for my body — this was very exciting. And this is part of loving yourself, the whole of you, you screwing just as much as you rushing round and helping the poor. And from that comes the ability to love and from relationships — from a position of strength.

I used to find dancing terribly boring. I couldn't understand why people enjoyed it. But my first dance with a guy! I really love dancing and spend all my time in night clubs and drinking in gay bars — totally trivial things that I despised all through my youth as being dreadful and worthless. So there's now this feeling that the ostensibly trivial is now of great importance to me. I love it just as much as I like arguing about Schopenhauer and J-P Sartre into the night, and all the other worthwhile things that society would label 'useful' or 'worthwhile'. Those are parts of me, sure, but so is me that goes dancing in the *Catacombs* and so on. It's the excitement of discovering yourself when you've denied an enormous side of yourself from your earliest years. Everything's exciting. Music — I've always liked music, but now I'm passionately fond of music. Once that part of you has been sorted out and can start growing, it frees you for other things.

Society does seem to me to be a very dull place. It's the restrictions people place on themselves. Part of the way to break out is to watch people who have. You may not have heard of the concept of 'gender fucking'. In the traditional gay scene you get drag pubs, and gay clubs, where all the jokes are about K Y jelly and 'cottages' — it's all based on the intrinsic humour of a man being dressed in women's clothes. It's very insulting to women, very self-parodying about gays. But in the Gay Liberation Front you get freaks who wear beards and eye make-up and dresses, and are not trying to be anything, just to deliberately outrage and wreck roles — that I find interesting. Sure, I'm anti-camp: I think it's based on self-hatred. I sometimes wear eye make-up, but it's me doing these things because I want to do them — not to look like a woman. I like not to be typed. Am I a butch guy or not? I never quite know. You get a lot of gays who put themselves in one of the two categories. I find that so depressing. It's so limiting.

One of the beautiful things about sex is its variety. You're free to be all sorts of things. There's great joy in being pursued and taken, and there's great joy in doing it as well — being the pursuer and the predator. It's so limiting to be a limp passive, who gets depressed because no-one chats him up, or to be one of the other kind — those typical Spaniards and people from very hung-up cultures — they get a lot of gays who never come to terms with it. They're terribly brutal, and strong and masculine and exploiting. And this is silly, where people are neither one way nor the other.

Luckily, this typing is dying out: you can't predict generally what someone's going to do in bed from the way he behaves. Versatility's very important. Another nice thing is coming to terms with your body. If you really like doing these sort of things, and they cut right across the whole concept of hygiene — you become less hung-up about your physical presence. And you're just not bothered about the great hygiene trip any more. Every part of us is sexually exciting — even sweat.

I feel my parents have missed out on so much. My father — desperate inferiority complex — and my mother despised him, and they wrecked each other's lives. Marriage is limiting, forcing people to be things they don't want to be.

You must order things for yourself. But I revel in the freedom of being beyond the pale. There are no norms for me, only a few sort of models that gays in the past have thrown up. I have to work it out for myself, to make sense to myself. I haven't a clue about the relationship between sex and falling in love, and meaningful relationships; and in a sense I don't want an answer, not even for myself, let alone prescribing a code of behaviour for anyone else.

Things happen to you and you become the sort of person that you are, and you look back and see it as a series of accidents. But yes, you can do something with people by making them face this.

Three themes ran (without any prompting) through the interviews: that their socio-sexual behaviour was not 'fixed'; that they were more impulsive and spontaneous and enjoyed life more than 'straights'; and that they delighted in extravagance, display and ceremonial. Even Jacob, the business executive who felt so oppressed, talked at length about the joy he felt when he accepted his sexuality in his late teens, and the wildness of his love for a Dutchman ('I was nineteen and he was twenty-nine but he told me he was twenty-three'): 'This was the great love of my life. I was wildly, deliriously happy.'

George, the railway porter, who lives a decorous suburban life with his friend, is deeply contemptuous of the boredom and banality of heterosexual domesticity:

> You go to the pub, and you see Fred and Alice and Bert and Mary sitting at a table having a drink, and they sit there all night and look at one another, and talk about the shopping and the washing and what Fred's done to his car. And there's no communication. They don't seem to enjoy themselves. But, you know, this girl was telling me she'd much rather mix with gay people, because you have more fun. You go out and enjoy yourself. What I can't really understand about straight people is, you know, they go out to the pubs ... I listen to their conversation, I'm nosey like that ... and they don't even enjoy it, don't even talk, they just stare into space. And there is no communication at all, none. They don't sit and talk to each other, not even that. And, you know, I just wonder why they got married in the first place.

Raymond, the thirty-eight year-old window-dresser, lives with his mother in a quiet street of red-brick semi-detached houses. He denied any fixed pattern of behaviour:

> We're versatile. It's not true that we have fixed ways of behaving, one the 'man' and the other the 'woman'. If someone says to me, 'What do you do?' I say, 'Come home with me and find out'. On the whole I'm passive, but I can meet the demands of any situation. In a way, though, I have to. After all, I'm thirty-eight. It's like everything else — you have to compromise. It's a butterfly existence.

But although he's thirty-eight, he claims to be unpredictable and spontaneous: 'And impulsive. Often we set off to go shopping in

Oldham and end up in Edinburgh or London. Most straight people wouldn't do that because of family responsibilities. But probably most of them wouldn't want to, either.'

There was an enormous bust of the Queen in Raymond's room, and he drew attention to it, giggling: 'That's another thing — the majority of homosexuals are fervent royalists. They love the ceremony and the splendour. It's the same with our taste in film stars and so on — the more flamboyant and outrageous the better. It's the glamour and the drama we love.'

Harold, the successful London artist, had actually got married when he was working in Greece: 'It was a marriage of convenience. Although I had sex with her, it was really impersonal. It was so she wouldn't be pushed back to Poland.' But it was worth it not for the sex but for the ceremony: 'It was really nice, though. We got married in the Cathedral, the Catholic Cathedral, with red velvet dias and two little-girl chairs, at the main altar. That's an experience, because I never thought I'd ever get married, especially in a Roman Catholic cathedral. It was gorgeous.'

At twenty-four Malcolm is still both delighted and bewildered by the openness and extravagance of the gay world, and by the wide range of behavioural styles that seem to be available. He has just graduated in modern history from a northern university. He married at eighteen and has a child: he also has a child by a fellow student ('And so I had these two women before I embarked on my homosexual career proper'). He is now getting a divorce. He took a younger male student into his marital home, as a lodger, and they had sex together. ('He really seduced me. We were making passionate love for about three weeks.') But he discovered that his boyfriend was also having sex with his wife, and both wife and boyfriend left him.

He has no regrets. His brief homosexual awakening was 'delirious': 'I really went overboard about it, you know. I was really happy.' He had vague feelings of being attracted to men even before he met his wife, but 'I still didn't realize what a ''queer'' was even when I met my wife-to-be at eighteen. But I've always been aware of the fact that, although I had this fantastic relationship with this girl, I've always been eyeing men up.' His first homosexual experience was a revelation and he has no wish to turn back: 'It was like taking a step … like getting married. There was no turning back. I didn't want to turn back. I was perfectly happy.' And yet he had an acute sense of isolation: 'I really did think I was queer at that stage. Really an abnormal freak.'

Four years later Malcolm is still on a voyage of discovery, exploring the infinite variety of the gay scene:

There are lots of differences in the gay world, I'm discovering. It was only two or three years ago that I realized there was such a thing as a drag queen who actually wanted to be in drag. I've done it a couple of times, just for fun. Lots of gays have more than one name. I've only got one. If you're going to have a feminine name it's usually similar to your masculine one. Actually it's not true in my case. They call me 'the wicked Jezebel', which is quite nice. Better than Myrtle. It's nice among intimate friends. Straight friends ask me if I think I'll ever settle down with a man. It's not as simple as that. I'd hate to think either of us was playing a passive role. I hate it when people see two men living together and assume that one will be the housekeeper: 'She's the wife.' I'm quite happy as I am in a male form, liking females but preferring males. There again, I prefer female company. I think women are much more shrewd, intelligent, interesting and humorous. But I'm still having to work out my ideas even at this stage. It's been fairly gradual and very baffling. When you reach a new stage in your gay development — like when I first went into the *Goya* and saw a drag queen on the stage, singing ... it didn't frighten me, it just surprised me — a pleasing feeling, really. Rather nicely naughty.

Malcom is pleased to be thought outrageous, but is still perplexed by many of the ambiguities of the homosexual world:

People think I'm a bit outrageous. I like the word, 'wicked'. Sarah, who's really John, is always using it. It really means 'nice'. I also like to call women 'scurrilous vixens' — that's nice. This is what a lot of gay people do — call people 'vixen' and 'hussy' and 'minx'. They're terms of endearment, really. Teasing ... So many men are 'size queens' — they're just after the biggest they can find. That's irrelevant to me. When they go into the *Goya* it's little more than a sex market. They're obsessed about clothes, a lot of them. Exhibitionists. I don't know ... In the end I'm just in a pea-green soup kind of fog.

Among the ambiguities and shifting definitions of the situation, he is still searching for what is 'real' and authentic:

I have a lot of lesbian friends. Lesbians are different again from gay men. A lot are prostitutes. They shock. I like that. I like people who have something to say, but not too belligerently. I think the inarticulate drag queens, transvestites, all the rest of them, might have more to say than the political gays. People ought to be what they are, rather than talking about it. I've heard what the radicals have to say — always the same. I'd rather hear a drag queen talking about herself. More spontaneous. People ought to live, not to talk about it. I think they should be outrageous and notorious. You can't be polite and pass fairy buns across the table all your life.

Shifting boundaries of self, society and time

Petula is twenty-five, an art school graduate who earns her living by working at a centre for severely mentally handicapped children. She attended a northern art school for four years, from sixteen to twenty. When she finally realized, by the age of twenty, that she was homosexual, she had a period of breakdown and some months in hospital following an unconsummated lesbian relationship. She came through this period of deep disturbance and travelled, on impulse, to Canada and California, earning her living by drawing and painting: 'I zoomed off to Canada, just on a moment's notice, with no money ... landed in Toronto, hitch-hiked across Canada to Vancouver ... and just knew thousands of people, and women, and I did a lot of pictures, got involved in women's farms and things like this.' In Vancouver she held 'a few exhibitions' and sold work on the streets. In San Francisco she lived among artists and sold her pictures, one for a comparatively large sum ('This woman wanted me to do her poodle, so I thought, well, you know, I need the bread...'). She was tempted to stay in California — 'seeing so much beauty, I mean — it was so incredibly beautiful.'

But she decided that her work was 'about people' and returned to England to work with subnormals — 'people that society is frightened of.' She paints, draws, and writes poetry in her spare time ('They're printing some of my pencil drawings and poetry in America this year') and feels that 'what makes my life important is these drawings'. She enjoys work at the centre:

Those kids are supposed to be cabbages. But I'm getting through to them, and I'm just learning from them every day: their experience is so different from ours, they don't see life the way we do. I mean, if you can get through all the snot and the shit, and get through all that — you have to allow yourself to switch on, be open to them — then you reach them, you know.

She has climbed out of the abyss and been reborn. 'I feel I've got such an important life, and yet I know I'm nobody.'

She was interviewed for two hours in her flat. The sitting room was sparsely furnished — there were no carpets, just rugs and trunks and benches. There were enormous brightly coloured paintings on the walls. There were easels with half-finished paintings, and a bench with tubes of paint and brushes. Petula sat on a mattress on the floor. It was impossible to give the interview even the lightest structure. She was asked about her present circumstances and invited to say what had led up to them. She talked...

Her story was in fact of *rites de passage* in their pure classic form: a progression from the secular-profane to the sacred, through a limbo of ambiguity, absence of status, marginality and symbolic death to rebirth and incorporation in a new world: through the passage described by Van Gennep as marked by the three phases of separation, margin and aggregation.[20] And, entirely without prompting, Petula talked of her experience of time — which went into reverse and began again when she rose from the dead: perhaps a symbolic replication of the social state.

Edmund Leach has argued that the sexual act provides the primary image of time and that the notion of time as oscillation and discontinuity (rather than a continuous straight line) rests on social shifts from the normal-profane to the abnormal-sacred, when social roles are inverted and everything goes into reverse. 'If time be thought of as alternation, then myths about sex reversals are representations of time.' The point at which the pendulum stops and swings back is: 'The marginal state. The moral person is in a sacred condition, a kind of suspended animation.' Men act as women, kings as beggars, servants as masters: 'In such situations of true orgy, normal social life is played in reverse, with all manner of sins such as incest, adultery, transvestitism, sacrilege, and *lèse-majesté* treated as the natural order of the day.'[21]

Petula had no knowledge of lesbians, or any notion that she might be one, until near the end of her art college course; but, looking back, she sees that as a young girl she was a 'tomboy', and recalls her father talking warningly of homosexuals:

I was a tomboy, you know, and I just loved the freedom that the boys had. And luckily girls are looked on as something great if they're tomboys, because the great masculine thing is all right. Parents are proud to say their daughter's a tomboy — until she grows up. And now my father's really worried when I go home and I'm still his tomboy...

As a child she gained an image of lesbians from her father, which she has had to unlearn: 'He'd warn us about homosexuals. And he'd say, there are women like that, too. And I had this idea of a lesbian as a woman who wanted to be a man, who wore a collar and tie. That was my idea of a lesbian. It really frightened me.'

At college she entered into normal heterosexual relationships:

I had my first sexual involvement with a man when I was seventeen, nearly eighteen. And I started, sort of, screwing guys. I was always bored after two weeks. I was bored with them, you know — thought there was something missing. But they were nice guys, gentle guys.

Then one day, one of the girls said about this tutor, 'I'll bet she's queer — the way she looks at the girls in modern dance'. And suddenly something inside me went 'Buzz' ... Anyway, I was in a college play, and I kept noticing this woman and realized I was getting incredibly excited, just looking at her. Of course my idea of lesbians was 'those dykey women', and there was this beautiful woman who was married, really sexy. I was having a good relationship with a guy, and emotionally good because he was older. Anyway, at the end of the play we had a party, and her husband was there, and it was all packed with students, and I was with my boyfriend. And I started talking to this woman. I hadn't drunk anything, but I was sort of drunk with this feeling that I'd never experienced before. And I was talking faster and faster to her, and my boyfriend just moved away out of the scene, because he knew something was happening. I noticed her eyes, and she was getting really worked up, and I don't know how I had the guts, but I said, 'Stop looking at me like that, you're really turning me on'. And she said, 'Oh God, you're not having me on, are you? Let's get out of here'. And I remember trying to get out, with all those people, wanting to touch this woman. Wow! it was incredible. And we eventually got out, but somebody asked her for a lift home. So I thought 'fuck', because all I wanted to do was to touch this female...

The affair was abortive:

I didn't even think I was a lesbian, even then. I just thought I was in love with this woman ... Anyway, it never came to anything sexual, except for a little cuddle once in the gym. But it just kept me going. My mind ... the excitement, the thought of what could happen, the thought of what you might do in bed with a woman ... I was doing drawings and sending them to her ... My physical relationship with my boyfriend had disintegrated completely. I couldn't sleep with him, couldn't bear him to touch me. And then she spread it around that I had lesbian tendencies. It really freaked me, really hurt me that she'd done that. And I started smoking, and I was going around with guys that I was sort of screwing, but all the time...

Petula 'died', and was slowly reborn:

I just deteriorated slowly. And eventually I got taken into hospital because I was smoking, I didn't want to know anybody. I stopped talking for about two weeks. And some friends just took me to a hospital. And I felt dead. You know, I was really dead inside. I just died. And all I could draw was a nose, an eye and a mouth. Lots of strange things happened during that time in hospital, when I went through this stage. I don't know what it was, but I died, and everything, you know. And then slowly I tried to get back. I was still in love with this woman. And I started to become her, be her, I started to be that person. And then I started to be anybody I wanted. Just anybody but me. I didn't know who I was. I was completely confused, frightened and alone: way out somewhere. I couldn't reach anybody...

She recovered slowly, began to face the nature of her sexuality, and when she finally did so was overcome with joy. This was her rebirth:

I went to a Gay Liberation meeting. I'd still never really met lesbians, and it just blew my mind to find there were lesbians who looked like me and not like dykes. I just felt wonderful. Here was someone else! Because all through this time I'd had the idea that I was the only one in the world. It was like being born. This was three years ago. I could be myself ... could put my arms round women in pubs ... For the first time in my life, just me. And I did a drawing and I wrote a poem. I'm not trying to be anything anymore: I've accepted everything, accepted my sexuality. And since that time three years ago I've felt so good.

There was a meeting of two hundred gays at Lancaster University, and that was marvellous. We all felt so protected by each other. And I've been through different experiences of being gay: sleeping with people. That was the main thing — being able to sleep with another body the same as yours. And suddenly I've come to the stage where I'm not lesbian, not heterosexual, or whatever. I'm just me. And I've experienced so many wonderful things as me.

'Liminal entities', says Turner, 'are neither here nor there; they are betwixt and between the positions assigned and arrayed by law, custom, convention and ceremonial ... Thus liminality is frequently likened to death, to being in the womb, to invisibility, to darkness, to bisexuality, to the wilderness, and to an eclipse of the sun or moon'. [22] Petula has emerged from liminality to 'communitas', and she feels not more restricted social bonds, but a wider kinship, a generic social bond. She has no wish to divide the world into two sexual camps:

I've moved so far away from men that I feel in danger ... I don't want to stop seeing men, but I could easily not be involved with them. And I think I'd miss out. There are two sexes living in this world, and I feel I mustn't cut myself off from one of them. Although I don't need men for anything ... It's very limiting to put an identity on everything. I'm a lesbian, so I'm part of a group. I'm not. I'm not a lesbian, I'm not a heterosexual, I'm not a bisexual. I want my life ... I want people just to be able to come into me, you know. I prefer, physically, women — but that is unimportant with the rest of life. Because there's so much going on. I feel I can't just cut myself off and say, 'I am this'.

She has no sense of belonging to a deviant, marked off minority: 'I know damn well I'm not deviant. It's such a beautiful thing. How can something so good be deviant?'
During her period of 'liminality', time went into reverse.

There's another thing where I thought I was the only one in the world. I was lying in bed reading Laing's *Bird of Paradise*. [23] And I read this book, and it's an account of a guy feeling he was going back in time — 'ten-day voyage'. And I jumped out of bed and said, 'Wow' There's somebody else experiencing it ... This is another minority group that I'm in. It's marvellous that there's someone else experienced this thing.

Of the stage of role-reversal (or marginality) Leach says: 'It is symbolic of a complete transfer from the secular to the sacred; normal time has stopped, sacred time is played in reverse, death is converted into birth.' [24] Petula is conscious of time as something with spaces in it, into which one should stray, opening oneself up to what is predestined:

I mean, what is time? We created time. This is something else. All my work deals with reality and fantasy, the whole thing. When we go to sleep, where do we go? You know this is what I'm trying to get at ... I try to live for today. Well, it's not exactly that. If I'm walking along a road to work, some intuition tells me to go down another road I've never been down ... I feel there's a reason for everything that happens. On a bus you might start a conversation, and you might learn so much. I sort of make time for that sort of thing. Like a lot of people jump out of bed, go to work, and don't see anything around them. I set off an hour earlier so I can walk and look at things and see things ... I'm no freak, and I don't believe in any religion, yet things have happened, I've been sent into people's lives. Why did I just leave and go to Canada like that? I didn't know anybody. I was protected right across that journey — I was looked after, I know it. There's a reason for everything that happens.

Time began again after her rebirth and stretches forward from this baseline into the future, marked by her drawings: 'It's like some people keep a diary, I keep drawings. I can look back over them, right from starting up as a lesbian.' Her pictures stretch into an infinite future but relate her to life: 'I got so much from that particular picture that I could go out and was ready to talk to people. I wasn't working for a diploma or to sell it to someone. Therefore I had all the time in the world to do this picture. It has become very detailed. It could go on and on until I died...'

Conclusion

Did the homosexuals described in this chapter 'really change' when they accepted their homosexuality and established relationships in the homosexual world? More than any other group discussed in this book they fit the symbolic interactionists' account of socialization through tentative and exploratory role-making as well as role-taking behaviour. As homosexuals they appeared not to occupy a 'status' with stable meanings and consensus regarding its rights and obligations; they enjoyed 'roles, which were more ambiguous, less fixed and institutionalized in character'. This clearly raised a problem of identity and promoted a constant search for 'genuine' behaviour and the nature of what and who they 'really' were. Like the parsons described in Chapter 3 they were preoccupied with the problem of being their 'real selves'. They themselves felt that accepting their homosexuality liberated them from the fixity of social roles, from programmed social behaviour, and made them less predictable, more spontaneous, possibly more 'outrageous', and certainly more interesting than they had been previously.

All the homosexuals interviewed had in some sense 'come home' and finally decided to be what they 'really were'; and yet in accepting all the implications of this 'home-coming' they often appeared to experience a genuine transformation of identity. A preceding period of 'liminality', when they felt lost and alone, seemed to be an important pre-condition of change. Taking a new name is a powerful sign that 'real change' has occurred; and like the English Sufis and Hare Krishna devotees described in the following chapters of this book, the male homosexuals had often adopted new, feminine names. When John responded to the name of Miranda he had accepted a new self.

'New selves' needed the support of new plausibility structures in the homosexual world. Plausibility is sustained by legitimacy, and parents and close friends were called upon to understand and approve the step the homosexual was taking and the life he was living. For some (especially the 'utopians' in CHE) legitimacy was conferred by an ideology which linked their position with other oppressed groups. And legitimacy also came through disproving the assumptions that straight society made about homosexuals and their activities. Legitimacy was gained by showing that the typifications used by straight society to characterize homosexuals were demonstrably invalid. But finally legitimacy lay for homosexuals — as it did for artists — in their simple and evident superiority over devitalized and debilitated 'straights'.

The significance of 'timetables' in conferring a sense of identity has been a recurrent theme in this book. Timetables and temporality were problems for homosexuals as they were for other groups that inhabited marginal worlds. For male homosexuals identity was based on a foreshortened timetable of sexual attractiveness. For the lesbian, Petula, temporality was seriously deranged when she struggled towards a new identity. Her experience appears to 'fit' the Durkheimian theory of symbolic replication of the social state. Much more extensive evidence from many situations of social 'rebirth' would be needed to give plausibility to this argument. Petula's experience of inverted time was very similar to the artist, Donald Elton's, described in Chapter 4. Both occurred at acute crises in their lives, when a sense of identity and everyday reality had dissolved. There is no warrant to explain these reversals of time as 'models' of the marginal state.

8 | Dervishes in Dorsetshire: re-alignment with reality

Secularization and the resurgence of sects

Modern identity, it is widely maintained, is distinguished above all by a secularized consciousness; and the most significant transformations of identity in our times have taken the form of 'de-modernization'. The 'counter culture' of the late 1960s and early '70s, at least in its mystical and anti-rationalist manifestations, has been seen as a symptom of the demodernizing impulse. The resurgence of occultism represents a counter-modern definition of reality and the self.

The secularized consciousness of modern man is a recurrent theme in the writing of Peter Berger who links the rediscovery of transcendence with the transformation of modern identity: 'In openness to the signals of transcendence the true proportions of our experience are rediscovered.' Personal identity is enlarged, rescued from triviality, and related to wider systems of meaning: 'A rediscovery of the supernatural will be, above all, a regaining of openness in our perception of reality.'[1]

Roszak interpreted the counter culture of the 1960s as essentially concerned with the expansion and transformation of consciousness, with a heavy reliance on LSD: 'If we accept the proposition that the counter culture is, essentially, an exploration of the politics of consciousness, then psychedelic experience falls into place as one, but only one, possible method of mounting that exploration.'[2] But more fundamentally the counter culture opposed the functional rationality of the modern world and — like Roszak himself — attacked the 'myth of objective consciousness' and sought new ways of knowing and understanding which did not sharply separate the knower from the thing known. Eastern mysticism (and 'phenomenological' sociology) no less than LSD have reinstated subjectivity and challenged the pretensions of objective consciousness.

This chapter reports a participant-observer study of an English commune of Islamic mystics in the Cotswolds, which was carried out in 1974.[3] The members opened themselves to signals of transcendence. They were young, highly educated upper-class English men and women. Their existence in a secular society presents a paradox that Andrew Greeley has discussed in an American context.

Greeley has observed the rise of 'neo-sacrilists' in the very best American universities. They are principally devoted to ancient Eastern religions, and they are inclined to renounce rational life-planning for divination by 'I Ching'. They are frequently outstanding students at great secular institutions devoted to scientific rationality, like the University of Chicago and even MIT. The neo-sacrilists are searching for what is 'really real'. Their interest is mainly in what Greeley calls 'the bizarrely sacred'. Demodernization has occurred in the very citadels of secularized, rational-scientific modernity: 'Furthermore, the "return of the sacred" has happened exactly where one would least expect it — among the elite students at the best colleges and universities in the land, precisely those places where secularization would presumably have been most effective and most complete.'[4]

The multiplication of sects in a secularized society is not really problematical. It is not a symptom of a breakdown of modernization. The 'pluralization' of modern complex societies, which has been an accelerating process since the seventeenth century, helps to explain both secularization and sect development: Berger argues that it has a secularizing effect,[5] and Wilson that it makes the emergence of sects — especially 'introversionist' sects — possible.[6] These are not incompatible positions. There is no need to argue that secularization is an inexorable and uniform 'master-trend' of modern history[7] in order to recognize that there is a general rationalization of modern consciousness, which tends to undermine the plausibility of religious definitions of reality and yet allows, and possibly provokes, a proliferation of fringe religious movements. Fringe sects have recently been widely observed in Britain as well as in America, from tin tabernacles in Stockport[8] to the 'Centre of Light' on the Moray Firth.[9] In a highly diversified society without a strong and binding central religious system, such religious (and cultural) pluralism is not so much problematical as self-evident.

From the point of view of the present study the Sufis in the Cotswolds (and the Hare Krishna commune described in the next chapter) in the mid 1970s were of interest not as a possible demonstration of the halt or reversal of secularization, but as a 'stage' in the transformation of the counter culture of the late 1960s and in the consciousness of the people who were involved in it. How did young, highly educated, upper-class English men and women change their definition of reality and their conception of themselves when they entered a commune devoted to an Eastern religion? And was there evidence that earlier personal experiences, perhaps in the 'classical' counter culture, had predisposed them to change? Had they been 'desocialized' before they were resocialized? Was the preceding counter culture perhaps their liminality?

In both communes there were obvious continuities with the earlier counter culture, but also sharp discontinuities and reversals. Were there corresponding continuities and reversals in the identities of devotees? The earlier counter culture had been considerably influenced by Eastern religions, and Roszak properly gave considerable attention to the 'journey to the East' in his account of how a counter culture was made: 'What began with Zen has now rapidly, perhaps too rapidly, proliferated into a phantasmogoria of exotic religiosity.'[10] But in the '60s the counter culture emphasized personal freedom and rejected all hierarchies;[11] and from Zen it extracted a 'wealth of hyperbolic eroticism'.[12]

Westhues found a greater discipline and sense of order in the American communes of the late '60s;[13] but the two religious communes described in this book are remarkable for the personal discipline they enjoined and the ordered routine of their days. In this sense at least they inverted the earlier counter culture as described by Roszak and Reich.[14] And yet many of their members clearly had strong sympathies with the older counter culture (especially, perhaps, with its aestheticism and rejection of ambition). Some had been deeply 'into counter culture' before they joined the commune. There were many indications that this was so in the Sufi commune, and even stronger evidence among the Hare Krishna devotees. New identities were being fashioned not only in relation to 'straight', orthodox, secularized society, but in relation to earlier phases of the counter culture itself.

The inquiry

Visits were made to a Sufi commune in the south-west of England in 1974 and during a period of residence a more intensive study made of the commune's members, their beliefs, daily routines and personal histories. This chapter is based on a diary kept at that time.

The commune has flourished since 1970. Its members change, but there are usually at least thirty men and women living in the commune: predominantly young (early twenties), English, Public School educated and upper-class. There is a sharp if unstated and informal division between the eight or ten young men and women who are relatively permanent in that they stay for at least six months and perhaps more than a year; and a larger, more variable penumbra of (slightly older and less upper-class) members who live there for a few days or weeks.

Members of the relatively stable inner core have no outside employment — although within a year or so most or all will have left to resume or take up normal (usually professional) careers. Occasionally one will move on to another commune, or travel in the East. They are engaged full-time in the work of the commune, which employs no domestic or ancillary help; they are unpaid but normally receive free meals and accommodation. They work hard: they preside over meditations, they lead study and discussion sessions on the texts of Sufi mystics and poets; they organize the work of short-stay residents and they themselves work in the gardens, look after the ducks, bees and hens, undertake construction work, collect, package and dispose of the commune's refuse. One of the girls is the commune's treasurer and another is secretary-receptionist (with typewriters, telephones, a duplicator and a filing system). The leader is the sheik.

The short-stay members typically have full-time jobs (as teachers, government scientists, secretaries, journalists) or are self-employed (as potters, writers and painters). Many come back again and again. They pay two pounds a day. Most of the twenty to thirty short-stay members, both men and women, are married, but none brings a spouse (though women bring their small children). None of the inner core members is married. The commune lives in an ancient and very beautiful stone farmhouse which stands by a trout stream a mile off a minor road, nine miles from the nearest small market town, forty miles from a (cathedral and university) city. The commune has a telephone and an old van. There is no television or radio. No-one brings a transistor. No-one is quite sure how mail is collected or despatched.

Religions hertiage

The Sufis are dervishes. (One of their most notable teachers and poets, Jalal al-Din Rumi, founded the Mevlēvi order of whirling or dancing dervishes in the late thirteenth century). They are Islamic mystics. But whereas Islam is cold, formal and legalist, Sufism is deeply subjective, ecstatic.

In the eighth and ninth centuries mendicant Arab mystics would appear in coarse woollen garments. The Arabic for wool is *suf*, and the fakirs, or ascetic holy men, were now commonly referred to as 'sufis'. The Koran repeatedly admonishes true believers to recognize Allah through the evidence provided by nature; for the fakirs such 'evidence' was an irrelevance. They held property in common and were notable for the zeal of their religious practices in a spirit of mortification and penitence. They diverged increasingly from true believers, and 'To distinguish themselves from other Muhammadans they took the name of Sufis'.[15]

Scholars have pointed to the deep inconsistency between Sufism and Islam. 'It might at first sight appear almost an impossibility for mysticism to engraft itself upon the legal system of the Qur'an ... The Sufis themselves admit that their religious system had always existed in the world, prior to the mission of Muhammad.'[16] Bouquet similarly maintains that Sufism was not a natural growth of Islam, 'but a foreign element which has worked its way into it, and is really inconsistent with the original dogmas'.[17]

The inconsistency is apparent in different forms and at various levels. Philosophically Sufism was influenced by Neoplatonism and preached absorption in the Divine. When the young Sufi mystic, Ibn 'Arabi, met the aging Moslem philosopher, Averroes, in Cordova in the late twelfth century, the conflict between mystical and natural theology was personified:

> He (Averroes) asked me this question: 'What manner of solution have you found through divine illumination and inspiration? Is it identical with that which we obtain from speculative reflection?' I replied: 'Yes and no. Between the yes and the no, spirits take their flight from their matter, and heads are separated from their bodies.' Averroes turned pale, I saw him tremble; he murmured the ritual phrase, 'There is no power save in God' — for he had understood my allusion.[18]

The Sufis established regular orders of dervishes until the middle of the eighteenth century. 'The Sufis are divided into unnumerable sects, which find expression in the numerous religious orders of Darweshes or Faqirs.'[19] The first order — the Alwaniyah — was established in the eighth century, and thirty major orders were established in the following millennium. One of the most notable was that to which Al-Rumi (1207-1273), the Persian poet who lived most of his life at Konia in Asia Minor, gave his name. This was the Mevlevi order (mawlana: master), later known as the order of whirling or dancing dervishes: 'The Mawlawis consider their dances a means to attain ecstasy and a representation of the movement of heavenly bodies.'[20]

The Koran denounces poetry (and is ambiguous on the subject of music), but 'The very essence of Sufism is poetry'[21] and Jalal al-Din Rumi was its greatest poet. Rumi formed a passionate attachment to a wild, mysterious, wandering Dervish, Shams al-Din. When Shams finally departed, Rumi in his anguish poured forth a torrent of poetry and 'invented the famous whirling and circling dance of his Mevlevi dervishes, performed to the accompaniment of the lamenting reed-pipe and pacing drum.'[22] A mid-nineteenth-century account describes the 'twenty performers, with high round felt caps and brown mantles ... They cast off their mantles and appear in long bell-shaped petticoats and jackets, and then begin to spin, revolving, dancing and turning with extraordinary velocity.'[23] Until the secularization of the Turkish state by Mustafa Kemal in the 1920s, the Dancing Dervishes enjoyed the privilege of girding each new Ottoman sultan-caliph with his sword.

The thirteenth century saw a remarkable poetical and philosophical flowering of Sufism. The Persian poet Jalal al-Din Rumi probably met the great Andalusian mystic, Ibn 'Arabi, at Damascus in the third decade of the century. Ibn 'Arabi left his native Seville in the year 1202, never to return. He visited Mecca, Baghdad and Cairo, and settled in Damascus. He systematized Sufism in his great work, *al-Futuhat al-Makkiyah*, and his central thesis was that all being is essentially one, a manifestation of the divine essence.

The Spanish mystic was undoubtedly the most influential one the Arabs produced. The impact of his teaching is manifest in Persian and Turkish followers. His theories of Logos and the perfect man are reflected in Jalal al-Din Rumi's poetry, one of the glories of Persian literature.[24]

In the thirteenth and fourteenth centuries the heresy of the Free Spirit swept through the great commercial cities of Western

Christendom from Cologne to Silesia. The adepts of the Free Spirit drew inspiration from Neoplatonism and sought direct union with God. The movement's historian, Norman Cohn, has pointed to the striking similarity with Sufism. While Sufism in its very early days was probably influenced by Christian mysticism,

> In turn it seems to have assisted the growth of the mysticism of the Free Spirit in Christian Europe. Certainly every one of the features that characterized Sufism in twelfth century Spain — even to such details as the particoloured robes — were to be noted as typical of the adepts of the Free Spirit a century or two later.[25]

Like the Victorian Anglican missionary T.P. Hughes, who compiled a monumental *Dictionary of Islam*, Cohn is inclined to focus on the 'immorality' of Sufism. The adepts of the Free Spirit acknowledged no authority save their own experience, and so embraced an eroticism which, far from springing from a carefree sensuality, 'possessed above all a symbolic value as a sign of spiritual emancipation'. The adepts were an elite of amoral supermen. And similarly, says Cohn, the Sufis:

> The novices among them were schooled in humiliation and self-abnegation ... But once they emerged from their novitiate, these Sufis entered a realm of total freedom ... They felt themselves united with the divine essence in a most intimate union. And this in turn liberated them from all restraints. Every impulse was experienced as a divine command...[26]

Hughes, in his *Dictionary of Islam*, concedes that many Sufis are doubtless earnest seekers after truth, but claims that 'it is well known that some of them make their mystical creed a cloak for gross sensual gratification'.[27] He also charges Sufism with elitism, digging a deep gulf between those who can know God, and those who must wander in darkness, feeding upon the husks of rites and ceremonies.

In fact the various orders of dervishes have varied considerably in their beliefs and practices. Like all mystics they maintain that division and separateness are unreal, that time is unreal, and that reality is eternal, not in the sense of being everlasting, but in the sense of being out of time. But actual social conduct has varied considerably among the orders: 'Some encouraged and practiced celibacy, which is frowned upon in the Koran.'[28]

There is a striking parallelism between 'ecstatic' social movements in thirteenth-century Europe, seventeenth-century England, and aspects of the Anglo-American counter culture of the 1970s. (The mid-seventeenth-century sect in England which was known by its enemies as the 'Ranters', was strikingly like both the Sufis and the adepts of the Free Spirit in its mysticism and some aspects of its social beliefs and conduct.[29]) It was not therefore with complete surprise that Dervishes were found, in 1974, in Dorsetshire.

Journal entries:

(1) *Orientations*

In the early afternoon I drove between dusty upland cornfields and turned down a narrow hidden valley to the farmhouse which houses the Sufi commune. The commune has existed for more than three years: its ten acres of land have been turned into flourishing vegetable gardens and an orchard has been planted. The stables have been converted into bedrooms and the Great Barn into a temple. (The large cruciform barn was built centuries ago, it seems, according to the proportions deriving from the Cabbalistic Tree of Life.) Extensive restoration and conversions of outbuildings are still being undertaken.

From the long drive the flanking gardens looked immaculate and the grass verges were cleanly trimmed. A large and ancient church bell hung from a wooden scaffolding before the barn. I entered the long, low sixteenth-century farmhouse built in local stone. It was empty of people but filled with eastern music from a record-player — dance music of the 'Whirling Dervishes'. A man walked across the lawn, greying, in his forties. He limped badly and walked with a stick. We talked. A year ago he was involved in a serious motorway accident. ('I was in hospital for a long time. I enjoyed it.') He has since stayed for periods in the commune. He was educated at Ampleforth, qualified and practised as a doctor, and was now, he said, a shepherd. (Actually, he had a large country house and an extensive hill-farm in Wales.)

A girl in her early twenties appeared, said she was Mary but known as Razieh, and took me to my room in the stables. It contained a chair and two mattresses on the floor. On the whitened walls were two large coloured posters: one was a circular Sufi calendar divided according to the signs of the Zodiac; the other was a picture of the Harem at Topkapi Palace in Istambul. There was no need for me to share the stable, Mary said: often there were some forty people altogether in the commune; for the next week or two, barely thirty. The first meditation was in the Great Barn at 6 o'clock; I must wash from head to toe beforehand; and I might need thick socks to wear in the temple, because I should have to remove my shoes.

At 5.30 I went to the ablutions. Some twenty people of both sexes were washing from tip to toe. At 5.50 the bell tolled. We went to the barn, collected woollen blankets from the doorway, removed our shoes, bowed to the altar, knelt motionless on low, slightly-angled stools for what was to prove an increasing physical agony for fifty minutes. The presiding Sufi lit an enormous altar candle and read a prayer from Ibn 'Arabi's *Treatise on Unity:*

> In the name of God, the Merciful, the Compassionate, and Him we ask for aid: Praise be to God before whose oneness there was not a before, unless the Before was He, and after whose singleness there is not an after, except the After be He. He is and there is with Him no after nor before, nor above nor below, nor far nor near, nor union nor division, nor how nor where nor when, nor times nor moment nor age, nor being nor place. And He is now as He was. He is the One without oneness, and the Single without singleness ... He is the First without firstness, and the Last without lastness. He is the Outward without outwardness, and the Inward without inwardness ... So that there is no first nor last, nor outward nor inward, except Him, without these becoming Him or His becoming them.

The president paused and lit another large candle. The twenty devotees remained completely motionless and rapt. The president continued the prayer:

> Understand, therefore, in order that thou mayest not fall into the error of the Hululis[30] ... It is necessary that thou know Him after this fashion, not by knowledge, nor by intellect, nor by understanding, nor by imagination, nor by sense, nor by the outward eye, nor by the inward eye, nor by perception ... He sent Himself with Himself to Himself. There was no mediator nor any means other than He. There is no difference between the Sender and the thing sent, and the person sent and the person to whom he is sent. The very existence of the prophetic message is His existence.

The prayer ended; we remained unmoving for another forty minutes, draped in our woollen blankets against the evening coolness of the large stone barn. And then, in unison, we intoned 'Hu', rose stiffly, bowed in turn to the altar with foreheads touching the ground, and went to put on our shoes.

We assembled for our vegetarian dinner in a long room with beams, a large open stone fireplace at one end burning logs, and a piano at the other. There were twenty-eight people to dinner, a dozen or so were new arrivals, and people said: 'I am Mary, from Ipswich. Have you been before. Where are you from and why have you come?' No-one indicated his function in the commune, but five young Englishmen were notable for their dark, neatly-trimmed, military-style moustaches, carefully pointed and turned up at the end.[31] They were addressed by Persian names and wore silver chains round their necks from which hung the Sufi symbol for unity, the 'Hu'. (Fifteen of the people who sat down to dinner were wearing these silver chains and the symbol for 'oneness'.) One of the men with a careful moustache, addressed as Mostaffa, sat at the head of the long table in a high carved chair covered with a sheepskin rug. I sat next to him. 'Where are you from?' 'Oh, the south-east of England. Actually, my home is the oldest castle in England. You know it? Did you know my mother, Lady Pamela?' Mostaffa was the youngest son of an English peer. But after the opening pleasantries, table talk was heavily about God and the meaning of 'Hu', the Divine Essence. Volunteers were invited for the washing up.

The evening study session began at 8.30 and lasted till 10. We took off our shoes and went in to a room which was empty apart from some thirty large cushions placed round the walls. We sat cross-legged on our cushions and a dark young man with a neat moustache suggested we talk about 'oneness', which is at the heart of Sufism.

The discussion was highly abstract and only three or four people spoke. One ventured: 'The prayer that was read at this evening's meditation appeared to be about the oneness of God, but it was a list of paradoxes and contradictory propositions.' 'How can we reconcile differences and plurality with oneness?' gently challenged another young man with a dark moustache. No-one was quite sure.

The discussion moved on to transcendentalism, God as the final source, and his love as the origin of all things. According to Ibn 'Arabi, we were told, God had created all out of love for himself, which was love of everything: 'I was a hidden treasure and I loved to be known.' But no specific personal morality was implied in God's love: there were very general moral implications, but no specific rules. The full circumstances of any action could not be known in advance: through Sufism one arrived at principles which informed personal action. But the nature and purpose of an action could not be known until it had been completed: rules of conduct laid down in advance were useless. The discussion was moving from transcendence to immanence.

'But how can we know oneness?' someone asked rather plaintively.

'The prayer we heard this evening said we could not know through understanding, or reason, or imagination, or the senses, or perception. What is there left?' A somewhat inconclusive discussion of the nature of knowing ensued, and the problem of knowing God without inter- mediaries (including reasoning and sense perception). Mostaffa, the peer's son, was floundering, suggested we should not forget the Lord's Prayer, and proceeded to recite the Creed.

The session concluded with the reading of a poem by Ibn 'Arabi on the transcendence of love. Love transforms all forms into the brilliance of a 'Fire which neither consumes itself nor consumes him, for its flame feeds on his nostalgia and his quest, which can no more be destroyed by fire than can the salamander.'

Mostaffa, the peer's son, took out his pipe and a tin of St Bruno. He was rather hard up, he said, 'until the end of the month, when my rents come in'; but anyway in a few weeks' time he was going to take a job as a forestry worker in the Highlands of Scotland. He gratefully accepted a fill of Balkan Sobranie Flake.

(2) *Of time and the essence of things*

This morning was leisurely. After early meditation and breakfast there were no programmed activities until the study group met at 11 o'clock. I walked by the trout stream talking to Pierre (Hasan), a long-stay member of the commune and son of a Belgian diplomat. Hasan had spent two years at Atlantic College before proceeding to the University of London to read Philosophy. He dropped out after two terms and travelled to the East. He was now twenty-one years old.

The English public school I went to was set on producing 'leaders' of the traditional mould — men to go off and serve the great multi-national corporations and so on. It was a heavy, pressurized study programme, and I began to take eight A-levels, but finally took four. But when I got to university, that wasn't really the right place for me at that time. I was trying to find myself amidst meaningless abstractions.

I don't think a university can lead you to truth, but I think that this place can. A university is based on the differentiation of know-ledge. But here, there is a unity, different areas of knowledge and understanding are not separated and segregated. The people here are whole. I came here first, about a year ago, for a few days. I saw what a powerful experience it was for the people who came — the way they appeared to be transformed by the experience. I decided to return for a longer stay.

We walked briskly in the sunshine. He was handsome, articulate and intelligent, with blue eyes and a beard. He had great physical vigour and moved everywhere with an easy grace. On the previous day I had watched him scythe the tall grass in the extensive orchard in the course of one afternoon.

I turned to the East, and arrived in Istambul. From there I might have gone anywhere — perhaps Africa, even Ceylon. I left myself open to accident, to chance ... I used the *I Ching* ... I moved towards a decision by making myself open to events. And finally I arrived high in the Himalayas. I went there to contemplate — but it wasn't really such a definite decision as that. Going up into the mountains was the point I was at. Contemplation followed. I realized that I must break through karma: I must break from my imprisonment within the cycle of birth, death, rebirth, death, rebirth ... I spent eighteen months on the mountain tops.

In this Sufi commune I've found a centre for my being. Being here promotes 'remembrance' — a constant awareness of oneness, of the unity of things. And when I'm in the outside world I have a great sense of serenity. And here I have a sense of wholeness and integrity. I even like washing up now. I used to hate it. It completes the experience of having food that is right with people who are right.

I've no career ambitions in the ordinary sense. I want to understand, so that I can be in some way involved in the transformation of society that is taking place. Although only a few people stay here and pass through here, they're contributing to the right-angled turn that contemporary history is taking. Hippies and 'freaks' and continental Marxists are also contributing to this right-angled turn. Marxism on the Continent is really the equivalent, in Catholic societies, of hippies in America and England — it is the opposition of a Cartesian, logical intellectual system to the dominant order, whereas hippies and communes are experimental, testing alternatives pragmatically, as we should expect in Protestant-positivist societies. And so Sufism really coheres in my mind with Marxism — it is all part of the contemporary social transformation: the right-angled turn.

It is not withdrawal from history. Even if people go off and sit in the forests and on mountain tops, and everyone else knows about them, general social awareness is extended. People who stay here, even for a short time, leave with a deeper self-knowledge and awareness, and they are an influence permeating society in a diffuse, non-specific way. They don't leave with any specific programme of social and political action, but they will have an influence.

I shall probably leave here at the end of the year. There's a commune south of London with some people who I feel it will be good to live with. They're really together people — really beautiful. I shall get a job of some sort ... I may be able to use my four European languages. The commune is setting up microbiotic food centres. And it has a 'crash-pad' and a 'busting fund' for people in trouble with the police. They're setting up another commune in Wales. One of the commune members has a Ph.D. in Physics and she's doing astrology. But I want to be with Amanda. She's forty and married but not living with her husband although he's in the commune. I knew when I first saw her that I'd known her before, although we'd never met...

In the study session before lunch we sat round the room on cushions while extracts were read from the works of Ibn 'Arabi dealing with time, causation and ways of apprehending reality. The following passage was read slowly and we tried to grasp its significance:

God predestines things in eternity but does not bring them into existence (eternity), or what is the sense in calling Him a creator if the created things are co-eternal with him. The universe is contingent and not-being; it always is and always will be.
It is idle to ask when the world was created. 'When' refers to time, and time is a product of the phenomenal world. There is no temporal succession between creator and created, but there is a logical order of before and after, not in time. The relation between God and the universe is analagous to that of yesterday and today. We cannot say that yesterday precedes today in time, since it is time itself. The non-existence of the world was never at any time.

We sat slightly dazed on our cushions. One or two thought they could see how logical connections could exist outside time. The discussion leader thought it might be helpful to consider Ibn 'Arabi's view of reality: 'Reality is what we do not directly know or perceive, but which, following our reason, we logically infer as we infer the existence of a substance when we perceive its accidents.' We began to move more easily among Platonic concepts of forms and appearances, essence and accident...

In the afternoon I weeded the cabbages with a young American who had visited the commune on numerous occasions and was leaving the following day to establish a commune in New Hampshire, and a young English research physicist from Southampton who was also leaving shortly to go climbing in Wales. No, he didn't think he'd come again: 'The discussion groups were disappointing. There was too much intellectualizing.' But he belonged to a group in Southampton which really reshaped your conception of reality: 'You begin by recognizing that you never see your own head...'

We were joined by Zahra, a slow dark girl from Sydney, a permanent member of the commune, who was totally silent in the discussion groups. 'Have you seen Trevor? Has he come this week? He said he was going to cast my horoscope.' I had not seen Trevor. 'What sign are you?' 'Sagittarius. Did you know?' 'No. I wish I knew astrology. Do you know anyone who could teach me?' I didn't. She talked about a time when people lived for nine hundred years. She wasn't sure whether she would like to.

After the 6 o'clock Meditation and the evening meal we met to read the poetry of the Sufi mystic, Jalal al-Din Rumi. The poems were moralistic, they told of encounters with the devil and counselled the way of the spirit and not the way of the flesh. They pointed the way to perfection by removing all desire from the heart: 'It is true greatness and felicity to close the heart to all human passions; the abandonment of the vanities of this world is the happy effect of the victorious strength given by the grace of the Holy Prophet.' This, we felt comfortably, we could understand. But the discussion-group leader turned our gaze from the phenomenal world and suggested we should look at the symbolism of the poetry — especially the recurrent symbolism of six. The poet had referred to 'the six dimensions of the world' and to 'the house with six doors from which we cannot escape'. Facile suggestions that the reference was to our senses were easily disposed of in a highly articulate discourse by the leader. We were awed by his erudition and apparent familiarity with the symbolic order of Islamic mysticism. We were rather relieved to end the session with a prolonged exhalation of 'Hu'.

'The devotees are flagging a bit', I said to Razieh, the secretary-receptionist, as we groped around for our shoes, 'There were only three people at this evening's Meditation'. 'I know', she replied, 'things are getting slack. We must have a blitz on discipline'.

(3) *A blitz on discipline*

Breakfast this morning was cheerful. A number of people had left the night before, and a companionable twenty sat round the table. As breakfast ended the permanent member at the head of the table, Jaffar, took from his pocket a sheet of paper with half a dozen headings written on it. He spoke to his paper in the caressing cadences of a Wykehamist accent which served only to reinforce the sternness of his reprimand:

I had intended that we should spend a little time taking stock of our study sessions, but instead I feel that I must bring a number of more important matters to your attention. We have become slack. People are not pulling their weight. It is vital, particularly now our numbers are smaller, that we all work together, and work hard.

The bathrooms and ablutions are a disgrace. They are untidy and unclean. It is distasteful to put your head inside. They must be cleaned up this morning. And kept clean. People are not volunteering as they should for the chores of cleaning, cooking and washing up. We cannot carry people who will not pull their weight. With our small numbers, everyone must give of his best and be more than usually willing and helpful.

People must talk to each other — make everyone feel at ease and at home. No-one should feel left out.

Everyone should align himself. Remembrance is a duty — you must remember the Divine Names. If you feel you are losing your alignment, if you are feeling astray, you should spend an hour in the contemplation room over the stable: sit quietly by yourself, or read the Bible or the Koran.

Discussion sessions are unsatisfactory. Arguments are not being followed through. Too many people are apparently satisfied with unsatisfactory answers. They give up the argument too readily. You must push the argument hard and insist on clarification and explanation.

Meditation is not sitting sleeping for an hour on a low bench. It calls for great effort. You must focus your minds. And you must let the world fall away. Ablutions before meditation have become perfunctory. They must be carried out thoroughly. They are essential for washing away the accumulations and accretions of the world and the day.

The bell is not being rung at the proper time by the appointed person. This slackness has thrown us all out of gear and cannot be tolerated.

Is there anything anyone wishes to say?

Nineteen people sat round the table looking crestfallen and sheepish. No-one spoke.

'Instead of the programmed study session, we shall all do an hour's meditation in the temple in the Great Barn.'

Silently, we all filed out, went punctiliously to our ablutions and then to the Barn, removed our shoes, and knelt motionless for an hour. At the end we gave two hundred chants. Three people had been taken on one side and asked to leave.

At lunch we recovered our gaiety. The day was hot and cloudless and we took a long, low trestle table down on to the lawn under the willow trees beside the river. 'Where's Hamid?' 'Oh, he's in the room of meditation. He's fasting today.' We talked about the way bread was baked in the commune. The ducks came up from the river and took food from our plates.

At 4 o'clock we met to read the works of the fourth-century (BC) Chinese mystic, Chuan Tzu. The poems seemed to contain common sense advice about the conduct of public affairs and the proper demeanour of a man holding high office. But the discussion leader resolutely turned our attention to the deeper implications, to the underlying concepts of the Perfect Man, of good and evil, and especially the concept of evil as nothingness. These ideas seemed to be echoed in the writings of Sufi mystics. We turned again to the works of Ibn 'Arabi:

> Evil is not a positive quality: pure evil is the same as pure not-being and pure darkness, and pure good is pure being and pure light. The difference between light and darkness is not one of contrariety, but that of existence and non-existence.

The distinction between good and evil seemed to be slipping away, since all is reduced to unity, and God is the author of all the acts of mankind. This seemed to be the inescapable conclusion from Ibn 'Arabi's contention:

> Logically a possible thing or action may be one or other of many alternative things or actions, but actually it is only one: the one God knows will take place. It is impossible for God to will what lies not in the nature of things. The intrinsic laws of man are the deciding factor in all that He does, good or evil.

No-one in the discussion group seemed inclined to pursue the argument and its implications with the vigour we had been told was required.

I washed up after dinner with a dark and strikingly attractive newcomer in her forties. Her eyeshadow was discreet and her gown expensive. She came from Hampstead and had been a teacher of handicapped children for twenty years. She was the daughter of a Swedish mother and Indian father. She had been before to the commune, and her twenty-year-old daughter, a student at Birmingham was coming in a few days' time. She had spent ten years in Transcendental Meditation and did an hour's (advanced) yoga before breakfast. She was very good at unblocking blocked up sinks.

(4) *Sundry conversations*
In *The Presentation of Self in Everyday Life* Erving Goffman offered 'a sort of handbook' to help in the study of 'the kind of social life that is organized within the physical confines of a building or plant'. As the days passed in the commune, I found Goffman's notions of 'front', 'backstage' and 'team' increasingly useful in interpreting what I saw and experienced. The 'team' was very unobtrusive and was difficult to pick out at all in the first crowded weekend; but it was effective and efficient and presented a united front for instance in discussion sessions. 'Backstage' I believe there was far less harmony: one of the team confided in me that there would have to be changes in the commune — there were difficulties (unspecified) among the long-stay members. The 'audience' of relatively short-stay members had no inkling of this.

The 'front' is quietly but effectively managed, and problems which arise seem to be referred very quickly backstage, processed and acted upon. The 'discipline blitz' was a notable example, but I found that stray comments I made about the conduct and content of study groups were acted upon by the team within hours. But team members are self-effacing, difficult to identify, although it is only they who take Persian names: they work with everyone else in the gardens and kitchens, they scatter themselves among the discussion groups, the women are remarkably silent. Team members sit at the head of the dining table, lead the study group and preside over Meditation, but they do not draw attention to themselves.

The distinction between the team and the rest is nevertheless deep and important. The distinction is not only in terms of function: the age of the ten team members (men and women) ranges only from twenty-one to twenty-six — their average age is about twenty-three. The age-range of the short-stay members is very much greater, extending from the early twenties to late forties, clustering around thirty, and averaging thirty-four or five. [32] Socially and educationally the difference also appears considerable. The team is upper-class, the rest middle-class. Schools at which team members were educated include Winchester, Eton, Ampleforth, Atlantic College, St. Mary's, Wantage; institutions of higher education attended include Cambridge, Oxford, Slade School of Art, Guy's Hospital, and the Universities of London and Sydney. Curiously there are no university students, although many have been students. A twenty-three-year-old girl who has been in the commune a year said she had been a medical student previously but had fallen seriously ill. When she recovered she visited the commune 'and realized this was the only thing I wanted to do'. She had no particular mystical leanings, 'but I had always read a lot of poetry'. Her father was prepared to pay her a small allowance 'provided there are no long-haired students there'. There were no students, long-haired or otherwise.

She has a strong sense that 'there are spaces in life'. Her values are those of a highly traditional aristocratic-gentry culture. She thinks that people who join the commune have a 'leisure notion of life through their upbringing': career success in the obvious sense of climbing ladders is not very important to them — but a sense of service is. People brought up in a tradition of leisure will feel at home here. They may find conventional, linear careers very constricting — without open spaces in which to breathe.

This morning, however, I planted rows of spinach with a woman in her early thirties who will shortly return to London where she is a self-employed artist. She has been here for three weeks: 'And I've been three times before, but I still feel I'm a visitor.' She has a strong sense of the difference between the commune's shifting penumbra and its more permanent core:

> I shall have to leave in a couple of days. I can't afford to stay any longer. There are some very well heeled people here, and some who have what used to be called 'breeding'. I've been three times before, for two or three weeks, but I have to count my pennies. Some never talk about leaving. They don't have to. They've got enough money to carry on — or their families have. They don't have to think about careers, like most of us, or making the right move at the right time.

The team members certainly display no signs of wealth — none has a car. They appear to pool their resources. At breakfast this morning it was announced: 'The treasurer is on call for too long. From today she will be available only between 10 o'clock and 11 for people to draw the money they need.' Some will return to orthodox careers: the Slade

School graduate said he had become disenchanted with the art scene, but will return to it before the end of the year. But a Cambridge graduate who read History ('for three meaningless years — until the third year, when I took an option in Chinese history') will move on to another commune.

A thirty-year-old teacher of ESN children who helped me to wash the breakfast pots has a sharp sense of the commune's social composition. She has a degree in Psychology, a feeling that education and society must change, 'and you've got to start somewhere'. The commune was a good place to start.

> In London I got very involved in Zen. I went to this fabulous lecture — very impressive. He said that if what you're doing doesn't feel right for you, you should stop doing it. So next day I went and resigned my job in a comprehensive school. And went off to Turkey. I was fascinated to see the Whirling Dervishes.
>
> I came back and visited this commune. I thought I might stay and study. But I didn't feel that involved. But I keep coming back. London is oppressive — but it's not just the fashionable anti-urban thing. There's so much wrong with education and society, but you can't change it all overnight. You've got to start somewhere — like here. Even a few people who come to know themselves can have an effect. But I don't feel entirely at home here. When I first came it seemed more socially mixed. There were always a lot of Public School people, but also a few like me who'd dragged themselves up. Now they all seem to be Public School.

After lunch I talked with Raza, a team member who had greatly impressed me as a study-group leader: fluent, erudite, cogent and penetrating in exposition and argument. He was dark, with a carefully trimmed moustache, rather serious and unsmiling, but with an air of serenity. He was an Australian (but spoke impeccable standard English) who had started to read Economics at the University of Sydney but dropped out after a term. 'I felt I must travel. I wanted to go to North Africa, but somehow never got there.'

Instead he became a bus conductor in Burnley. He liked England: 'I immediately felt England was right for me: that I'd come home.' But when he went to work in London he felt trapped in a pointless routine. 'It always seemed important to be somewhere else. I felt I should always be moving on. But here I've found a centre or stillness. There's no need to keep moving on.'

The commune was not a retreat: it strengthened you ('But it's not psychotherapy — that's no answer'). After his first short stay in the commune he returned to London: 'But at that time I just couldn't get it together. I was unemployed and had no money. I was almost starving. And then I got fifty pounds from my father in Australia — it was my twenty-first birthday. That kept me going for some weeks, and then I lived somehow from day to day.'

He returned to the commune for a longer stay, and then went back to London, 'And now I found I really could get it together. I set myself up making leather goods and was soon making thirty pounds a week. People were coming in all the time. And there were parties. I was enjoying myself. I had a sense of unity with everything.' But when he was invited back to the commune to help to run it, 'I felt that was right'.

He has a strong sense of the accidental in life, and finds it meaningless to talk of 'causes':

I can't really say what brought me to this commune and why I am here. That would involve a conception of causation and linked temporal sequences which does not correspond with reality. I am very aware of the way my experience of time varies: sometimes it goes very slowly, sometimes it is very fast. Something that happened two weeks ago can be further away than something that happened five years ago. We have to think in vertical, not horizontal terms. We have to find vertical solutions to problems, and that makes time and temporal succession and sequence irrelevant.

When he arrived in England he was looking for a personal solution to his sense of futility.

But now I realize that it is a much wider — almost an infinite — problem that has to be solved. Trying to solve personal relationship problems at the personal level can't work — that's horizontal, there's no way out. You can only keep going round and round. Solutions are vertical — through oneness with the Essence. We don't discuss people's personal problems here, although a lot of people with personal problems come in for help — with mental problems, drug problems, and so on. But here we're seeking religious answers, not psychological cures. Meditation has the effect of bringing people together, but it's not group dynamics or group therapy — all have an intuition of union with a higher essence, the ultimate reality. We let go of ourselves. But this is not a negative thing, it is a way to completeness. Sufism doesn't cut you off from society — quite the contrary, it unites you with it, through oneness with the Essence.

My talk in the evening with a short-stay man of forty from Norwich was comparatively boring. He was an ardent conservationist, a partner in a firm of surveyors who spent his weekends at organic farms. He was an active supporter of 'People', a new political party dedicated to reducing the population, controlling pollution, decentralization, making Britain agriculturally self-sufficient, and imposing taxes to encourage craftsmanship. I felt dispirited. I had been here before.

(5) *Of archetypes and divine love*

Our readings this morning began with Ibn 'Arabi's account of his encounter with Khidr and led to a discussion of the place of inter-mediaries in our approach to reality. We were side-tracked into some consideration of the archetypal Green Man.

The leader read from Ibn 'Arabi's *Futuhat:*

> When he was in Tunis, on a warm night of full moon, Ibn 'Arabi went to rest in the cabin of a boat anchored in the port. A feeling of uneasiness awakened him. He went to the edge of the vessel while the crew was still plunged in sleep. And he saw coming toward him, dry-shod over the waters, someone who approached and talked with him for a moment and then quickly withdrew into a grotto in the mountain-side, some miles distant. The next day in Tunis a holy man unknown to him asked him: 'Well, what happened last night with Khidr?'

The Arabic words *khidr* and *khadir* (like the Persian *khezr*) mean the verdant one or the green man. Khidr in some sense called Ibn 'Arabi to God, but his precise role as intermediary (or teacher) is unclear. Perhaps Khidr is the same archetypal figure that we find in *Sir Gawain and the Green Knight?* The Green Knight is not merely a vegetation myth, though he fights Sir Gawain, and recovers from his injuries in the New Year; he is also testing out Sir Gawain's chivalric conduct and ideals, keeping him in 'alignment'.

No-one in the study group felt that this reference to archetypes really explained anything. The story of Khidr, it was suggested, raised the problem of 'where does one start from in order to know?'. Do we start from where we are and progress by stages? But such step-wise progression in knowledge implies a sequence in time and ends up by being circular knowledge, turning back on itself. We must start vertically, with alignment on the ultimate and absolute.

A team member referred us to the identification of Khidr and Elijah in the Koran and Koranic commentaries: sometimes they are linked as a pair, sometimes they are identified with one another. But they seem to stand outside historical time, as in the episode when Khidr-Elijah meets Moses as if they were contemporaries.[33] Relationship with Khidr invests the disciple with a trans-historical dimension: it is more than incorporation into the brotherhood of Sufism.

One of the team members tried to illustrate this point by telling the story of Sufi testing and initiation:

> A young man served as a menial in the Palace kitchens for 1,001 days. The chief of the kitchen said he would now take him out of the kitchen to the Sheik. He attached a silken thread to himself and the man, and led off towards the Sheik's apartments. The silken thread had to be taut but not so taut that it would break; and not slack either. If the silken thread broke, or if it slackened, the man was not ready to go to the Sheik, and would be returned to his menial tasks in the kitchen for a further 1,001 days.[34]

The silken thread, it was suggested, symbolizes 'vertical alignment' and takes the relationships out of time.

Man's relationship with God or the Essence is union: it is an expression of God's love of Himself, and it allows of no intermediaries. We ended the discussion session with a reading from Runi's book, the *Masnavi*, which makes this essential point:

> One knocked at the door of the Beloved, and a voice from within inquired, 'Who is there?'. Then he answered, 'It is I'. And the voice said, 'This house will not hold me and thee'. So the door remained shut. Then the Lover sped away into the wilderness, and fasted and prayed in solitude. And after a year he returned, and knocked again at the door, and the voice again demanded, 'Who is there?'. And the Lover said, 'It is thou'. Then the door was opened.

After lunch I talked to a woman of about thirty who had recently arrived. She was a primary school teacher from Derby, a psychology graduate and married. She had left her husband and children at home. I asked her why she had come.

> I've been before, a few weeks ago, just for the weekend. I found it a very remarkable experience. Let me tell you about it.
>
> I've always read lots of poetry, and a few years ago I became

interested in yoga, but I never got the hang of meditation. Recently I've been reading Colin Wilson and the new existentialists, but a book by Christmas Humphreys, *Zen — A Way of Life*, seemed the most whole and together expression of all these things. And then I heard about this commune, and where it is, and it seemed very attractive and exciting. As far as I could gather the Sufis were a mystical group with little connection with their Islamic source, and really very similar to Zen in their thinking. So I came.

I arrived late one Friday afternoon and they were all in Meditation. A long-haired Austrian was wandering about carrying a baby who turned out not to be his but belonged to an American girl who was in Meditation. We sat in the dining room and he told me about his experience of the commune. He said he'd learned to use words like 'love' and 'God'; before he'd found it difficult to say them.

When they came out of Meditation I was given one of the stables and I changed and went back to the dining room where people were standing in groups, talking. The supper was good — fresh salad and eggs and fish and fruit and coffee. Everyone sat for ages afterwards, and I wished something would happen. I felt tired and confused. A suave Sufi man was arguing with a large, ugly, genteel woman of about sixty. She'd been to Iona and Glastonbury and seemed to want assurance that being a Christian did not exclude her. The suave Sufi man said the Sufis encompassed all religions and ways.

Later we all sat in the front room. There seemed to be lots of small dark men with moustaches. The leader said that since there were lots of newcomers, people with more experience should say what it meant to them. One girl said she'd learned a lot about herself, cast off old concepts, and this was just the beginning of possible future growth. The Austrian said he had not at first understood much of the works they studied, but gradually the words attracted him and he kept reading. He had come to know God. A moustached man said he stayed because he liked it. Another man said he kept coming back but didn't know why. The moustached man said it often happened that people came without knowing why: people reached a stage of development and questioning at the same time that knowledge reached out to them.

It was clear that self-knowledge of the individual was more important than group harmony, and that anyone who needed booting out would assuredly be booted out.

The leader said that ideally people should go back to everyday life with a sense that barriers between themselves and everything else were gone. They might behave oddly and be misunderstood, but they would feel at one with everything and everyone.

On Saturday we were awakened early. It was nice waking up in the sunshine and finding the place still real.

In the morning we read 'Arabi's writings about different kinds of knowledge, and then some poems. Jane felt she hadn't contributed much to the discussion. It was the only one I ever contributed to, and I felt pleasantly integrated. In the afternoon I planted chicory seeds. I got muddy and tired. It was nice.

At supper there was talk of having a jolly evening. I thought, My God, games? charades? I felt utterly depressed and disillusioned about Sufis, and aware of my own unsociability and limitations. But we escaped charades and read the *Thousand and One Nights*. I went to bed feeling chastened and purified by my own awareness, as if my bones had been bleached in the desert.

On Sunday I woke up feeling better and sad at the thought of leaving. After Meditation, as we walked from the barn, the Austrian and another man fell into each other's arms and kissed and walked on arm in arm. They looked round and smiled at me. I think they had really recognized the 'Hu' or oneness in each other. New people arrived, meeting people they'd known before. They embraced and kissed with a sudden, spontaneous delight in recognition.

When I left, I felt I'd changed a bit — not into a mystical or ecstatic state which I'd half expected, but intellectually a few ideas were clearer, and as a whole I felt a bit stronger. Strength of the bleached bone, a deep resilience which had always been there but I hadn't always known. I'd probably forget it, or lose it again and again, but it would be easier to get back to it, the route to the true self was opened a bit. Yes, I said as I left, I would come back again.

In the evening study session we reverted to time and the essence of things. We considered Ibn 'Arabi's statement about time: 'That whose existence is infinite: it comprises eternity, everlastingness and what lies between them; it is identical with the divine Essence. Time is an eternal now. That which guides the whole knows the future as present.' There followed a discussion of time as spaces analagous to the silences between notes in music, and the illusory nature of time as the interval between birth and death. We were reaching the conclusion that birth and death are contemporaneous, and beginning to doubt the efficacy of argument by analogy.

Some people were becoming impatient of abstractions. One newcomer asked what social or personal implications, of a fairly prosaic kind, there might be in all this. The question sounded slightly blasphemous. But the leader rose to the challenge. Certainly Sufism was not concerned with any facile adjustment therapy at a personal level, or with revolutionary social and political programmes. 'But the belief that the true Sufi *is* God sounds like an extreme form of spiritual elitism — indeed, an amoral elitism. A man, being God, does his own thing?' No, through Sufism one arrived at principles of action, but not specific and limiting formulae. 'But', said the leader, 'if his principles took a man off to be a mercenary soldier in Africa, I would respect that'. 'We are not the Divine Light Mission', said another long-stay member: 'They just want to make people happy.' 'No', rejoined the leader, 'but if someone from the Divine Light Mission walked in through the door, we would respect them and try to understand them, because that's where their principles have taken them'.

We left the session a little more ruffled than usual. A rather homely girl wearing glasses came up to me and handed me a piece of paper. She had no make-up on and wore a rather inexpertly home-made skirt. She was always the first to volunteer for the more unpleasant chores. She smoked a lot of Menthol cigarettes. 'Read this', she said, 'I think it will help you'. (My growing impatience with abstractions must have been more obvious than I'd thought.) It was a poem she had written. She had been unable to sleep the night before, and had spent the long night writing it. It was called 'Together' — a simple, poignant poem about loneliness, and God in every man.

(6) *Leaving*

As I was leaving today a bearded young man carrying a rucksack walked wearily up the drive. He had a sharp, dark face, and moving, intelligent eyes. Could he stay here for a time? for nothing? There was a conference between two long-stay members. The man with the rucksack has successfully failed all fourteen papers in his final Sociology examinations at the London School of Economics. He was now a student of Theology. Yes, he could stay. Meanwhile a very smart American woman in her forties had arrived in a Citroen. She unloaded expensive luggage; she wore green eyeshadow and an elegant, high-collared trouser-suit. Yes, she could stay, too. Together they entered the old farmhouse with a verse of Rumi's inscribed over the door:

Come, come, whoever you are,
It doesn't matter whether you are an infidel,
    an idolator, or a fire-worshipper.
Come, our convent is not a place of despair.
Come, even if you have broken your vow a thousand times.
Come, come again, come.

I drove slowly along country lanes and reflected on the continuities and discontinuities between the commune and the world. The discontinuities were striking. But there was no local hostility to the commune, of the kind that has been reported in America.[35] Indeed, some local people came in to Sunday services in the temple; and some weeks previously the commune had held a garden fête and had staged a folk-play on the lawn. Local people had flocked in, and the profits from a modest entrance fee were fifty pounds. Curiously, students in the university forty miles away showed no interest.

Conclusion

The Sufi commune was, indeed, 'high status marginality' both in terms of the social background of members and the view they had of themselves. And, of course, it was entirely voluntary, enjoyed by people predisposed to open themselves to new experiences. It was 'discontinuous' in de-emphasizing external domestic and marital ties, but was certainly not committed to even temporary celibacy.

Contemporary American communes have been depicted as 'intentional social islands',[36] their deliberate apartness and non-political stance emphasized, their similarities with monasticism highlighted. [37] The Sufi commune is not a social island: its boundaries with the wider society are highly permeable. People cross and recross the boundary, and the commune's wider social and indeed political purposes and implications, though non-specific, are real and important to most members, both 'inner core' and peripheral.

But discontinuities with the 'straight' world are sharp. There is the underlying conception of non-linear, non-cumulative life-styles with 'open spaces', detours, but a strong sense of service. Most striking, however, are the intellectual and conceptual discontinuities, especially with regard to concepts of time and causality.

Had the members of the commune significantly changed? Had their identities been transformed? Had they (as Berger's argument would suggest) regained, through their rediscovery of the supernatural, an 'openness' in their perception of reality? In the absence of any systematic follow-up or 'longitudinal' data, only very tentative answers can be given. But the strong impression gained from close observation and conversation is that the answer to all these questions — at least with regard to the long-standing members — is: Yes.

The deeply committed, permanent members had changed their names, and they had changed their appearance by adopting disciplined hairstyles (sharply contrasted with the uncontrolled and luxuriant hairstyles of hippies) and by wearing the Sufi symbol of unity. Changes in 'hair behaviour' have been extensively discussed as signals of change in social position and orientation.[38] In the way they presented themselves to their fellows, the committed members of the commune signalled their separation from both 'straight' and hippie cultures. They announced a new self.

Certainly the long-standing members claimed that they had changed significantly, even fundamentally, through involvement in the commune's life and rituals. They claimed that they had found serenity, calm and repose after experiencing life as frenetic and disjointed. But far from feeling apart from the world, they had a sense of all-embracing order and unity: there were no 'intermediaries' in the form of persons, institutions or ideologies which separated them from 'reality' and their fellow men.

Some of the committed members had been deeply into the hippie counter culture but had apparently wholly renounced it (Mostaffa referred to the 'scene' he had formerly been in in London, but said that the people he had been with then he now 'wouldn't want to know'), but others, like Hasan who had followed a 'classical' counter-culture career of drop-out, drugs, 'crash-pads', and the journey to the East, were not so finally disengaged from their past. Raza had come to the commune from a familiar disorganized, counter-cultural career, but appeared to have reversed his former aesthetic-anarchistic orientation and to have found a firm, calm centre for his life.

The hippie counter culture — or some deep disturbance like serious illness or bereavement — seemed to have been a prelude to entering the commune. These 'neo-sacrilists' were not recruited from a source quite outside the hippie counter culture (though some had been mainly in its aesthetic-environmentalist fringe), as Greeley suggests has been the case in America. Greeley recognizes a relationship between counter culture and neo-sacrilists but denies identity or continuity of personnel: 'The new religious enthusiasts clearly owe a major debt of gratitude to the hippies. Indeed, one might even consider them to be merely one wing of the hippie movement ... Both are a search for "experience" and for a specific kind of experience — one that "takes one out of oneself".' But Greeley claims that those who become hippies and those who become neo-sacrilists are quite different people: 'One hesitates to say it, but the neo-sacrilists appear to be much more "respectable" than the hippies.'[39] The Sufi commune in the English Cotswolds suggests much more overlap; and the Hare Krishna commune described in the next chapter provides still stronger evidence that many neo-sacrilists may have found 'communitas' after a prior, liminal phase of hippiedom.

9 | Demons and devotees: Hare Krishna and the transformation of consciousness

The key point of this chapter is to take further, through an account of a Hare Krishna commune, an issue that emerged in a rather tentative way in the last: that a period of 'desocialization' may be an important preliminary to the effective resocialization of adults. This is not necessarily a period of abasement and mortification, which has been reported in accounts of initiation into 'total institutions',[1] elitist regiments,[2] and tribal offices,[3] although such experiences might have a similar desocializing effect. It is a period of lostness, disorientation or being adrift which corresponds closely to the ambiguities and uncertainties of Van Gennep's 'liminality'.

Becoming a 'freak' (in the counter culture of the late 1960s and '70s) has been convincingly examined principally as a process of desocialization: self-initiated desocialization and disengagement from ordinary institutions and interpersonal networks, rather than socialization to a set of standards. On the route to the counter culture ordinary, conventional, socialized behaviour is defined as 'hang-ups', neurotic symptoms which must be overcome. Desocialization is difficult (and may be helped by drugs): 'Of course, positive socialization does take place, but it appears to us to be casual and takes little effort, in contrast to the deliberate effort devoted to obtaining freedom from conventional societal constraints.'[4] But after resocialization and becoming a freak, a wide range of identities may be available:

> Moreover, we should note that the more general subprocesses of desocialization and disengagement can make an individual not only free to be a freak, but also render him free to be or become a Jesus

Freak, a follower of Hare Krishna, a wandering holy man in the Indian style, a dope dealer or an active revolutionary, or the like.[5]

Victor Turner cites contemporary hippies and historical Sufism and the Hindu religion of Krishna as examples of 'communitas'. In fact, counter-cultural hippiedom more closely resembles a preceding phase of liminality or transition. Turner highlights the abasement of hippies, who have opted out of the status-bound social order and acquired the stigmata of the lowly, and their emphasis on spontaneity and immediacy, which contrasts sharply with 'structure'.[6] But the religion of Hare Krishna, at least in its current Anglo-American manifestations, enjoins a disciplined and rule-regulated life. Moreover the evidence presented in this chapter, and the research in America carried out by J. Stillson Judah,[7] indicated that in many respects Hare Krishna is an inversion of hippiedom. And yet it is from among the hippies that many — perhaps most — of its devotees have been drawn.

The inquiry

The material on which this chapter is based was collected during a period of residence in a Hare Krishna temple in 1974, when the researcher was treated essentially as a postulant.[8] He worked alongside other members in cleaning and maintaining the premises, joined in their ceremonies and devotions, accompanied them on a preaching expedition, and was able to tape-record many hours of conversation and discussion.

The commune is to be found in a country-house in a well-to-do outer suburb of London. It is the temple of an Eastern religion, and its forty to fifty members are young English men and women. The devotees shave their heads (except for a tuft of hair which is a handhold for God), wear saffron robes, take new, Sanskrit names, and live a regulated life of austerity. Their music has strange rhythms. The God Krishna dances on their tongues and his footprint, the 'tilak', shaped like a tuning fork, is stamped on their foreheads in clay. They have an unvarying vegetarian diet of boiled rice, curried vegetables, fruit, yoghurt and milk. For the devotees the local suburbanites are 'demons' and the whole world beyond the temple is 'nonsense' and 'stool'.

In 1974 the temple had in residence some thirty-five males and fifteen females, mostly in their mid twenties, but ranging in age from late teens to early thirties. There were ten married couples and six young children.

The temple is one of some seventy centres of the International Society for Krishna Consciousness which have been established in America and other parts of the Western world in the last ten years. (About half of these centres are in America.) The organization has a flourishing business in the manufacture and sale of incense (with a large factory in Los Angeles). But it was immediately apparent in the temple in suburban London that the International Society for Krishna Consciousness proposed a new view of the world: it offers new rules for interpreting events and performing actions and giving plausibility to an unusual way of life. The devotee experiences, on the one hand, tension between the material reality in which he is living and a spiritual and transcendent reality to which he aspires; and on the other, between the enclosed world of the commune and the mundane world outside. His problems are boundary problems, and through rituals and rules he manages and maintains the boundary between alternative realities. He also appears to create and sustain a new self.

Religious heritage

The International Society for Krishna Consciousness was established in New York in 1966 by Abhay Charan De. It is a puritanical sect (with many similarities to Calvinism) which looks back to the ancient and highly erotic Indian religion of Vaisnavism. Abhay Charan De had graduated from the University of Calcutta and retired in 1954 from his position as the manager of a chemical firm. In 1965, at the age of 70, he went to America and started his mission to the West by chanting the names of the God, Krishna, while sitting under a tree in a New York park. In Tompkins Park on the Lower East Side he preached the religion of the cowherd deity, Krishna. Abhay Charan De took the title A.C. Bhaktivedanta Swami Prabhupad ('Prabhupad') and the Centre he established in New York was devoted to spreading the message of the early sixteenth-century Hindu prophet, Caitanya. The International Society now sends missionaries from America to India.

Krishna is eternal and transcendental and the religion — if Krishna is a religion — of bliss. The reality to which it gives access unites all opposites and differences. Krishna loved Radha the milkmaid; but he united with her to form one being, neither male nor female, neither duty nor pleasure. This being which unites opposites is held by devotees to be embodied in the prophet Caitanya: human completeness represented in bisexual form which transcends all distinctions of sex, culture and caste.

The ancient religion of Vaisnavism had for many centuries found an extensive following in India and especially in Bengal: it was the religion of the cowherd deity Krishna who engaged in erotic play with Radha and other (married) milkmaids. Caitanya arose as a charismatic prophet in the sixteenth century who gave the ancient religion a powerful new impetus and reformulated it in more ascetic but socially popular terms: it transcended the barriers of caste and offered adherents religious ecstasy in a pious, self-disciplined life of service to a personal God.

The Krishna Consciousness Movement, like the historical religion of Vaisnavism, is based on ancient Sanskrit texts like the *Bhagavad-gita*, but it is centrally concerned with Caitanya's life and teaching (as found in the seventeenth-century biography, *Caitanya Caritamrita*). Early Vedic texts like the *Puranas* emphasized the ecstatic eroticism of Krishna's relationships with the *gopis* (milkmaids); Caitanya reinterpreted Krishna's sexual activities as a religious sacrament. In the earlier literature Krishna charmed the milkmaids by playing on his flute in the forest so that they left their homes, husbands and families and fled to him in the night. The religious rituals of Caitanya and his followers culminated in the act of sexual intercourse between fully initiated devotees who simulated the love-making of Krishna and Radha. This was an act of ritual intercourse between a devotee and the wife of another. But it was not sensual indulgence: it was preceded by meditation and self-denial — an outward sign of spiritual grace.

Like the members of the Sufi commune, the Krishna devotees have become heirs not only of a powerful religious tradition, but of the social attitudes out of which it grew and which it helped to shape. Like the Sufis (and early Calvinists) the followers of Krishna form a spiritual elite which has inevitable social connotations. In neither the Sufi nor the Hare Krishna commune was there any sense of social stigma, although members of the latter encounter much ridicule and often active hostility. In both the communes women are somewhat subdued and self-effacing, but in the Hare Krishna commune more explicitly relegated to an inferior status and regarded as somewhat unclean.

Both the Sufis and the followers of Krishna have accepted a tradition of disciplined thought and behaviour, both engage in rituals which concentrate the mind. In the Krishna commune the mind must be 'kept in place, properly situated'; in the Sufi commune it must be 'in alignment'. In the former, chanting is a powerful aid to this end, in the latter protracted periods of meditation and the prolonged exhalation of 'Hu'. The Sufis seek 'oneness with the Essence' and the Krishna devotees wish in some sense to be 'part and parcel of Krishna'. But there is a crucial difference: the Sufis become God, but Krishna's devotees remain distinct. The devotees of Krishna do not make a dualistic distinction between instances and essence; for them the Godhead resides in concrete, immediate objects as well as in remote abstractions. The God of the Sufis is highly abstract, but Krishna is concretely personalized: the food he prefers is butter, his favourite bird is the peacock, and the musical instrument that gives him most delight is the flute.

Both the Sufis and the Krishna devotees take from a rich religious heritage a new relationship to time; but whereas the former deny the distinction between past and future and stand outside time, for the latter time is an eternal present, enclosed in the tight boundary of 'regulative practices'. Krishna Consciounsess is detachment from 'karma', the futile search for sense gratification; it is purification through chanting and dancing, through austerity and a scripturally regulated life. Devotees briefly and lightly dismissed their previous biographical selves and generally de-emphasized the past. And the future is depersonalized, merely a succession of 'spiritual platforms'.

The devotees take their temporal bearings from a long tradition of religious thought and practice. Krishna is an escape from both karma and the effluxion of time: from the cycle of reincarnation, from birth, death and rebirth. As one devotee said: 'Krishna *is* time; he is before and after time; he transcends times.' But a recent recruit to the temple pointed to the detailed timetable of chanting: 'It seems like a job of work, all that clock-watching. I mean, that's what I came to the temple to get away from, all that nine-to-five routine — "Do this by such-and-such a time or else..."' He was firmly reproved: 'That is what the Vedic life is like: a routine. After all, Krishna *is* time, the controller of time. Krishna is time itself.'

Maintaining a new consciousness

The religion of Caitanya rejects philosophical dualism for an all-embracing unity which accepts no distinction between subject and object and finds God in diversity; and yet inevitably — and even dramatically in Western industrial societies — it locates the devotee in one of two sharply contrasted social 'sides': there is the devotional world of the devotee and the impure world of the 'karmis'. The social world is, after all, deeply dualistic: it has a right hand and a left; it contains a boundary which marks off the inferior side and affords protection against defilement. The devotees derive from their teaching, their rituals and their sacred texts a strong sense of the importance of the right hand and the inferiority of the left. Their temple is on the right. The left hand is for wiping the backside with; only the right hand conveys food to the mouth.[9]

The boundary with the outer world is strong and holds firm. When the children in the commune reach the age of five they have to go to school in America, at Dallas. One young mother was in deep distress because her child was rising five:

> We're really worried about it, and we've been praying to Krishna. You see, if you just send them off, they're officially adopted, aren't they? And you have to sign away everything. You could never see them again. I know we're not supposed to have 'attachments', but if you've never had children you don't know how it feels.

Acceptance of this rule, however grudgingly in the event, is a measure of the great strength of devotees' commitment, of the allegiance that the sect exacts, and of the power of the commune's boundary with the outside world.

The temple is very sharply marked off from the world: it is separate, contemptuous of 'karmi', the ordinary world in which everyone is uptight, anxious, frantic, 'puffed up', stupid, unclean. It has a strong sense of its superiority and apartness, which is reinforced in daily ritual and routine; and the body's boundaries are scrupulously cleansed and maintained and its orifices controlled. *The Hare Krishna Cookbook* lists forbidden foods. There are carefully prescribed methods of conveying food to the mouth without using the left hand or the index (or 'poking') finger; and the poking finger must never touch the sacred 'japja' beads. 'Stool' is passed only once every day (at the same time), and only a narrow spiritual passage, the 'jiva', leads outwards, from the heart to the spiritual platforms. The body's exits and entrances are elaborately protected, and shaving the head is one means of cleaning up the body's boundaries. The devotees are encircled in Krishna's protective embrace: those in the outer world who mock and despise them have a way of ending up mutilated or dead under lorries and buses. But the boundary with the outer world is not wholly impermeable: this is not an 'introversionist sect' but a 'utopian sect'[10] which sends its itinerant preachers to make converts in the world.

The outer world is in many ways the inverse of their own, in its values and personal behaviours: 'You need only to look at their faces: they're so much anxiety, the karmis. They look so worried and unhappy, just trying to plan some enjoyment or other.' By contrast they themselves are purified and at peace: 'We're blissfully free of all that.'

The local inhabitants are 'demons' and the commune's grounds are patrolled at night to ward off their attacks. 'We get a lot of intruders … the villagers. Most of them are demons and they want us out … They're just demonic, you know. They're frightened of Krishna; and the property values have gone down here, since we came.' The devotees' noise sometimes gives offence:

> Sometimes we go out into the village and chant Krishna's name. And the demons can't bear to hear it. So they try and attack us. Prabhupad wants us to take over the entire village. Just think of it … a whole village of devotees. All for Krishna. So Prabhupad tells us to make our 'kirtan' dancing as loud as possible, so that the demons will not be able to stand it and leave. Then we can start buying up all the houses. Only the devotees will be left.

A devotee's social life shrinks to the confines of the temple. Trebubanath observed:

> We have social life only here, with devotees. We have no other friends, really. My parents don't really understand, but they've come to terms with it. They visit me sometimes. It's a really nice atmosphere here, really strong. Krishna Consciousness is so ecstatic. We're putting on a really nice play tonight; you must come along.

Boundaries with the spirit world are correspondingly tight, and difficult to negotiate. A devotee's aim is to reach Krishna's abode, 'Krishnaloka', but the transit is difficult and dangerous. In one of the study sessions a girl asked for enlightenment on the way transference from material to spiritual platforms could be achieved. It was patiently explained to her that there was, in the human body, a kind of bridge, a tiny passage, along which this dangerous journey could be made. This passage, the 'jiva', was only one ten thousandth of the width of a hair; it was situated in the heart and floated on 'airs'. Through these airs, part spiritual, part material, the vital transition could be made. The discussion group members listened with rapt attention.

Within their tightly bounded world the devotees abide by 'regulative principles' and enact rituals of purification:

We all try to follow the rules here, because we want to purify ourselves of attachments to material nature, from the idea of enjoying
ourselves on our own, apart from Krishna. Eating meat ... that's a
kind of pollution, a pollution of our sense of compassion and
mercy. Smoking and taking intoxicants — that pollutes the mind,
destroys the best thing we have, our reasoning power. And they
destroy our health, too. Illicit sex life: that's an offence against our
cleanliness, and a pollution of our austerity, too. And gambling —
well, obviously, that's an offence against truthfulness. So we try not
to do any of these things, because we want to purify and spiritualize
ourselves. These austerities are necessary to being transcendentally
situated ... Chanting is the easiest way of spiritual advancement.
When we chant Krishna's name he is with us directly. You see,
Krishna is not different from his name.

The boundaries of their world are protected not only by nightly patrols
but by Krishna himself. The greatest offence against Krishna is to
offend his devotees. Many stories were told to illustrate this protective
embrace. Mahabhuja explained:

All the people who come up to us in the street and insult us ... I'm
always telling them to stop: 'Please, stop! You don't know how
great an offence this is.' There was one drunken boy who came up
to us and said something awful. It was in Glasgow. And he stag-
gered off, and was straightaway run over by a car ... You see, that's
how strong Krishna is. His vengeance will find people out sooner or
later. His vengeance is never direct. He uses car crashes and
thunder-storms and things like that as his agents. That's what he
means when he says, 'I'm *in* everything'. That is what Krishna is
like.

The daily round is closely regulated: it is in all its aspects and
phases, however apparently mundane, a devotional routine. Its
purpose is the attainment of eternity and to this end the devotee is
immersed in the immediate present, shorn of longer perspectives and
forgetful of deeper histories. Through his ever-busy life in 'material'
time he is freed from karma and transcends time itself.

A meticulous timetable regulates an eighteen-hour day: little more
than six hours are allowed for sleep (9.30 p.m. to 3.45 a.m.). Devotees
murmur a prayer before rising and taking a cold shower; they then
make twelve clay marks on their bodies, Krishna's footprints drawn
out of clay 'taken from Krishna's bathing place in India'. The most

elaborate clay mark is on the forehead. After robing, everyone assembles in the temple for 'mongalarti': offerings of incense, flower bloom and conch-shells are made to an image of Krishna, music is played and Sanskrit prayers intoned. A scripture class follows before breakfast is served.

Four and a half hours after rising the devotees break their fast and take 'prasadam' sitting cross-legged in a circle on the floor. They eat after praying: 'Oh my Lord, the material body is a lump of ignorance, and the senses are a network of pathways leading to death ... But you, dear Lord Krishna, have sent me this nice prasadam to help me conquer my tongue.' Food is eaten with the right hand.

Practical activities extend throughout the day until 6 o'clock, allocated and supervised by the Temple Commander who reproves and instructs. After the evening meal 'arti' extends until bedtime at nine: kirtan dancing and offerings to the deities followed by a study of sacred texts. The temple world had its own internally regulated rhythm: events were not placed on a numbered time-scale, but located on internal co-ordinates: 'Come and see me after prasadam', 'We'll do it before arti', 'He told me during jappa'.

Chanting goes on throughout the day and holds the world in place. It is an activity of supreme importance:

> Must chant your rounds, you know. It's really important. I some-times think I won't bother this morning, but then I notice the difference. My mind keeps wandering all day. I can't get engaged. I forget what it's all for, you know. When you've said your rounds you feel great: it fixes you up for the day. It lasts all day.

Rules reduce individual differences, enable everyone to play his part, and prevent anyone getting 'puffed up':

> There are rules for everything here. There are strict rules for the rhythms and beats you should use with these drums, so it's not a question of talent. Krishna plays the flute, but that's very difficult. If we had a flute player he would be bound to get puffed up. If you have a great talent it is difficult to be a good devotee. I don't envy people with talent.

A new spiritual consciousness is thus created, sustained and protected through rituals, regulations and rules which give everyday routines of social relationships, working and eating a spiritual signifi-cance. The great danger lies in sleep: this is a condition of extreme vulnerability, difficult to regulate and integrate conceptually in a scheme of life that is called spiritual. Ritual observances enable the devotee to relabel the gross material act of eating as a devotional service. It is not so easy to prescribe rituals which will incorporate the bodily ease and indulgence of sleep and dreams within Krishna consciousness. The regulative machine that sustains Krishna consciousness is temporarily halted and the sleeper is off-guard, wide open to supernatural intrusion.

The marginal world of sleep and dreams is only precariously bracketed with the massive reality of the temple's everyday life. One devotee talked of ghosts in the night:

There *are* such things as ghosts, you know. There are ghosts here, too. I've felt them sometimes in the night. It's a weird feeling. They try and get in your body while you're asleep. Have you ever had that feeling? Like, you wake up, and it feels very cold, and there's something really heavy pressing down on your chest. It's really terrifying. You have to try to chant Krishna's name. You mustn't let them in. But it's night, you see: there's nothing happening. Everyone's asleep, and their minds are all over the place, dreaming, you know? So ghosts can get in and catch you.

And in sleep and dreams a devotee may fall from grace. He may even forget Krishna's name. One young man answered a cheerful morning greeting with a worried reflection on his dreams:

I'm all right, thank you, *prabhu*. But I feel a little disengaged this morning. I had a terrible dream last night. It was the Third World War, and the bomb had gone off. I was trying to think of Krishna and I just couldn't. You know that sort of dream? It was terrible, you know.

Sleep is regulated as far as possible by prescribing its duration and placing it under the surveillance of the temple authorities who carefully keep watch on individuals who oversleep the limits. The Temple Commander prodded one sleeper with his toe: 'Come on, now, Mahabhuja, *prabhu*.' His voice was chiding. 'Oh, Mahabhuja! You've had enough rest now, surely? You can't go on like this, sleeping all the time. You've had too much rest.'

Sleeping and eating are often closely associated in the talk of devotees: oversleeping and dreaming may be considered the result of over-indulgence in 'prasadam'. Sleep at its entrance and exit is guarded by prayer, but it is never wholly secure: it represents a dangerous hiatus in the massive operation of regulative practices which sustain a new consciousness.

The 'regulative principles' appear to be quickly and effectively internalized. It is true that the temple has a hierarchy and a division of labour among its members; but the hierarchy is not obtrusive. There is a President and Treasurer, but only the Temple Commander is in evidence: 'They are all of them just for administration, you see, to keep things running, the practical side of things. We obey them because there has to be a leader in that way. But it doesn't mean that they're spiritually different from us. It's not like that.' Important in the division of labour are the 'pujaris': 'They look after the deities, clean the temple, and each day wash Krishna and his partner Radha, and change their clothes. And they are the ones who make the offerings at arti and mongalarti.'

A new member is given jappa beads to chant on and receives a new, Sanskrit name. After six months he becomes a full member. By this time he has learnt that the key to control is his tongue:

> Controlling your tongue is very important. It easily gets lusty and wants to eat too much. It wants to enjoy. But if you can control your tongue you can control your stomach, too. And if you can control your stomach, you can control your genitals. So if you control your tongue you control everything. But if you let it do just as it wishes, you will end up trying to satisfy your genitals. The tongue is very hard to satisfy unless you've got a good engagement for it, like chanting the Holy Names.

Post-hippiedom

It would be wrong to equate membership of a Hare Krishna commune with the 'counter culture' and hippiedom. Devotees are rejecting the basic ground rules of Western society; and they are — often quite explicitly — rejecting hippiedom, too. Many appear to have been 'in the drug scene' a year or two before; their present life is strikingly discontinuous with their hippie days. Conceivably a period of hippie life 'desocialized' them so they were open to still more extraordinary experiences. They had been 'loosened up'. They have turned hippiedom on its head; and in the process have discovered 'pure nectar'.

The devotees had formerly worked in a wide variety of occupations: they included a former teacher, a clerk ('just an office nobody'), electrician, a photographer and a probation officer. One had joined the commune immediately after taking a degree in physics at a southern university. When they (rarely) talked about their life before conversion, they spoke of its being 'heavy'; and some recalled with amusement the time when they were 'offenders', taking drugs, selling drugs, and involved in fights with authority. It is impossible to say how many had spent a time as hippies; but there was frequent talk of pop festivals:

I always remember at the Isle of Wight, I'd been looking forward to the festival for weeks, you know, saving up. Bob Dylan was actually going to be there. And when it came to it, I slept right through the act. Slept right through Bob Dylan!

I was there, too. I slept right through Jimi Hendrix. I was so wiped out. All I remember is this girl trying to wake me up.

There seemed to be no hankering for their former style of life: 'I shall never leave here. It's nice. I'm a bit of a rascal, you see. I was a great offender, always lots of girls, drugs and things. But I really want to get away from all that karma. It's too heavy outside...

Hare Krishna devotees still visit pop festivals, but now for a different purpose: to help people who are 'smashed' and to make converts. One member of the commune recalled his conversion:

I was tripping, really out of my mind with this acid we'd got hold of. I really didn't know where I was. And suddenly all these people came by with bald heads. And they were singing and chanting and playing this really far out music. They started preaching. It seemed wonderful, and I just couldn't tear myself away. I just followed them around all day.

The electrician who is now called Satya Gopal had worked in a northern town and his conversion had also been sudden:

I was into a really heavy scene: drugs, rock music, a bit of radical politics. It was really heavy. I must have been insane, all that non-sense, trying to be hipper than anyone else. Then I just happened to run into the devotees one day, and I've never looked back. It took me a while to surrender completely, but you know there's nothing so completely satisfying.

An ex-public schoolboy (Madhava) has been in the commune three years:

When I left my public school I travelled a lot. I went to lots of countries. I was a sort of hippie figure. I took drugs ... I took an awful lot of drugs. All sorts of drugs ... And then I just sort of

met the devotees on the street, you know, and went to a temple.
And I've been here ever since.

The speed of conversion is stikingly different from that of the men
who became Anglican parsons after first embarking on secular careers
(see Chapter 3). The difference, perhaps, is that the parsons had
experienced no such prior 'liminality' as hippiedom. In the case of the
Krishna devotees, a somewhat disorganized life, which included
drugs, appeared to be a common preliminary to conversion. A young
art school graduate from Blackburn, who had been employed in
graphic design and had been in the commune two years, explained the
change in his life:

> My life changed completely. Before this my life was very unhappy,
> I felt very dissatisfied with myself. I went to art college and after
> that worked in graphic design; but I really wanted to be an artist. I
> got this design job but was never really into it. Nothing gave me any
> satisfaction at all. I sort of drank a lot with friends, smoked a bit of
> pot, and had affairs with girls. I did actually go to a sort of Buddhist
> commune in Scotland for about a week, but you had to leave when
> your money ran out.
> And then one day I was sitting in Picadilly Gardens in
> Manchester, opposite Woolworth's, you know ... It was a sunny day
> but I felt very low and not knowing what to do with myself. And I
> heard this music, so I just crossed over into the gardens, and there
> they were, with their shaved heads and yellow robes. I didn't know
> what to make of it, but they all looked so happy. I went back with
> them to the temple; I ate some 'prasadam' and heard them preach,
> and I began to feel really great, for the first time in years. Anyway,
> within a week I shaved up and became a devotee myself. I was sure
> I'd have to surrender sooner or later, so I thought it might as well be
> straight away. It was just the happiness, really ... You become
> purified, you see ... I no longer look beyond the moment, 'bhakti-
> yoga', the instant happiness of Krishna's service ... If we chant his
> name he is dancing on our tongues.

The break with hippiedom appears to be final and complete: the
first few weeks in the commune establish a sharp break with the past.
One devotee recalled: 'They sort of take all your ideas away, everything you think, and smash them all up. They're really merciless. You
feel terrible. But at the same time you can feel foundation stones
going down for something else, something better.' But there are

attitudes to 'straight' society which converts certainly share with hippies, and vestiges of hippiedom remain, especially in casual attitudes to work tasks. The Temple Commander felt constrained to reprove a work party: 'Great! So you finally got it together. You hippie types! It's great when you actually do something.'

The parents of at least one ex-hippie — 'they're very strict, old-fashioned people' — heard that their son had joined the commune with heartfelt relief. The young man had smoked his last packet of Benson and Hedges on his walk to the commune ('I remember I was smoking like a chimney all the way up here on the train'). He finished his last cigarette at the gate.

From liminality to communitas

Hippiedom is liminality and the Krishna temple itself is communitas. Victor Turner has singled out the Hindu religion from which the Hare Krishna movement has sprung as a supreme 'example of communitas'. (He also places Sufism in the same category.[11]) He compares the ecstatic communitas of Krishna with that of Dionysos: he emphasizes the passion and the absence of 'structure'.[12] Turner highlights the absence of hierarchy, the weakness of boundaries, the magic and spontaneity of life outside 'structure'. Caitanya promised that even low-caste, ignorant and humble people would float on the sea of love. The Hare Krishna commune in outer London exhibited many of these characteristics of 'communitas'; but it differed from the historical sect in its strong sense of external boundaries, and above all, perhaps, in its control and suppression of sex.

But in spite of the rule-regulated life and the watchful eye of the Temple Commander, there was little sense of hierarchy in the commune in the London suburb:

> You're free here, you know. I've had lots of jobs — there was always somebody on your back. Somebody telling you what to do all the time. Here I work hard, but I do it because I want to. I can walk out of here tomorrow if I want. It's the freedom ... I was working on the railways before I came here. And I just left. Didn't even wait for my wages. I just drew all my money out of the bank and gave it to Hare Krishna. It was only a few quid. They're welcome to it.

The morality plays frequently staged in the commune disparage the structure of the life of 'karmis' — especially the structure of formal education, careers and suburban domesticity. Bosses are ridiculed, and the pursuit of educational qualifications which secure well-paid but routinized jobs.

Members of the commune experience high emotion when dancing in the temple: there is great excitability, and leaping and dancing reach a pitch of high fever. Devotees strip off their shirts and their faces are running with sweat. A devotee appears with fire in a brass vessel and dancers pass their right hand through the flame. The climax is almost intolerable, but subsides into prayer murmured to the accompaniment of a tiny bell.

Life in the commune is 'bliss' and 'pure nectar': 'We do not have to wait to taste the bliss that will be ours when we take our place with Krishna in the spiritual sky. We can taste this nectar here, in devotional service to him. And it *is* such nectar. If you drink this you will never thirst again.' The devotees describe their state in a way, and in terms remarkably reminiscent of the way homosexuals had described theirs. And homosexuals and Krishna's devotees used strikingly similar terms to describe the staleness and sheer boredom of 'straight' society, of life lived in structure.

But there is one important difference between the Hare Krishna commune in London and the historical religion from which it has sprung: the original religion was highly erotic, the commune exercises severe sexual control. Turner appears to regard this eroticism as an essential ingredient of communitas. Krishna made love to a group of milkmaids who were charmed beyond caring by the sound of his flute. Sacred dances celebrate Krishna's relationship with the milkmaids, and Indian art portrays a ring of girls between each of whom is the blue and beautiful form of their divine lover. This is the symbolic expression of communitas: 'Communitas is the link between the *gopis*, the blue god between each milkmaid.'[13] And religious ceremonies culminated in the act of ritual sexual intercourse between devotees.

There are no such rituals in outer London. Sexual appetites are rigorously subdued, and women are seen as temptresses and somewhat unclean. One young devotee (Rohini Nandan) explained the situation:

> Women are always tempting you into committing impurities, you know. It's not really their fault. They want to marry, and all that. They are very powerful, actually, because they are so attractive to men. They can make a man do anything they want him to, once they have aroused his lust. They make men attached to them. Take

me ... before, I used to do all right with girls, I suppose I was a bit of a dandy figure, really. You know, long hair, fast car, nice clothes. I went to a public school so I was quite, you know, well-spoken. It made it so easy with women. It was *too* easy, really. They would let you do anything. I'd go out with a girl and then we'd go back to my flat and play nice music, and I'd think, 'Well, just this once more'. And she'd always let me and we'd end up in bed ... Women really dominate men that way. And that's why the scriptures say they should be strictly controlled.

In the commune there is wild dancing and everyone talks of ecstasy and bliss; but there is no ritual copulation to crown their dancing. The source of nectar is elsewhere ... in chanting the Holy Names.

Conclusion

Mary Douglas argued in her book *Purity and Danger* that the state of social boundaries influences (or determines) ideas of pollution, categories of clean and unclean food, and concern (or otherwise) for the body's orifices: '... when rituals express anxiety about the body's orifices, the sociological counterpart of this anxiety is a care to protect the political and cultural unity of a minority group.'[14] 'If we treat ritual protection of bodily orifices as a symbol of social preoccupations about exits and entrances, the purity of cooked food becomes important.'[15] More generally: '... the only way in which pollution ideas make sense is in reference to a total structure of thought whose keystone, boundaries, margins and internal lines are held in relation by rituals of separation.'[16]

The account given in this chapter of the society and concepts of a Hare Krishna commune appears to support more than any other material in this book the central thesis advanced by Mary Douglas. There is a striking correspondence between the firmness of social boundaries and the sense of pollution. In other respects, too, one might argue for the symbolic replication of the social state: time is tightly encircled in the present and mirrors, perhaps, the tight perimeter of the commune's social world.

There are considerable difficulties, however, in sustaining this argument. The young English men and women who have become devotees have entered a community in which these concepts already prevail and are expounded and illustrated in ancient Sanskrit texts that have come from afar. Categories of the clean and unclean, and concepts of time and causality, are not the outcome of the devotees' experience of new social structures: present-day recruits have 'taken over' conceptual schemes which originated in other times and in quite different social conditions. It is doubtless much easier to embrace strange concepts by moving from 'straight' society into marginal worlds; but that is a different argument, which has no bearing on the actual origin and 'cause' of concepts.

But there can be no doubt that experience of life in the temple was a cause of a profound change of consciousness which had many of the features of conversion. The devotees had changed their style of life in a major and dramatic way; they had taken new names and felt that they had taken a new identity. J. Stillson Judah reached a similar conclusion after investigating two Krishna temples in California. Throughout his book he refers freely to 'personal transformation' and maintains that: 'To understand the power of Krishna to change lives is to learn more about basic human needs and at least one way in which they can be resolved.'[17]

Judah examined the continuities and discontinuities with the hippie counter culture and concluded that for many devotees the life and religion of the temple was an arrangement of their long-standing counter-cultural values in a more meaningful context. Joining the temple was both a progression from hippiedom, for most devotees, and at the same time a reversal. It involved a rejection of drugs and of 'illicit sex'; and instead of 'doing your own thing' it involved a closely rule-regulated life.

Most of the devotees in the Californian temples had formerly been hippies, and those who had not had experienced a period of profound disorientation: 'I can't begin to describe how empty I was feeling. I had no association ... I considered myself completely mad.'[18] The devotees were of generally superior education (70 per cent had had at least one year of college studies) and were 'largely upper-middle-class youth' with fathers in business and the professions; but before joining the temple they had often felt lost and distressed.

Judah emphasizes three background characteristics of the devotees: their superior social origins and education; their previous counter-cultural careers; and their age. The overwhelming majority of the devotees with whom Judah made contact were twenty-five years of age or younger; only a very small number were over thirty. Authentic personal transformation might occur at any age, but Judah considers that it is probably much easier at twenty-five than forty.

Nevertheless, Judah quotes one striking instance of a man in his forties whose life had been utterly transformed by joining the temple. He had counter-cultural inclinations previously, but 'Krishna Consciousness changed my life a thousand per cent.' He thinks he would probably have committed suicide if he had not come to the temple. He has given up drink, drugs, and sex, even though 'Sex was the biggest thing in my life'. But he feels that he doesn't do quite as much chanting as he should, and that his age is perhaps an impediment: he doesn't quite fit in.[19] The evidence of both the Sufi and Krishna communes suggests that anyone interested in personal change in adult life will be well advised to focus attention on the perhaps strategic significance of the ten years between twenty and thirty.

10 | Can adults really change?

People who carry out research in the field of adult socialization usually regret the absence of any well-developed theory to guide their inquiries and help them interpret their results. The concept of socialization itself lacks precision: the distinction between socialization and maturation is as treacherous as the distinction between nurture and nature (and equally unhelpful if too rigidly drawn). And then there are serious moral worries in using the term at all, especially in the context of social policy-making: it makes policies of indoctrination or worse seem not only natural and perhaps inevitable, but respectable and actually 'scientific'.[1]

There are probably few behavioural scientists today who would endorse an earlier view of some psychoanalysts that one can predict most of subsequent behaviour from a knowledge of the first few months or years of experience. But theory is especially silent on the relationship between early and later influences — between primary and secondary socialization. A few recent empirical studies, which differ considerably in method and scale, have addressed themselves to this problem, but without clear-cut or safely generalizable results.

The connection between primary socialization and later socialization experiences is usually seen in simple terms of congruence and reinforcement, or of discontinuity and non-fit. Conventional marginal man theory (in the tradition of Stonequist) is based on the assumption that unfortunate consequences and personality dislocation arise from a lack of congruence between primary and secondary socialization. Peter Berger's interpretation of the counter culture of the late 1960s is based on the same simple model: permissive child-rearing practices in middle-class homes were followed by bureaucratic socialization at work and in mass universities. There was a sharp disjunction between the 'new childhood' and the increasing bureaucratization of all forms of life; and the result was the hippie.[2] This interpretation has considerable plausibility — although there is a good deal of evidence that those who embraced a counter-cultural life had often to fight hard against their earlier socialization and transcend an essentially 'straight' upbringing which had emphasized not freedom and autonomy but compliance.[3] And the further change to the disciplined post-hippiedom described in this book would not fit the simple disjunction model at all. Permissive child care is not an obvious prelude to the free choice of a closely regulated communal life.

The theory of adult socialization which we hold, will greatly influence our approach to a wide range of important social issues, from the construction of multi-racial societies and the absorption of immigrants, to the scope and nature of continuing education and prison reform. Perhaps one of the best — certainly one of the clearest — illustrations of the influence of a particular socialization theory on a set of educational proposals is to be found in Bertrand Russell's book *Education*, which was published in 1926. In the light of currently fashionable psychoanalytic theory, Russell declared that education of character 'ought to be nearly complete by the age of six'. Courage was an important virtue, but there was nothing that schools could do about this — it had already been done in the home, and 'One generation of fearless women could transform the world...'

British anthropologists who, in the wake of Malinowski, studied 'culture contact and change' might have been expected to make a significant contribution to the field of adult socialization; but they generally stood aloof from such a seemingly psychological enterprise and pointed to the involved complexities and difficulties of social change. More recently ambitious (mainly American) studies of the 'modernization' of developing countries have made an important contribution to research into secondary socialization (one such major study — by Inkeles — is reviewed below). At one extreme we have today small-scale intensive studies of a handful of housewives or convicts, and at the other global inquiries which compare seven or eight countries and inevitably invite the charge of superficiality, with very little in between.

There is little doubt that adults in industrial societies will be called upon to change to an unprecedented degree as society changes — and are already failing to do so, often with bizarre consequences for the running of the national economy. But they must change not only to 'fit in', but equally importantly not to fit in: to demand further and perhaps different changes as well as responding to them. This raises in acute form the problem of socialization even if this is defined in very basic terms as the 'acquisition of interactional competences'. Interactional competence may be as important to effective not-fitting-in as to smooth adaptation to change. And beyond the acquisition of interactional competences lies the problem of finding new meanings — quality, even Greek 'virtue' and excellence, and honour — in an unfamiliar scene. The creative 'role-maker' of the symbolic interactionists may be only another name for a quack. The key problem of social change for the people involved is not competence but integrity. The central concern that runs through the case studies reported in this book is a moral issue: knowing and being one's 'real self'.

Some recent studies of adult change

Among recent empirical studies and accounts of change in adult life, four — which differ greatly in scale and methods — seem particularly relevant to the theme of this book and provide a context in which its materials can be reviewed. They are studies of long-term prisoners in an English gaol; a wide-ranging cross-cultural study of modernization; a study of married women's participation in work; and an account of a kidnapped American heiress. The prisoners appear to demonstrate the capacity of adults to withstand a massive and prolonged assault on their sense of identity; the cross-cultural study claims to demonstrate fundamental change in adult life; the story of the heiress shows a remarkably rapid overthrow of an established self; and the study of young married women indicates a more complex relationship between early and later influences but suggests possibilities of 'metamorphoses' in adult life.

Cohen and Taylor's study of prisoners in the maximum security block of Durham gaol is not, they assure us, just 'another book about a prison'. They say they are concerned with a person's symbolic universe in the sense employed by Berger and Luckmann and they refer explicitly to socialization as Berger and Luckmann understand it: 'Socialization involves giving the individual conceptual machineries to maintain his universe. He has to develop a picture which is not just orderly but which is plausible and explains or justifies his experience.' Through their weekly visit to the prison (to teach a class of prisoners) over a period of some four years they aimed to construct a phenomenology of the security wing and discover how life was given meaning: 'What we are interested in is how, under extreme situations, people cope with universes changing, (conceptual) machineries being sabotaged and pictures being blurred or wholly obliterated.'[4]

The prisoners did not change. The 'screws' were not powerful 'significant others' who changed their definition of reality and conception of themselves: they were contemptible (but with real power to punish); the prisoners were an elite. Systematic degradation did not strip them of their identities. They were preoccupied with the possibility of 'deterioration': 'Central to this conception (of himself) was the wish to be the same person on leaving prison as on arrival.' Without privacy, and facing a deep abyss of empty time before them, they constructed sustaining ideologies and short-term timetables with 'bench-marks' and 'stages' to mark progress (for example in weight-lifting). Cohen and Taylor state their conclusion in unequivocal language:

> We have asserted that the men in E-Wing hardly lost their identities as a result of being processed through the prison system. Being pro-cessed did not seem to have significantly changed them. They fre-quently joked about the labels that others had attempted to fix upon them, they asserted their superiority over their guards, and developed ways of dealing with attacks upon their self conceptions.[5]

But there are difficulties in interpreting this study. We are given surprisingly scant information about the prisoners studied — we do not know their ages, how long they had been in prison, their previous record of imprisonment, or even their numbers. This study is based, perhaps, on thirty-five prisoners and none had been inside for many years. The one prisoner they knew (a little) who had been inside for fourteen years had retreated to a world of phantasy and showed obvious signs of 'deterioration'.[6]

In spite of many obvious differences, this prison study invites comparison with the account given above of the Cheshire Home (Chapter 5). There is a general congruence. The Cheshire Home residents are really in for life; but they showed a similar concern and ingenuity in sustaining their 'true' (historical) self. In neither the prison nor the Home did the 'inmate culture' have the transforming properties that the writing of Goffman has led us to expect.

In the cross-cultural studies of modernization it is the factory which appears to have remarkable transforming properties. Alex Inkeles constructed a scale of 'Overall Modernity' and administered it to adults in six modernizing countries (Argentina, Chile, East Pakistan, India, Israel and Nigeria) and in two already-modern countries (Britain and Greece) for comparative purposes. Scale scores were correlated with a wide variety of circumstances and regression equations and other sophisticated statistical techniques were used to assess the relative contribution of early and later socialization to 'modern' attitudes. Later socialization experiences were everywhere highly important, and in three countries apparently of greater importance than childhood experiences.

Modernity scores measured the attitudes that the researchers assumed to characterize industrial-urban man: openness to new experiences; orientation to the present and future rather than the past; a sense of being in control of the environment; and confidence that the world is rational and calculable. Scale scores were positively related to exposure to the mass media, to period of urban residence, to schooling, and above all to factory employment. 'It seemed clear that men learned to be more modern, year by year, after they entered the factory.' [7] There appeared to be no 'psychological price-tag' attached to modernization. A Psychosomatic Symptoms Test was administered but there was no indication that modernization was associated with psychological maladjustment. Modernization did not produce the classical marginal man but, if anything, a more stable individual.

Inkeles draws very wide and firm conclusions from this research: 'No man need be permanently limited to the attitudes, values, and modes of acting he develops in his early life.' However traditional a man's upbringing, 'his later experiences may transform him' into a modern man. Inkeles regards his evidence as conclusive:

> We read the evidence as showing conclusively that an individual's personality, at least on the dimensions measured by the O M (Overall Modernity) scale, can be substantially changed after adolescence if he comes into sufficient contact with those institutions which inculcate modernity in mature men.[8]

Inkeles regards his research as a rebuttal of Bloom. Fundamental change in adult life is not the virtual impossibility that Bloom had suggested, after reviewing an extensive research literature in his book, *Stability and Change in Human Characteristics* (1964):

> The O M scale measures some patterns of response which lie at the core of personality ... Modern psychology considers these attributes as basic, in the sense that they are assumed to be laid down in

childhood and adolescence, and thereafter to be stable or relatively unchanging, certainly much more so than are mere opinions. Consequently, our critics were led to express the same views as Benjamin Bloom ... Bloom had in mind mainly such attributes as intelligence and cognitive capacity, but a large segment of the community of personality psychologists takes essentially the same pessimistic view of the prospects of bringing about significant change in basic characteristics of personality after the age of 16 or 18.[9]

In fact, there is no warrant in Inkeles' data for these large statements about 'adults'. It is difficult, among the dense and abundant statistics of his tables, to discover how old his subjects actually were; but apparently the research assistants were instructed to select no-one over thirty. In fact the research tells us something about men between twenty and thirty. The average modernized man about whom Inkeles is writing grew up in a traditional village, moved to a town in his teens, is now twenty-six and has worked in factories for ten years.

But even this more limited conclusion has very important implications for the present study: indeed, it's very limitation is its importance. There is no doubt that the subjects on this present study often changed in quite radical ways; but the late twenties (and perhaps early thirties) are a time when for many there may be most openness to new modes of experience. This is an issue that will be taken up again later in this chapter.

Patty Hearst was kidnapped from the University of Berkeley by the Symbionese Liberation Army on 4 February 1974; before the end of March she had changed her name (like homosexuals, Sufis and Krishna devotees described in this book). Patty had become Tania, the name of Che Guevara's mistress. On 15 April, less than three months after being kidnapped, she took part with the 'Army' in a bank raid. In tape-recorded messages she had explicitly rejected her former identity and loyalties and redefined her position as a member of an embattled army. Her father, a millionaire newspaper proprietor, announced that he had known her for twenty years and knew that she could not have really changed.[10]

There was little in Patty's earlier history to herald such a conversion, and kidnapping would not seem calculated to secure it. A conventional upbringing in a well-to-do Catholic home, membership of the country club and an education at private schools, had produced a young woman not wholly unlike Jane Austen's Emma: 'handsome, clever, and rich ... and had lived nearly twenty-one years in the world with very little to distress or vex her.' She was apparently apolitical, though it is true that she lived with her fiancé and had smoked pot. On the Berkeley campus this was such a modest history as to be almost reactionary.

The extent, reality and speed of the 'transformation of identity' are so well attested in tape-recordings and actual behaviour as to be virtually incontrovertible. After the initial shock and restraint involved in the kidnapping, there is no evidence of coercion or intimidation; but for nine weeks she lived in a small room with eight deeply committed members (three men — one black — and five girls) of the SLA. In that time she acquired a powerful ideology to sustain an alternative reality. But again the focus must be on her age and her relative 'disengagement' as a student. Berger's 'conversion-prone' modern identity probably has a quite limited and specific age and social base.

The fourth and final study (by the Rapoports) is far less dramatic. It is a questionnaire study of some three hundred married women graduates with children in their late twenties and their attitudes to following a full-time career. It is a complex study of the interaction of early and contemporary influences: the influence of birth order (and the early socialization experiences that it implies), of family relationships in the family of origin, of relationships in the family by marriage, and husbands' attitudes to working wives. There was some evidence of the effects of 'reinforcement' (when the attitudes of husbands were congruent with earlier experiences), but the final picture is far from clear-cut, and the Rapoports point to complex interactions which release hidden potentials and reverse the expected course of action. They conclude with a familiar plea for better theory:

> Taking all this into account, it would seem that a sophisticated analysis of the ways in which early and late socialization experiences combined to influence adult behaviour depends on a dynamic theory — one that articulates psychological and sociological concepts better than any now in existence.[11]

What do these case studies tell us?

Certain conclusions seem clear from the case studies. The historical self has a rock-like endurance and yet adults are capable of fundamental change. Two other conclusions seem clear: that the importance of 'significant others' in the maintenance or transformation of the self has been exaggerated by many social psychologists; and the importance of 'liminality' as a prelude to change insufficiently recognized. Other general conclusions are more speculative, but it seems possible that change which is towards society's centre may occur at any age; but change which is away from the centre is largely age-based, occurring most easily and commonly between the early twenties and thirties.

The studies in this book were addressed to fairly precise and reasonably well-defined propositions about adult change that are to be found in books written by Peter Berger and Berger and Luckmann over the past ten years. In these writings change tends to be phrased as 'transformation of identity' and a strategic role in promoting these transformations is given to a particular form of 'marginality' and the support of significant others.

The case studies bring seriously into question the importance of significant others in personal change, and they make abundantly clear the importance of the historical self. Contemporaries (even when they are part of the 'reality-processing machinery') do not have the power and importance that Berger claims; and the 'inmate culture' of institutions has a trivial influence (contrary to Goffman's thesis) on adults' conceptions of themselves.

The importance of the historical self is most apparent in the studies of adults who went blind or entered a Cheshire Home: these studies are in line with the general picture and interpretation offered by Cohen and Taylor in their study of long-term prisoners in Durham goal. The adult personality does not appear to have the fragility suggested by Erving Goffman and theorists who have drawn heavily on his work. 'Transformations of perspective' do not, as one such theorist suggests, follow so readily from the 'displacement of significant others'.[12]

Bruno Bettelheim's classic account of a German concentration camp has given powerful support to the thesis that significant others — in this case camp guards — are able to promote fundamental changes in mature adults. Bettelheim was himself a prisoner in Dachau and Buchenwald, where everyone apparently changed but himself. (His own immunity arose from his detachment as a social scientist.) They became like their guards. They progressed through three or four stages from the first shock of arrest and transportation to a final stage when they learned to think, feel and act like their gaolers. Their former selves dissolved: new inmates boasted of their 'civilian' occupational statuses but soon ceased to mention them. Bettelheim concluded that they had become unimportant.[13] Precisely the same conclusion might have been drawn from observation of the Cheshire Home. Talking about previous occupational statuses was discouraged: you had to forget that you had once been a big-shot. But in fact they did not. When they talked to an interviewer who had come in from outside, they could often talk of little less. The talk (and silences) of inmates among themselves is not an infallible guide to what they 'really are'.

But the consciousness of some of the people described in this book was profoundly modified: the relationship between the knowing and perceiving self and the surrounding society was greatly changed and new realities negotiated.

The case studies suggest that marginality in the sense of 'liminality' may be an important prelude to deep-seated personal change. This book began by making a distinction between three senses in which the term marginality is currently used (see Chapter 1). It is in the sense employed by Victor Turner (following Van Gennep), as a stage or phase in a social process, that the concept has particular value in this study. In the simple sense used by Berger (in effect as 'subculture') it is of comparatively little use.

The homosexuals, the Sufis, the Krishna devotees, and the artists, experienced personal change which approximates to a 'transformation of identity'; and they had emerged from a period of social uncertainty and ambiguity which corresponds closely to Turner's notion of liminality (at least, 'life-crisis' liminality as distinct from the 'calendrical' liminality in which an entire society may be involved[14]). And now, after their liminal phase, they seemed to experience something strikingly like Turner's 'communitas'.

The ceremonies and rituals of both the Sufis and the Krishna devotees are rich in the symbolism of transition and change. In the Sufi commune ritual cleansing before meditation signalled the sloughing off of one's former self; and the account of kitchen-boys who were led by a silken thread to the sheik reinforced the idea of personal change involved in entering the Mevlevi order. In the Hare Krishna commune teaching centred on the 'jiva', the tightly constricted passage which led to spiritual platforms. And through chanting, man was in a constant process of becoming God.

In the post-liminal stage change may be a return to, or equally a turning away from, society's centre. (The pregnant woman returns to the centre after the birth of her child, the homosexual who decides to come out turns away.) Van Gennep distinguished between post-liminality which took the form of an aggregation to a new condition, and re-aggregation to the old. Turning away from the centre appeared, at least in the case studies reported above, to be age-based; the evidence that we have on turning back to the centre (for instance on 'reformed characters') suggests that it may be independent of age.

Studies of Alcoholics Anonymous have many striking points of similarity with the case studies of change in this book, and especially with the account of the Krishna commune. Studies of reformed alcoholics provide some of the best evidence that we have that 'real change' can occur in adult life, and that it is preceded by a liminal phase with most of the critical characteristics described by Victor Turner — the experience of degradation, abasement and humility, a sense of reaching the limit and 'hitting rock bottom' with reality unstable and in disarray.

Entry into Alcoholics Anonymous is a rebirth and creation of a new self.[15] (It also appears to be entry into 'communitas'.) But there are two crucial differences between recruits to Alcoholics Anonymous and a Hare Krishna commune: the former are typically in their forties and the latter in their twenties; the former have turned back to society's centre, the latter have turned away. However difficult the alcoholic's 'conversion' might be, it is at least supported by the massive weight of society's dominant values and institutions, which are regained to bring order from chaos and hold terror at bay.

The recruit to Alcoholics Anonymous commonly constructs a new calendar for his life which dates from his 'conversion': his birthdays are counted from the day that he joined. In this book personal change has been conceived as modifications of consciousness, and the experiencing of time has appeared repeatedly as a crucial constituent of consciousness and aspect of an ordered reality. At the heart of our modern consciousness are progressive and tightly interlocking timetables by which we live our lives and keep ourselves 'in line'. The younger people among the blind perhaps illustrate most clearly the importance of maintaining 'proper' temporal structures and sequences for keeping consciousness normal and intact. In the communes the nature of time was the subject of systematic, abstract and sophisticated reflection. It seemed that in reconceptualizing time one constructed a new self. And in two dramatic instances — the lesbian, Petula (described in Chapter 7), and the artist, Donald (described in Chapter 4) — the collapse of self in a liminal phase was inseperable from the dissolution and inversion of time.

There is no warrant in the materials in this book for supposing that reconceptualizations of time are Durkheimian 'models' of changed social states — or that concepts generally are modelled on society's boundaries and margins (as Mary Douglas claims). In the Hare Krishna commune ideas of time and pollution (and perhaps the significance of the left hand) might be seen as symbolic replications of the social state. But as Vieda Skultans, who examined this same theory in the context of spirit possession, concluded: 'Explanations in terms of boundaries can be dangerous.'[16] She expressed grave doubt about their explanatory value. In the present study the evidence is too slight, and open to more obvious and plausible psychological explanation, to justify even a highly tentative conclusion concerning the symbolic replication of the social state.

The importance of being one's real self

In the five groups which had voluntarily embraced a new life, change was a moral quest for one's real and authentic self. (In the two groups which experienced involuntary change, holding firm to one's historic self had a similar moral purpose.) Peter Berger has postulated one crucial aspect of modern consciousness as the decline of honour and the rise of dignity: 'the obsolescence of the one and the unique sway of the other.'[17] (Like other aspects of modern consciousness it is probably in considerable measure age-based, found most often among young adults, and commonly expressed as a protest against 'alienation'.[18]) The case studies in this book support Berger's thesis: they show the concern for dignity and authenticity as both an aspect of modernity and a powerful reason for rejecting it.

Honour is found in the great institutional orders of society; dignity in escaping from them to be one's real self. Honour is an attribute of 'me' rather than 'I'; in rejecting honour for dignity, 'me' finds its way back to 'I'. The men who left conventional careers to become parsons and artists had decided to be true to themselves. And so had the men and women who accepted their homosecuality, and especially those who decided to 'come out'.

Parsons, artists and homosexuals were preoccupied with the problem of what their true selves really were. They were also afraid of being trapped in new roles which were not their true home; and partly for this reason resisted the definitions that 'significant others' (like the parsons' parishioners) placed on them. They were engaged in a moral quest without end.

In Chapter 2 the problem was raised: why should homosexuals who could easily 'pass' decide to 'come out'? The decision to come out in spite of attendant social risks and penalties is difficult to explain in terms of hedonistic theories of social behaviour (although Lemert has attempted to do so[19]), or in terms of the distribution and redistribution of social power. It is true that homosexuals in some social positions and occupations (like politics and industrial management) face social penalties which effectively discourage them from coming out; but others who will certainly not come out with impunity decide to do so. They are not in principle different from accountants and architects who decide to become parsons although they know they will be poor.

Honour has become rather ridiculous, and few would now die for it or avenge their dishonoured sisters. Personal dignity, with its basis in genuineness and authenticity, is not to be found in the performance of institutional roles which only hide or distort the true self. The lack of a sense of personal worth is no longer a private misfortune but a public injustice and legitimate base for a social movement. The behaviour of homosexuals who come out must be interpreted in the light of a modern consciousness in which authenticity has been redefined not as a private and optional luxury but as a moral imperative and a public right.

Some implications for lifelong education

The studies reported in this book arose out of an interest in the possibilities of change in adult years and the implications for 'life-long education'. The book will end on a speculative note concerning educational provision and personal change in adult life. It will suggest, picking up admittedly inconclusive clues from the case studies, that our educational effort should be massively redeployed from the teenage years to the decade of life between twenty and thirty.

Clearly people in middle age and beyond are able to progress intellectually and socially and acquire difficult new skills: the account of the blind gives instances of remarkable developments in middle and later life. These developments reinforce an established self. But there are strong indications in these case studies (especially of the communes and homosexuals) that fundamental change of perspectives occurred most readily between the early twenties and early thirties. The openness to change in this age-range is consistent with both the Patty Hearst story and the cross-cultural study by Inkeles of personal change. Becoming counter-modern, no less than becoming modern, is probably largely age-based.[20]

Change in the sense of non-stock and principled response to new circumstances is most likely when two conditions are met: firstly, when there has been a period of disengagement from the major institutions of society (amounting to 'liminality'); and secondly when moral reasoning is at the level of Kohlberg's 'post-conventional morality'. And it is in the twenties and early thirties that these two kinds of stage — a social process stage and a psychological stage — are most likely to intersect.

Most of the individuals in the 'voluntary' groups on which this book is based, especially those in the communes, are probably representative of the post-conventional stage of moral reasoning. This can be no more than an informed guess, but the terms in which they justified and accounted for the actions of themselves and others generally accord with Kohlberg's definition of highly principled moral reasoning. This level of reasoning will never be reached by the majority of people; but between sixteen and twenty there occurs (according to Kohlberg's research) a significant moral regression — what Kohlberg aptly calls the 'Raskolnikoff Syndrome': a relapse into more conventional (and even pre-conventional) modes of moral reasoning.[21] It is true that Kohlberg finds that most of these young Raskolnikoffs eventually return to the developmental track at approximately the point where they dropped off; nevertheless, the age group for which we now provide higher education may be particularly unsuited to benefit from it.

Earlier ages were usually quite clear that adolescence was an unfortunate time for education, but could see no practical alternative. It was Rousseau who propounded the special virtues of adolescence as the period for serious educational endeavour. Dr Arnold never accepted this view and always regretted that educational effort was concentrated on this period of life. But we have now proceeded to mass schooling in the adolescent years and are in danger of creating a great waste of spiritual desolation. We may be wise to concede to adolescents not only the right to schooling but the right to work.

It is ten or even twenty years later that many young people may be at the point where they can respond most openly and creatively to the changing problems of our world. It is then, too, they are likely to perform most effectively in traditional academic pursuits, if this is what some of them want to do. Studies of the academic performance of mature university students suggest that the highest levels of attainment are probably reached around the age of thirty.[22]

Creative responses will be needed to a wide range of social changes, and the massive 'redundancy' of adults — perhaps, by the end of the century, some 15 to 20 per cent of people between twenty and sixty — may be taken as illustrative. It is increasingly obvious that in industrial democracies human beings will become too expensive for their economies to use on an extensive scale. Non-creative responses include both over-manning and 'job creation'. The problem is less one for social policy than social philosophy: what is at issue is a redefinition of social membership in modern societies and an exploration of new bases of identity and definitions of personal worth. Administrative solutions like retraining schemes, early retirement and short-term contracts instead of tenure for life will doubtless be tried: but the solution lies in a profound modification of consciousness. If no such modification occurs, large and often highly gifted segments of the adult population will be labelled layabouts and parasites. The most formidable change that we face is a redefinition of the significance of work and its contribution to a sense of identity.

The educational experiences that must be provided for adults, and especially for younger adults, will constitute an essentially moral education — not in the sense of propounding a particular morality, but in the sense of affording time, opportunity, and preferably a range of real-life experiences, for exploration of the moral universe and one's conception of self. These two fields of exploration are closely related, for as Berger says: 'Definitions of identity vary with overall definitions of reality.' [23] (The huge sales of Robert Pirsig's *Zen and the Art of Motorcycle Maintenance* indicate the extent of the need and some ways in which it might be met.) Adults can change in quite fundamental ways paradoxically as they seek their 'true selves'.

Notes to chapters

Chapter 1

1 See F. Musgrove, 'New Hope for Adult Education', *Universities Quarterly* (1959, 13) and 'A Uganda School as a Field of Culture Change', *Africa* (1952, 22).

2 B.L. Neugarten points to 'the enormous difficulties of conceptualization', as well as the lack of systematic data, as problems facing the development of an adequate psychology of the life-cycle: see *Middle Age and Aging* (1968, University of Chicago Press), p. 75.

3 See H.C. Lehman, 'The Creative Production Rates of Present versus Past Generations of Scientists', *Journal of Gerontology* (1962, 17) and W. Dennis, 'Creative Productivity between the Ages of 20 and 80 Years', *Journal of Gerontology* (1966, 21).

4 See V. Skultans, 'The Symbolic Significance of Menstruation and the Menopause', *Man* (1970, 5) and B.L. Neugarten *et al.*, 'Women's Attitudes towards the Menopause' in op. cit.

5 E.g. T. Parsons, 'Age and Sex in the Social Structure of the United States', *American Sociological Review* (1942, 7). Parsons thought that middle-aged men were distinguished by a preoccupation with depersonalized, physical sex, but was otherwise largely silent about the middle years of the life-cycle. Depersonalized physical sex was in no sense a 'natural', invariant developmental 'stage', but a functional prerequisite of stable, monogamous marriage.

6 E.g. R.F. Peck and R.J. Havighurst, *The Psychology of Character Development* (1960, Wiley: New York).

7 L. Kohlberg, 'Stage and Sequence' in D.A. Goslin, *Handbook of*

Socialization Theory and Research (1869, Rand McNally: Chicago).

8 K. Keniston, 'Moral Development, Youthful Activism and Modern Society', *Youth and Society* (1969, 1).

9 E.H. Erikson, *Childhood and Society* (1965, Penguin Books: Harmondsworth), pp. 239-66.

10 L. Terman's celebrated longitudinal study has followed up 'gifted' Californians since 1922 when they were eleven years of age. Scores on the Strong Vocational Interest test, for instance, have proved to be 'surprisingly constant': see 'Are Scientists Different?', *Scientific American* (January 1955).

11 P.M. Symonds and A.R. Jensen *From Adolescent to Adult* (1961, Columbia University Press: New York).

12 B. Bloom, *Stability and Change in Human Characteristics* (1964, Wiley: New York), pp. 167-230.

13 Of course there are many major exceptions among sociologists and different schools of sociological thought. Karl Mannheim's thesis of 'generational consciousness', for example, appears to entomb the individual in his generation for life: 'Early experiences tend to coalesce into a natural view of the world. All later experiences tend to receive their meaning from this original set, whether they appear as that set's verification and fulfilment or as its negation and antithesis': see 'The Problem of Generations' in *Essays in the Sociology of Knowledge* (1952, Routledge & Kegan Paul: London).

14 F. Musgrove, 'The Invention of the Adolescent' in *Youth and the Social Order* (1964, Routledge & Kegan Paul: London).

15 P.L. Berger and T. Luckmann, *The Social Construction of Reality* (1971, Penguin Books: Harmondsworth), p. 117.

16 Ibid., p. 155.

17 G.H. Mead, *Mind, Self and Society* (1934, University of Chicago Press), p. 161.

18 P.L. Berger and T. Luckmann, op. cit., p. 155.

19 E. Goffman, *The Presentation of Self in Everyday Life* (1971, Penguin Books: Harmondsworth), p. 21.

20 Ibid., p. 244.

21 M. Speier, 'The Everyday World of the Child', in J.D. Douglas, *Understanding Everyday Life* (1973, Routledge & Kegan Paul: London).

22 R.W. Mackay, 'Conceptions of Children and Models of Interaction' in R. Turner, *Ethnomethodology* (1974, Penguin Books: Harmondsworth).

23 A. Strauss, 'Transformations of Identity' in A.M. Rose, *Human*

Behaviour and Social Process (1962, Routledge & Kegan Paul: London).

24 H.S. Beeker, 'Personal Change in Adult Life', *Sociometry* (1964, 27).

25 I. Rosow, 'Forms and Functions of Adult Socialization', *Social Forces* (1965, 44).

26 P.L. Berger, *Invitation to Sociology* (1966, Penguin Books: Harmondsworth), p. 119.

27 P.L. Berger *et al.*, *The Homeless Mind* (1974, Penguin Books: Harmondsworth), p. 73.

28 P.L. Berger and T. Luckmann, op. cit., p. 177.

29 P.L. Berger, *Invitation to Sociology* (1966, Penguin Books: Harmondsworth), p. 118.

30 See R.E. Park, 'Human Migration and the Marginal Man', *American Journal of Sociology* (1928, 33) and Everett E. Stonequist, *The Marginal Man* (1937, Scribner's: New York). These works inspired a series of psychological studies of the personality characteristics of 'marginal men', e.g. A.C. Kerckhoff and T.C. McCormick, 'Marginal Status and Marginal Personality', *Social Forces* (1955, 34) and J.W. Mann, 'Group Relations and the Marginal Personality', *Human Relations* (1958, 9). The psychological concept of marginal man as a personality type had fallen into disrepute by the 1960s: see A. Antonovsky, 'Towards a Refinement of the Marginal Man Concept', *Social Forces* (1956, 35) H.F. Dickie-Clark, *The Marginal Situation* (1966, Routledge & Kegan Paul: London) and Ralph H. Turner, *The Social Context of Ambition* (1964, Chandler: San Francisco).

31 E. Durkheim, *The Elementary Forms of the Religious Life* (1971, George Allen & Unwin: London).

32 A. Van Gennep, *The Rites of Passage* (1960, Routledge & Kegan Paul: London, trans. M.B. Vizedom and G.L. Caffee).

33 See A. Schutz, 'Don Quixote and the Problem of Reality' in *Collected Papers*, vol. 2 (1964, Martinus Nijhoff: The Hague).

34 M. Douglas, *Purity and Danger* (1970, Penguin Books: Harmondsworth).

35 V. W. Turner, *The Ritual Process* (1974, Penguin Books: Harmondsworth).

36 P.L. Berger and T. Luckmann, op. cit.

37 W.I. Wardwell, 'A Marginal Role: The Chiropractor', *Social Forces* (1952, 30).

38 E. Shils, 'Centre and Periphery' in P. Worsley, *Modern Sociology* (1970, Penguin Books: Harmondsworth).

39 M. Douglas, op. cit., p.115.

40 See M. Douglas, *Natural Symbols* (1973, Penguin Books: Harmondsworth), in which she follows very closely the 'symbolic replication' thesis in E. Durkheim and M. Mauss, *Primitive Classification*. For criticisms of this thesis see E. Benoit-Smullyan, 'The Sociologism of Emile Durkheim and his School' in H.E. Barnes, *An Introduction to the History of Sociology* (1966, University of Chicago Press), and R. Firth, 'The Right Hand and the Wrong', *Times Literary Supplement* (21 February, 1975), who speaks of Durkheim's 'staggeringly simplicist conclusion'.

41 V.W. Turner, op. cit., p. 81.

42 Ibid., p. 92.

43 Ibid., p. 119.

44 Ibid., p. 127.

45 Ibid., p. 120.

46 P.L. Berger, *A Rumour of Angels* (1971, Penguin Books: Harmondsworth), p. 95:

47 P.L. Berger and T. Luckmann, op. cit., p. 114.

48 Ibid., p. 167.

49 Ibid.

50 P.L. Berger, *Invitation to Sociology* (1966, Penguin Books: Harmondsworth), p. 152.

51 P.L. Berger and T. Luckmann, op. cit., p. 185.

52 P.L. Berger, *A Rumour of Angels* (1971, Penguin Books: Harmondsworth), p. 96.

53 P.L. Berger *et al.*, *The Homeless Mind* (1974, Penguin Books: Harmondsworth), p. 62.

54 Ibid., p. 73.

55 Berger places the study of consciousness at the centre of the sociology of knowledge. Consciousness is about 'meaning' and 'reality': 'The consciousness of everyday life is the web of meanings that allow the individual to navigate his way through the ordinary events and encounters of his life with others.' Consciousness is not theorizing: 'Consciousness ... does not refer to ideas, theories or sophisticated constructions of meaning. The consciousness of everyday life is, most of the time ... pre-theoretical consciousness.' (Ibid., p. 18).

56 A. Strauss, 'Transformations of Identity' in A.M. Rose, op. cit.

57 O.G. Brim, 'Adult Socialization' in J.A. Clausen, *Socialization and Society* (1968, Little, Brown: Boston).

58 A. Strauss, op. cit.

59 I. Deutscher, 'Socialization for Postparental Life' in A.M. Rose, op. cit.

Chapter 2

1 For a statement (but not a resolution) of this problem see M. Clarke, 'On the Concept of Sub-Culture', *British Journal of Sociology* (1974, 25).

2 B.R. Wilson, 'A Typology of Sects' in R. Robertson, *Sociology of Religion* (1969, Penguin Books: Harmondsworth).

3 E. Goffman, *The Presentation of the Self in Everyday Life* (1971, Penguin Books: Harmondsworth), p. 110.

4 H. Garfinkel, *Studies in Ethnomethodology* (1967, Prentice-Hall: New Jersey), p. 165.

5 E. Goffman, *Stigma* (1968, Penguin Books: Harmondsworth), p. 117.

6 Ibid., pp. 100-1.

7 P.L. Berger and H. Kellner, 'Marriage and the Construction of Reality: An Exercise in the Microsociology of Knowledge', *Diogenes* (1964, 64).

8 E.M. Lemert, *Human Deviance, Social Problems, and Social Control* (1967, Prentice-Hall: New Jersey), p. 18.

9 E.g. H.S. Becker, *Outsiders* (1963, Free Press: New York). 'The deviant is one to whom that label has been successfully applied; deviant behaviour is behaviour that people so label' (p. 9).

10 E. Goffman, *The Presentation of Self in Everyday Life* (1971, Penguin Books: Harmondsworth), pp. 19-27.

11 T. Parsons and E. Shils, *Toward a General Theory of Action* (1961, Harper and Row: New York). Chapter 2: 'Personality as a System of Action'.

12 G.H. Mead, *Mind, Self and Society* (1934, University of Chicago Press), p. 210.

13 E. M. Lemert, op. cit., p. 63.

14 Ibid., p. 75.

15 Ibid., p. 91.

16 P.L. Berger *et al.*, *The Homeless Mind* (1974, Penguin Books: Harmondsworth), pp. 74-6.

17 P.L. Berger, *Invitation to Scociology* (1966, Penguin Books: Harmondsworth), p. 118.

18 Carlos Castaneda, *A Separate Reality* (1973, Penguin Books: Harmondsworth), p. 16.

19 Ibid., pp. 225-6.

20 A.K. Kerckhoff and T.C. McCormick, 'Marginal Status and Marginal Personality', *Social Forces* (1955, 34) and J.W. Mann, 'Group Relations and the Marginal Personality', *Human Relations* (1958, 9).

Chapter 3

1 See D. Martin, *The Religious and the Secular: Studies in Secularization* (1969, Routledge & Kegan Paul: London). Especially Chapter One: 'Towards Eliminating the Concept of Secularization'.

2 W.S.F. Pickering, 'The Persistence of Rites of Passage: Towards an Explanation', *British Journal of Sociology* (1974, 25).

3 T. Luckmann, *The Invisible Religion* (1967, Macmillan: London).

4 B.R. Wilson, *Religion in Secular Society* (1966, Watts: London), p. xiv.

5 R. Towler, 'The Social Status of the Anglican Minister' in R. Robertson, *Sociology of Religion* (1969, Penguin Books: Harmondsworth).

6 Wilson, op. cit. 'going to church is one of the values of American life; having faith is expected of all upright citizens' (p. 91).

7 P.L. Berger, *A Rumour of Angels* (1971, Penguin Books: Harmondsworth), p. 119.

8 J.B. Bury, *A History of Freedom of Thought* (1913, Thornton Butterworth: London), p. 243.

9 See M. Moore, 'Demonstrating the Rationality of an Occupation', *Sociology* (1974, 8).

10 H. Kearney, *Scholars and Gentlemen* (1970, Faber: London), p. 33.

11 Ibid., p. 33.

12 C.A. Anderson and M. Schnaper, *Public Schools and Society in England*, (1952, Annals of American Research, Public Affairs Press: Washington DC), p. 24. See also D.H.J. Morgan, 'The Social and Educational Background of Anglican Bishops — Continuities and Change', *British Journal of Sociology* (1969, 20) for evidence that bishops have come increasingly from clergy

families: only 14 per cent in the 1860s, 54 per cent in the 1960s.

13 C.A. Anderson and M. Schnaper, op. cit., p. 19.

14 The number of Anglican clergy declined from 23,670 to 18,749 in the first 60 years of this century. In 1901, 18 per cent were over 65, in 1961, 27 per cent. See B.R. Wilson, op. cit., p. 77.

15 L. Paul, *The Deployment and Payment of the Clergy* (1964, Church Information Office: London), p. 91.

16 Cf. P.L. Berger *et al.*, *The Homeless Mind* (1974, Penguin Books: Harmondsworth), p. 63.

17 R. Robertson, *The Sociological Interpretation of Religion* (1970, Blackwell: Oxford), pp. 68-9.

18 R. Towler, 'The Social Status of the Anglican Minister' in R. Robertson, *Sociology of Religion* (1969, Penguin Books: Harmondsworth).

19 B.R. Wilson, op. cit., p. 137.

20 P.L. Berger *et al.*, *The Homeless Mind* (1974, Penguin Books: Harmondsworth), p. 70.

21 H.R. Stub, 'Education, the Professions and Long Life', *British Journal of Sociology* (1969, 20).

22 See O.G. Brim, 'Adult Socialization' in J.A. Clausen, *Socialization and Society* (1968, Little, Brown: Boston).

23 As conceived in the older literature on marginality, e.g. in E.V. Stonequist, *The Marginal Man* (1937, Charles Scribner's: New York).

24 See M. Moore, 'Demonstrating the Rationality of an Occupation', *Sociology* (1974, 8).

25 For a seminal treatment of 'paradigm' see T.S. Kuhn, *The Structure of Scientific Revolutions* (1970, University of Chicago Press). Kuhn raises questions about the acceptance of scientific paradigms as socialization into the community of (currently orthodox) scientists (p. 209).

26 R.K. Jones, 'Sectarian Characteristics of Alcoholics Anonymous', *Sociology* (1970, 4).

27 P.L. Berger *et al.*, *The Homeless Mind* (1974, Penguin Books: Harmondsworth), p. 69.

This chapter is based on: F. Musgrove, 'Late-Entrants to the Anclican Ministry: A Move into Marginality?' *Sociological Review* (1975, 23).

Chapter 4

1 P.L. Berger and T. Luckmann, *The Social Construction of Reality* (1971, Penguin Books: Harmondsworth), p. 194.

2 Cf. P. Aries, *Centuries of Childhood* (1973, Penguin Books: Harmondsworth), p. 393.

3 Cf. J.H. Goldthorpe *et al.*, *The Affluent Worker: Industrial Attitudes and Behaviour* (1968, Cambridge University Press), pp. 144-9.

4 J.M. and R.E. Pahl, *Managers and their Wives* (1972, Penguin Books: Harmondsworth), p. 107.

5 P.L. Berger *et al.*, *The Homeless Mind* (1974, Penguin Books: Harmondsworth), p. 63.

6 See P. Burke, *Culture and Society in Renaissance Italy 1420-1450* (1972, Batsford: London), pp. 53-70.

7 N. Birnbaum, *The Crisis of Industrial Society* (1969, Oxford University Press), p. 162.

8 These interviews were carried out by Roger Middleton.

9 J. Barzun, 'The Arts Today: Consolation or Confrontation', *Journal of the Royal Society of Arts* (1972, 120).

10 E.R. Leach, 'Two Essays Concerning the Symbolic Representation of Time' in E.R. Leach, *Rethinking Anthropology* (1966, Athlone Press: London).

Chapter 5

1 P.L. Berger and T. Luckmann, *The Social Construction of Reality* (1971, Penguin Books: Harmondsworth), p. 168.

2 J.A. Roth, *Timetables* (1963, Bubbs-Merrill: Indianapolis).

3 S. Cohen and L. Taylor, *Psychological Survival* (1972, Penguin Books: Harmondsworth).

4 D. Nelkin, 'A Response to Marginality: The Case of Migrant Farm Workers', *British Journal of Sociology* (1969, 20).

5 E. Goffman, *Asylums* (1961, Doubleday: New York), pp. 6-7. Goffman claimed to be using the 'method of ideal types' to facilitate inter-organizational analysis, but his model is useless for understanding systematic variation among types or organization. Goffman confuses classificatory, polar and ideal types and so renders the 'total institution' valueless for comparative analysis. See N. Perry, 'The Two Cultures and the Total Institution', *British Journal of Sociology* (1974, 25).

6 A.R. Edwards, 'Inmate Adaptations and Socialization in the Prison', *Sociology* (1970, 4).

7 E. Goffman, op. cit., pp. 127-169.

8 Ibid., p. 169.

9 Ibid., p. 164.

10 P.L. Berger and T. Luckmann, op. cit., p. 175.

11 Ibid., pp. 118-9.

12 Ibid., p. 168.

13 E. Goffman, op. cit., p. 155.

14 Ibid., pp. 151-2.

15 Cf. J. Rose, 'A Very Rare Couple', *The Observer Review*, (18 August, 1974). 'Homes for the disabled have been set up, often by religious foundations, in pleasant rural surroundings where the disabled could be out of sight, cared for with great devotion, but cared for like children ... The moral ethos of the homes effectively curbs most of the possibilities of meeting and mating with the opposite sex' (p. 22).

16 See A. Schutz, *The Phenomenology of the Social World* (1972, Heinemann: London, trans. G. Walsh and F. Lenhert). Schutz conceded that all pastness is not equally past, and with regard to a particular experience 'its meaning is different depending on the temporal distance from which it is remembered and looked back upon' (p. 74).

17 For a refreshing commonsense critique of Schutz see D. Martin, 'The Sociology of Knowledge and the Nature of Social Knowledge', *British Journal of Sociology* (1968, 19).

18 P.L. Berger and T. Luckmann, op. cit., p. 42.

19 E. Goffman, op. cit., p. 164.

20 S. Cohen and L. Taylor, op. cit., p. 148.

Acknowledgement is due to Yvonne Stride (former postgraduate student in the University of Manchester) who helped with the interviewing on which this chapter is based.

This chapter is also based on: F. Musgrove, 'A Home for the Disabled: Marginality and Reality', *British Journal of Sociology* (1976, 27).

Chapter 6

1 A. Schutz, 'The Stranger' in A. Brodersen, *Studies in Social Theory*, Collected Papers 11 (1964, Martinus Nijhoft: The Hague).

2 P.L. Berger and T. Luckmann, op. cit., p. 59.

3 A. Schutz, 'Don Quixote and the Problem of Reality' in *Collected Papers*, vol. 2 (1964, Martinus Nijhoff: The Hague).

4 E. Goffman, *Stigma* (1968, Penguin Books: Harmondsworth) p. 52.

5 Ibid., p. 51.

6 P.L. Berger and T. Luckmann, op. cit., p. 110.

7 See ibid.: horizontal integration means 'relating the total institutional order to several individuals participating in it in several roles', while vertical integration concerns 'the totality of the individual's life, the successive passing through various orders of the institutional order....' (p. 110).

8 Cf. E. Goffman, *Asylums* (1961, Doubleday: New York), for a discussion of the mental patient's 'pre-patient career' reconstruction (p. 145).

9 P.L. Berger and T. Luckmann, op. cit., p. 115.

10 V. Skultans, *Intimacy and Ritual* (1974, Routledge & Kegan Paul: London).

Chapter 7

1 A.V. Cicourel, *Cognitive Sociology* (1973, Penguin Books: Harmondsworth), p. 28.

2 R.H. Turner, 'Role-Taking: Process Versus Conformity' in A.M. Rose, *Human Behaviour and Social Process* (1962, Routledge & Kegan Paul: London).

3 A. Schutz, *Collected Papers II. Studies in Social Theory* (1964, Martinus Nijhoft: The Hague), pp. 29-30.

4 Cf. the theme of V. W. Turner, *The Ritual Process* (1974, Penguin Books: Harmondsworth).

5 Limen = threshold.

6 V.W. Turner, op. cit., p. 83.

7 E. Durkheim, *The Elementary Forms of the Religious Life* (1971, George Allen & Unwin: London, trans. J.W. Swain), p. 218.

8 R. Linton, *The Cultural Background of Personality* (1947, Routledge & Kegan Paul: London), p. 50.

9 E. Goffman, *The Presentation of Self in Everyday Life*, (1971, Penguin Books: Harmondsworth), p. 21.

10 T.R. Sarbin, 'Role Theory' in G. Lindzey (ed.), *Handbook of Social Psychology*, Vol. I (1954, Addison-Wesley: Massachusetts).

11 R.K. Merton, 'Role-Set: Problems in Sociological Theory', *British Journal of Sociology* (1957, 8).

12 D.J. Levinson, 'Role, Personality, and Social Structure in the Organizational Setting', *The Journal of Abnormal and Social Psychology* (1959, 58). See also S. Stouffer and J. Toby, 'Role Conflict and Personality', *American Journal of Sociology* (1951, 56).

13 W.J. Goode, 'Norm Commitment and Conformity to Role-Status Obligations', *American Journal of Sociology* (1969, 66). If role is simply the enactment of status obligations, 'then there is little point in studying role behaviour ... Necessarily, all the important data on roles, would then be contained in a description of statuses'.

14 'However, the crucial difference between a simple role relationship and one that is based on status is that the obligations and rights of the status are much more firmly backed by the approval or disapproval of others who are in a more or less direct relationship with ego and alter' (ibid).

15 V.W. Turner, op. cit., p. 127.

16 Ibid., p. 119.

17 M. Douglas, *Purity and Danger* (1970, Penguin Books: Harmondsworth). 'For the only way in which pollution ideas make sense is in reference to a total structure of thought whose key-stone, boundaries, margins and internal lines are held in relation by rituals of separation' (p. 54).

18 V.W. Turner, op. cit., p. 82.

19 E. Durkheim, op. cit., pp. 215-6.

20 See A. Van Gennep, *The Rites of Passage* (1960, Routledge & Kegan Paul: London, trans. by M.B. Vizedom and G.L. Caffee).

21 E.R. Leach, 'Two Essays Concerning the Symbolic Representation of Time' in E.R. Leach, *Rethinking Anthropology* (1966, Athlone Press: London). Leach's notion of alternating and contrasted social opposites, 'formality' and 'masquerade', are strikingly like Turner's notions of 'structure' and 'communitas'. His state, or phase, of 'role reversal' corresponds to Turner's (and Van Gennep's) 'liminality'.

22 V.W. Turner, op. cit., p. 81.

23 See R.D. Laing, *The Politics of Experience and the Bird of Paradise* (1967, Penguin Books: Harmondsworth), Chapter 7, 'A Ten-Day Voyage'. A ten-day voyage backwards in time was an experience related to Laing in 1964 by a well-known sculptor and war-time Commander R.N. The experience had occurred almost

thirty years previously. The sculptor 'suddenly felt as if time was going back'. He was taken to a mental hospital and had the feeling 'that I had died'. And yet: 'Everything seemed to have a much greater — a very much greater significance than normally.' When, after ten days, he came back to normal forward-moving time, he 'suddenly felt that everything was so much more real than it — then it had been before. The grass was greener, the sun was shining brighter, and people were more alive, I could see them clearer.' Laing speaks of 'ego loss' which seems very similar to the experience of 'liminality' as described by anthropologists. Laing considers that a 'voyage' such as that described by the sculptor is a response to 'ego loss' and is not something requiring a psychological 'cure', but 'is itself a way of healing our own appalling state of alienation called normality' (p. 136).

24 E.R. Leach, op. cit., p. 136.

Chapter 8

1 P.L. Berger, *A Rumour of Angels* (1971, Penguin Books: Harmondsworth), p. 119.
2 T. Roszak, *The Making of a Counter Culture* (1970, Faber: London), p. 156.
3 This study was undertaken by Frank Musgrove.
4 A.M. Greeley, 'There's a New-Time Religion on Campus' in B. Berger (ed.), *Readings in Sociology* (1974, Basic Books: New York).
5 P.L. Berger *et al.*, *The Homeless Mind* (1974, Penguin Books: Harmondsworth), p. 76.
6 B.R. Wilson, 'A Typology of Sects' in R. Robertson, *Sociology of Religion* (1969, Penguin Books: Harmondsworth).
7 D. Martin attacks the interpretation of secularization as a 'master-trend': see *The Religious and the Secular: Studies in Secularization* (1969, Routledge & Kegan Paul: London).
8 See B. Hickman, 'Steady Growth of Sects on the Fringe', *Guardian* (20 December, 1974), p. 20.
9 A. Rigby, *Communes in Britain* (1974, Routledge & Kegan Paul: London), pp.107-38.
10 T. Roszak, op. cit., p. 139.
11 R. Cochrane, 'The Measurement of Value Systems in Deviant Groups' (Paper to the British Psychological Society Annual Conference, 1972).

12 T. Roszak, op. cit., p. 136.

13 K. Westhues, *Society's Shadow* (1972, McGraw-Hill Ryerson: Toronto).

14 C.A. Reich, *The Greening of America* (1971, Allen Lane: London). See also F. Musgrove, *Ecstasy and Holiness* (1974, Methuen: London).

15 T.P. Hughes, *A Dictionary of Islam* (1885, Allen: London), p. 116.

16 Ibid., p. 609.

17 A.C. Bouquet, *Comparative Religion* (1941, Penguin Books: Harmondsworth), p. 220. Cf. P.K. Hitti, *Islam: A Way of Life* (1970, University of Minnesota Press: Minneapolis), pp. 54-5.

18 Quoted in H. Corbin, *Creative Imagination in the Sufism of Ibn 'Arabi* (1969, Routledge & Kegan Paul: London, trans. Ralph Mannheim), p. 42.

19 T.P. Hughes, op. cit., p. 608. 'The doctrines of the darwesh orders are those of the Sufi mystics, and their religious ceremonies consist of exercises called *zikrs*, or "recitals"' (p. 116).

20 P.K. Hitti, op. cit., p. 63.

21 T.P. Hughes, op. cit., p. 617. 'To Sufis music was a means to achieve the emotional, ecstatic state that preceded revelation' (p. 173).

22 A.J. Arberry, *Discourses of Rumi* (1961, John Murray: London), p. 6.

23 T.P. Hughes, op. cit., p. 118.

24 P.K. Hitti, op. cit., p. 62.

25 N. Cohn, *The Pusuit of the Milennium* (1970, Paladin Books: London), p. 152.

26 Ibid., p. 151.

27 T.P. Hughes, op. cit. 'A sect of Sufis called *Mahabiyah*, or 'revered', maintain the doctrine of community of property and women, and the sect known as *Malamatiyah*, or 'reproached', maintain the doctrine of necessity, and compound all virtues with vice. Many such do not hold themselves in the least responsible for sins committed by the body, which they regard as the miserable robe of humanity which encircles the spirit' (p. 620).

28 P.K. Hitti, op. cit., p. 65.

29 N. Cohn has given an excellent account of their literature and the way they were regarded by contemporaries: see N. Coh, op. cit., pp. 287-330: 'Appendix. The Free Spirit in Cromwell's England: The Ranters and their Literature.'
    For a comparative study of 'ecstatic' social movements see

F. Musgrove, *Ecstasy and Holiness* (1974, Methuen: London).

30 Who believe in the incarnation of God.

31 Cf. T.P. Hughes, op. cit.: 'Generally, all the dervishes allow their beards and moustaches to grow. Some of the orders ... still wear long hair, in memory of the usage of the Prophet and several of his disciples' (p. 120).

32 The author has argued elsewhere that the contemporary 'counter culture' in the West is not a teenage phenomenon, but 'cuts off' at an average age of about thirty-six. See F. Musgrove, *Ecstasy and Holiness* (1974, Methuen: London).

33 For a discussion of this see H. Corbin, op. cit., p. 59.

34 This same account, but without the silken thread motif, is given by T.P. Hughes as initiation into the Mevlevi Order of Whirling Dervishes: 'The aspirant is required to labour in the convent or *takyah* 1,001 successive days in the lowest grade, on which account he is called *karra kolak* (jackal). If he fails in the service only one night, or is absent one night, he is required to recommence his novitiate. The chief of the kitchen, or *ashjibasha*, one of the most notable of darweshes, presents him to the shaikh, who, seated in an angle of the sofa, receives him amid a general assembly of all the darweshes of the convent.' See T.P. Hughes, op. cit., p. 121.

35 See M.E. Brown, 'The Condemnation and Persecution of the Hippies', *TRANS-action* (September, 1969).

36 See K. Westhues, op. cit.

37 See R.M. Kanter, 'Commitment and Social Organisation: A Study of Commitment Mechanisms', *American Sociological Review* (1968, 33).

38 See E.R. Leach, 'Magical Hair', *Journal of the Royal Anthropological Institute* (1958, 88), and C.R. Hallpike, 'Social Hair', *Man* (1969, 4).

39 A.M. Greeley, op. cit.

This chapter is based on: F. Musgrove, 'Dervishes in Dorsetshire: An English Commune', *Youth and Society* (1975, 6).

Chapter 9

1 E. Goffman, *Asylums* (1961, Doubleday: New York), pp. 14-15.

2 S.M. Dornbusch, 'The Military Academy as an Assimilating Institution', *Social Forces* (1945-5, 33).

3 M. Fortes, 'Ritual and Office' in M. Gluckman, *The Ritual of*

Social Relations (1966, Manchester University Press). See also
V.W. Turner, op. cit., p. 159.

4 D.L. Wieder and D.H. Zimmerman, 'Becoming a Freak: Pathways
into Counter-Culture', *Youth and Society* (1976, 7).

5 Ibid.

6 V.W. Turner, op. cit., p. 99.

7 J.S. Judah, *Hare Krishna and the Counter Culture* (1974, Wiley:
New York).

8 The fieldwork on which this chapter is based was carried out by
Roger Middleton.

9 Cf. R. Hertz, 'The Pre-eminence of the Right Hand: A Study of
Religious Polarity' in R. Needham, *Right and Left* (1973, University of Chicago Press).

10 See B.R. Wilson, 'Typology of Sects' in R. Robertson, *Sociology
of Religion* (1969, Penguin Books: Harmondsworth).

11 V.W. Turner, op. cit., p. 147.

12 Ibid., p. 144.

13 Ibid., p. 146.

14 M. Douglas, *Purity and Danger* (1970, Penguin Books: Harmondsworth).

15 Ibid., p. 151.

16 Ibid., p. 54.

17 J.S. Judah, op. cit., p. 11.

18 Ibid., p. 164.

19 Ibid., p. 6.

Chapter 10

1 Cf. S. Andreski, *Social Sciences as Sorcery* (1974, Penguin Books:
Harmondsworth), p. 174.

2 P.L. Berger and B. Berger, 'The Blueing of America' in B. Berger
(ed.), *Readings in Sociology* (1974, Basic Books: New York).

3 D.L. Wieder and D.H. Zimmerman, 'Becoming a Freak', *Youth
and Society* (1976, 7).

4 S. Cohen and L. Taylor, *Psychological Survival* (1972, Penguin
Books: Harmondsworth), p. 58.

5 Ibid., p. 148.

6 Ibid., p. 110.

7 A. Inkeles and D.H. Smith, *Becoming Modern* (1974, Heinemann,
London), p. 167.

8 Ibid., p. 277.

9 Ibid., p. 154.

10 D. Boulton, *The Making of Tania: The Patty Hearst Story* (1975, New English Library: London), p. 139.

11 R. and R.N. Rapoport, 'Earlier and Later Experiences as Determinants of Adult Behaviour', *British Journal of Sociology* (1971, 22).

12 T. Shibutani, 'Reference Groups and Social Control' in A.M. Rose, *Human Behaviour and Social Process* (1962, Routledge & Kegan Paul: London).

13 B. Bettelheim, 'Individual and Mass Behaviour in Extreme Situations', *Journal of Abnormal and Social Psychology* (1943, 38).

14 V.W. Turner, *The Ritual Process* (1974, Penguin Books: Harmondsworth), p. 157.

15 R.K. Jones 'Sectarian Characteristics of Alcoholics Anonymous', *Sociology* (1970, 4).

16 V. Skultans, *Intimacy and Ritual* (1974, Routledge & Kegan Paul: London), p. 86.

17 P.L. Berger *et al.*, *The Homeless Mind* (1974, Penguin Books: Harmondsworth), p. 80.

18 See R. Turner, 'The Theme of Contemporary Social Movements', *British Journal of Sociology* (1969, 20).

19 E.M. Lemert, *Human Deviance, Social Problems, and Social Control* (1967, Prentice-Hall: New Jersey), p. 74.

20 For evidence on age and the rising wave of occult participation in America, see P.A. Hartman, 'Social Dimensions of Occult Participation: The Gnostica Study', *British Journal of Scociology* (1976, 27).

21 Reported in K. Keniston, 'Moral Development, Youthful Activism, and Modern Society', *Youth and Society* (1969, 1).

22 P.Walker, 'The University Performance of Mature Students', *Research in Education* (1975, 14).

23 P.L. Berger *et al.*, op. cit., p. 85.

Index

Also available from Methuen and Tavistock:

METHUEN

ECSTASY AND HOLINESS
Counter culture and the open society
Frank Musgrove

Frank Musgrove's enormously readable study of the values and activities of the counter culture in England relates the contemporary movement to those that accompanied major periods of economic transformation in the past. The counter culture, he argues, is the outcome of opportunity not alienation, of openness not bureaucracy or technology.

TAVISTOCK

MYSTICS AND MILITANTS
A study of awareness, identity and social action
Adam Curle

'It is a simple, profound and compassionate book ... if it is accused of lacking complexity, subtlety or substance, the defence must be that it starts at exactly the point at which the sincere generation to whom it is addressed begin to discuss their problems.'
The Times Literary Supplement

FAMILIES AND FAMILY THERAPY
Salvador Minuchin

Family counselling and therapy is a swiftly growing subject. In recent years the importance and value of this particular branch of therapy has been increasingly recognized.
'This will undoubtedly be a classic in family therapy, useful for both the experienced family therapist and the beginner.'
Geoffrey Goding, Mankind

TAVISTOCK WOMEN'S STUDIES SERIES

Tavistock Women's Studies is a new series of empirical studies designed to cover all aspects of the position of women in modern society. The books will range over a variety of interests and are intended to meet the needs of undergraduate students of sociology and other related subjects.

WOMEN AT WORK
Lindsay Mackie and Polly Pattullo

From farm labourers to barristers, from machinists to MPs, the authors of this book spoke to hundreds of women all over the country, bringing together both the facts and figures, and the often disregarded personal experiences of working women.

WOMEN AND THE WELFARE STATE
Elizabeth Wilson

The author looks at the development of State welfare intervention from the early 19th century to the present day and relates it to the changing position of women, children and the family. She defines the Welfare State as the State organization of domestic life and argues for an emphasis on the ideology of welfare.

ON BEING A WOMAN
Fay Fransella and Kay Frost

This book delineates and explains the ways in which women are influenced and coerced socially, commercially, and culturally into their traditional roles, their subsequent internalization of this definition, and their consequent perception of themselves.